Northern Scotland

VOLUME 6 2015

Edited by Alastair Macdonald and David Worthington

Edinburgh University Press

Subscription rates for 2015

One volume per year, published in May

		Tier	UK	EUR	RoW	N. America
Institutions	Print & online	1	£38.50	£41.70	£43.85	$74.50
		2	£49.00	£52.20	£54.35	$92.50
		3	£60.50	£63.70	£65.85	$112.00
		4	£73.00	£76.20	£78.35	$133.00
		5	£82.50	£85.70	£87.85	$149.50
	Online	1	£33.00	£33.00	£33.00	$56.00
		2	£41.00	£41.00	£41.00	$69.50
		3	£51.50	£51.50	£51.50	$87.50
		4	£61.50	£61.50	£61.50	$104.50
		5	£69.50	£69.50	£69.50	$118.00
	Additional print volumes		£34.00	£37.50	£39.65	$67.50
Individuals	Print		£24.00	£27.00	£29.50	$50.00
	Online		£24.00	£24.00	£24.00	$42.50
	Print & online		£31.00	£34.00	£36.50	$62.00

Postage

Print only and print plus online prices include packaging and airmail for subscribers outside the UK.

Payment options

All orders must be accompanied by the correct payment. You can pay by cheque in Pounds Sterling or US Dollars, bank transfer, Direct Debit or Credit/Debit Card. The individual rate applies only when a subscription is paid for with a personal cheque, credit card or bank transfer from a personal account.

To order using the online subscription form, please visit www.euppublishing.com/nor/page/subscribe

To place your order by credit card, phone +44 (0)131 650 4196, fax on +44 (0)131 662 3286 or email journals@eup.ed.ac.uk. Don't forget to include the expiry date of your card, the security number (three digits on the reverse of the card) and the address that the card is registered to.

Cheques must be made payable to Edinburgh University Press Ltd. Sterling cheques must be drawn on a UK bank account.

If you would like to pay by bank transfer or Direct Debit, contact us at journals@eup.ed.ac.uk and we will provide instructions.

This publication is available as a book (ISBN: 9781474406628) or as a single issue or part of a subscription to Northern Scotland, Volume 6 (ISSN: 0306-5278). Please visit www.euppublishing.com/nor for more information.

CONTENTS

CONTRIBUTORS   v

ARTICLES

Thomas Brochard, The Integration of the Elite and Wider Communities of the Northern Highlands, 1500–1700: Evidence from Visual Culture   1

Silke Reeploeg, Northern Maps: Re-negotiating Space and Place in the Northern Isles and Norway in the Eighteenth Century   24

David Alston, A Forgotten Diaspora: The Children of Enslaved and 'Free Coloured' Women and Highland Scots in Guyana before Emancipation   49

REPORT

Colin Miller, Bennachie, the 'Colony', Balquhain and Fetternear – Some Archival Sources   70

OPINION PIECE

Sir Crispin Agnew of Lochnaw Bt, Crofting: A Clean Slate   84

REVIEWS

Alasdair Ross, *The Kings of Alba, c.1000–c.1130*
Neil McGuigan   98

Peter Anderson, *The Stewart Earls of Orkney*
Ian Peter Grohse   101

David Worthington, *British and Irish Experiences and Impressions of Central Europe, c.1560–1688*
Martyna Mirecka   104

Barry Robertson, *Lordship and Power in the North of Scotland: the Noble House of Huntly 1603–1690*
Alexander D. Campbell   107

Allan Kennedy, *Governing Gaeldom: The Scottish Highlands and the Restoration State, 1660–1688*
David Worthington — 110

Karen J. Cullen, *Famine in Scotland. The 'Ill Years' of the 1690s*
Richard W. Hoyle — 112

Anne Macleod, *From an Antique Land. Visual Representations of the Highlands and Islands 1700–1880*
Alastair J. Durie — 114

Aaron Hoffman, *The Temperance Movement in Aberdeen, Scotland, 1830–1845: 'Distilled Death and Liquid Damnation'*
David Beckingham — 116

John H. McKay, *Scotland's First Oil Boom. The Scottish Shale-Oil Industry, 1851–1914*
Robin Mackie — 119

Alexander Fenton with Mark A. Mulhern (eds), *A Swedish Field Trip to the Outer Hebrides: In Memory of Sven T. Kjellberg and Olof Hasslöf*
Andrew G. Newby — 121

Iain J. M. Robertson, *Landscapes of Protest in the Scottish Highlands after 1914: The Later Highland Land Wars*
James Hunter — 124

Simon J. Potter, *Broadcasting Empire. The BBC and the British World, 1922–1970*
Marjory Harper — 126

John A. Burnett, *The Making of the Modern Scottish Highlands 1939–1965: Withstanding the 'Colossus of Advancing Materialism'*
Catriona Mackie — 129

CONTRIBUTORS

Thomas Brochard is an Honorary Research Fellow at the University of Aberdeen.

Silke Reeploeg is a Researcher and Lecturer in the Centre for Nordic Studies, University of the Highlands and Islands.

David Alston is Councillor for the Black Isle ward of The Highland Council.

Colin Miller is an independent scholar.

Sir Crispin Agnew of Lochnaw Bt is an Advocate and Chair of the Crofting Law Group.

THE INTEGRATION OF THE ELITE AND WIDER COMMUNITIES OF THE NORTHERN HIGHLANDS, 1500–1700: EVIDENCE FROM VISUAL CULTURE[1]

THOMAS BROCHARD

Introduction

The integration of the Scottish northern Highlands into wider Scottish and British society did not occur within a vacuum.[2] Rather, it took place in a specific cultural context. This cultural dimension served at the same time as both source and receptacle of the reforming policies and measures of the crown. Governmental actions were explained away and validated by a so-called 'civilising' leitmotif. Conversely, the clans and families of the region were not mere passive objects of study to be reformed by the various institutional authorities. Within the field of visual culture, they projected themselves as actors for their own culture.[3] Furthermore, the cultural perspective cannot be restricted to an opposition between the central powers and northern Highland society. One needs to consider a transversal culture, that is, cultural elements coming from the community at large or from abroad and not solely from the centre. These in turn created a hybrid culture with its mixture of all these cultural aspects originating in both the centre and periphery and from external sources.

First, this article will examine the pictorial framework within which the concepts of the northern Highlands and of northern Highlanders developed. This will establish the intellectual background to their culture, as conceived and imposed primarily from outside and from above, with correlated relevance to that of Highlanders in general.[4] In the second and main part of this paper, various cultural elements, as produced and consumed both in the area and outside, will be examined in order to unravel the relationships between that intellectual framework and the visual culture *in situ*, in which women took an active role. The premise is to set a perceived 'barbarism' against actual cultural achievements and consumption on the ground. The methodology adopted for this approach is to look into various visual elements of that culture, namely architecture, heraldry, and paintings. These will be shown to reveal cultural facets in which these people had a significant input/control of output to a degree. This local/internal measure certainly emphasises a cultural and, by extension, integrative model from below then in operation and valid for the northern Highlands, defined in the present case as the shires of Ross, Sutherland, and Caithness, and the Outer Isles, in the sixteenth and seventeenth centuries, but with variations in terms of people, location, and time.

The articulation of northern Highland culture: the visual rhetoric of an identity

In a parallel to contemporary Irish and European cases, the terminology of savagery and barbarity contributed, in Scotland, to the formulation of a 'segregation policy' so as to establish a clear distinction between civility and wilderness within wider civic discourse.[5] This rhetoric constituted a trenchant rejection of the aristocratic politics of violence with a view to the 'civilising' regimentation of the elite. As a propagandist tool, it further justified and eased the passing of repressive legislation against 'uncivil' subjects. It was also integral to the wider discourse of the *via negativa* of cultural denigration, this marking a constant and common feature of the European articulation of civility as gradually accreted from classical Antiquity. But the commonplace of the 'wild man' combined multiple and indeed contradictory historical and cumulative nuances in its manifold depictions and representations. In the constitution of Western identity, the wild man indicated the separation between nature and culture that characterised the notion of civility. This conception accorded with Scottish/British identity with the Highlander/Islander cast as the wild man.[6] Language was also a powerful tool of governance and was integral to the panoply of governmental containment of the *Gàidhealtachd*.[7] Needless to say, Gaelic views jarred with such a representation.[8]

Turning to the visual, the projection of an image could be calibrated to send desired signals of status and identity at the expense of the local population as the key point lay in the control of these visual productions. Interestingly, the *topoi* of northern Highlanders, and of Highlanders in general, were not confined to a literary or secular context. Medieval and early-modern topography and visual arts made full use of the readily available template.[9] The full force of the articulation of 'mountaineers' as 'beasts', grounded upon an Aristotelian 'civilising' model of the city, comes to the fore in late-medieval Tuscan accounts and in cartographic representations showing terrifying sea monsters off the coasts of Ireland and northern Scotland on William Bowyer's map of the British Isles of 1567, reminiscent of Olaus Magnus' 1539 'Carta marina' of Scandinavia. The northern part of Eddrachillis did not fare any better, being shown as an 'Extream wilderness' with 'verie great plentie of wolfes too haunt in this desert places'.[10] The 1595 map of the Jesuit priest William Crichton attested too to the religious and indeed pan-confessional propaganda at work *vis-à-vis* the more remote parts of Scotland, as could further be found in Ireland, the contemporary Mezzogiorno, and late-medieval Tuscany.[11] Crichton linked the men under the earl of Sutherland with those under the Hebridean chiefs as, together, 'barbarorum et semiinermium' (savage and semi-clad), whereas the earl of Caithness's men, though still 'semiinermium', were 'semibarbarorum'. Perhaps, this was an allowance of Caithness' better Catholic receptiveness. Crichton might also well have felt that Gaelic speakers were worthy recipients of the Irish mission as things then stood.[12]

This axis of barbarism extended to other pictorial representations, in itself a long-established European tradition, both at home and abroad. At the Bayonne tournament of 1565, organised for Catherine de' Medici and Charles IX, knights clothed as wild Scotsmen, demons, Turks, and nymphs. glorified monarchical rule over the savage, the mythic and the demonic. The baptismal celebrations at Stirling in December 1566 indirectly borrowed from the Bayonne fête, but with goatskin-clad 'wild Highland men' in charge of the fireworks in the Scottish royal burgh as opposed to moors in the Basque locality.[13] Alternatively, the Stewart monarchs and courts accoutred *à la* aboriginal but not necessarily within a context of tensions inherent in mock battles and tournaments.[14] In 1633, King Charles I recognised the identity of the Gaels during his visit to Edinburgh.[15] This society, in the process of being integrated into a wider Scottish/British entity, was thus perceived in mixed ways, but was still distinctive enough to command a certain specificity, as was similarly projected in Languedoc or England's north-east at the time.[16] Even though this was not the sole means at the disposal of the crown for the recognition of Highland and Hebridean identities, the 1617 and 1633 royal visits underlined a distinct regal perspective too on that particular topic, if not a different attitude altogether. As in Elizabethan England, the tradition of the wild man was instrumental in courtly discourse and, via a wider dimension, in the artistic imagery of the time.[17]

The visual culture of the northern Highlands

The study of local visual culture in the region assumes an importance in that it was an area in which northern Highlanders themselves had a direct influence on the projection of an image, identity, and status to the family, the clan, and the wider world. Unduly underrepresented in early-modern Scottish history, this visual anatomy or grammar of the northern Highlands provides evidence of these communities gradually immersing into the broader ambient late-Renaissance and Baroque culture.[8] In this respect, the triptych of architecture, heraldry, and painting will be examined. It is well worth emphasising that the progress was only a gradual one and was by no means universal both in its geographical and societal coverage.

Architecture

such houses [fitt for nothing else but as a place of refuge in the time of trouble, wherin a man might make himselfe a prisoner] truly are worn quyt out of fashione, as feuds are, which is a great happiness.[19]

Art historians have recently rejuvenated the traditional historiography of Scottish architecture of the late medieval period and the Renaissance. The revised perspective on country seats has moved away from a perception solely of their preparedness for war to a focus on status, display, and symbol, and the notion of lifestyle and comfort that came with the expansion of domestication. Overall, the so-called castles of that period were not purely functionally defensive but also, rather, metaphorically so. They amalgamated the appearance and substance of martial nobility but also combined manifold cultural and socio-economic considerations. Noble estates would have been surrounded by the wherewithal to survive, expressed architecturally in the form of walled gardens and enclosures often on a very extensive scale.[20] The relatively dynamic and sustained period of construction of châteaux in Easter Ross, Sutherland, and Caithness, in particular, attested to the comparative wealth of the landlords and their engagement with the wider Scottish and European Renaissance.[21]

The few extent building contracts within the Sinclairs' sphere of influence, for example, demonstrated the landlords' vision, at least in part, for contemplation and a more pleasurable lifestyle.[22] George, fifth earl of Caithness, and probably Jean Gordon, the countess, were themselves amateur architects who stipulated directions to follow complete with technical terms as they undertook, in 1616, the repair of the 'new wark' at Castle Sinclair. They notably outlined the installation of a platform and the conspicuous use of ashlar – a dressed stone that was then expensive. As a regional cynosure, the structure emulated the wider Renaissance architectural designs in vogue in contemporary Scotland with some finely carved corbels to support angle turrets and windows. It further signalled the participation of women in the management of the estates and buildings as elsewhere in Scotland.[23]

The multiple fields of application affected by Renaissance architectural influences in these lands testified to its wide-ranging effect. Contemporary maps of Ross certainly reveal the impressiveness of the multiple-structured country seats of Cadboll and Tarbat/Ballone and the five- to six-storey high Milntown Castle, which embraced the Renaissance avidity for verticality.[24] Visual grandeur was *de rigueur* as a reflection of status and as a statement of one's sphere of influence over the landed estate. Architecture visually encapsulated the sensitivity of the elite towards status, hierarchy, and especially precedence.[25] This architectural panache also demonstrated the smaller lairds emulation of the great houses of Scottish magnates.[26] Their patronage crossed architectural fields too, as regards secular benefactions for chapels and ecclesiastical sites. In 1616, George Munro of Milton and his second wife, Margaret Dunbar, erected the easterly chapel at Kilmuir

Easter with a country seat-style circular bell-tower capped by a conical roof. These secular elements expressed the worldly status of the patrons.[27]

Engaged with the Renaissance enthusiasm for carved wood panels and as a testimony to foreign influences, largely in the form of continental pattern-books, Sir Thomas Urquhart of Cromarty showcased a series of thematic politico-religious panels which illustrated the theological and cardinal virtues, the four evangelists, the so-called nine worthies, Scottish monarchs, Samson, and the Albanian nationalist, Skanderbeg. These bear comparison with, among others, those at Crathes (Aberdeenshire) and Earlshall (Fife).[28] Taken together, the renovation and extension work of Sir Rory Macleod, in 1622–1623, and of his grandson, Iain Breac, from 1664 to 1666, at Dunvegan Castle, similarly underlined their embrace of contemporary designs and materials with a southern rural and urban influence.[29] This stood in marked contrast to the general state of the built environment in the Isles. Traditional historiography depicts its overall basic nature in terms of stonework and masonry, alongside the additional smallness of the windows and other openings as well as the prevalent absence of vaults and mural fireplaces.[30] Against this background, though, the addition of a crow-stepped gable complete with a chimney to the hall at Caisteal Chiosmuil (Kisimul Castle) in the seventeenth century, reflects the appreciation of Renaissance design, albeit belatedly, and the appeal of greater comfort.[31] Feasting halls too were modified to accommodate domestic apartments and illustrate the expansion of domestication. Ameliorations to domestic accommodation, storage, and services were likewise the order of the day for those that could make them. In essence, local landlords were trying to emulate Lowland patterns through additions to their feasting halls, initially with a tower and, later, with other embellishments.[32] Indeed, at least in the case of Caisteal Ormacleit on South Uist, local tradition assigned to a woman, Penelope Mackenzie, suggests that the incomplete earlier structure, erected by Allan, captain of Clanranald, at the close of the sixteenth century, had failed to meet her required standards.[33] Thus, overall, there is a sense that the castellar renovation and remodelling in the Isles did not reach the full potential of Renaissance architecture with its more refined elements, as seen in the Lowlands, until a later period from the 1650s and 1660s onwards. Despite its gradual nature this qualified the categorical view prevalent among the literati of a mythified barbarity which irretrievably grounded Irish and Highland communities in a culture of apathy towards Renaissance comfort and refinement.[34]

Local materials, like the flagstones of Orkney and Caithness, contributed to the individuality of the northern Scottish townscape. Equally significant for building materials along the northern coasts and on the islands were materials from Norway and Scandinavia. Additionally, what made the area even more dynamic in terms of architecture were the flows and counter-flows between these northern lands and the Lowlands in terms of building material and personnel. Works on royal castles and ships in the Lowlands produced a demand, at times, for Caithness slate and Ross timber respectively.[35] Wood resources on the west coast were used for internal consumption to help local building projects and shipbuilding developments.[36] Private architectural projects outside the region further relied on the import of Caithness slate which was used on the very best buildings.[37] Likewise, nobles had access to, and hired, qualified craftsmen of national stature, albeit presumably in a limited way as the vast majority of the work-force tended to be of a local/regional origin. Perhaps the most outstanding example is the employment of the English carver, Ralph Rawlinson, by George, first marquess of Huntly, in 1633, who was recalled from his work at the Chanonry (Fortrose) to dedicate his services to Holyroodhouse.[38] Renaissance architectural designs were gradually and innovatively incorporated into the buildings of the area. However, this was an ongoing process which should be viewed over the long term.[39] The overall balance between the necessity for the Scottish nobility and gentry to adhere to an interpretation of feudal tradition, to establish, stabilise, or reinforce their landed rights, alongside a quest to embrace wider contemporary fashion, was present in the region too. Thus, with the creative tension between tradition and innovation, a dynamic of architectural hybridity or multiculturalism characterised the built environment in the region.[40]

Heraldry

Northern Highlanders adopted the foreign system of heraldry, which originated in north-eastern France in the twelfth century, to display their identity and status. This was relatively rapidly used within the sphere of the kingdom of the Isles.[41] Heraldry was a dynamic process and an outlet to cast in marble, in a sense, family relationships and tensions, an ostentatious statement of a person's views.[42] The Mackays of Farr under Hugh and Sir Donald Mackay, lord Reay, experienced frictions in their relations with the earls of Sutherland. Their armorial achievements illustrated no connection with the comital family whereas, in 1503, the arms of this Strathnaver landlord bore the trademark three stars of the Sutherland earl.[43] Yet, one should not underplay the propagandist nature and *raison d'être* of some of these armorials.[44]

Satellite families associated themselves with more powerful regional clans, a move reflected in the adoption of heraldic charges to their coats of arms.[45] Moreover, minor and cadet families only managed to have their heraldic achievements come to official prominence later on, in the 1660s and 1670s, as was the case for the Baynes of Tulloch and of Logie or the Munros of Balconie. This indicated an aspiration to the recording of one's escutcheon as a mark of gentility.[46] However, this should not distract from the fact that, on the ground, these cadet families, and even less wealthy members of this society, had long joined their clan peers in a visual bonding and sense of belonging epitomised by carved heraldry on various monuments, particularly those of a sepulchral nature.[47] Elsewhere on the European periphery, noble families on the eastern shore of the Adriatic, mainly Croatians and Bosnians, had their faked medieval arms confirmed by the Italian and Austrian authorities in the seventeenth and eighteenth centuries.[48] Moreover, the relative paucity of heraldry documented for the Gaelic Irish should not be extrapolated to the Scottish northern Highlanders in general.[49] Significantly, there is a scantiness of records in contemporary armorials concerning the heraldry of the Macneils of Barra, which has been compounded by a sustained misattribution of their arms.[50]

Heraldic arms permitted the visual re-enactment and actualisation of one's pedigree and, to some extent, mythic ancestry. These were the pictorial match to written genealogies.[51] Interconnections between visual, aural, and written/oral media need to be highlighted, albeit not being *sui generis*.[52] Elsewhere, Serbian and Croatian epics seemingly influenced the way in which some family crests were depicted.[53] Clans from the Western Isles and Highlands shared in a pan-Gaelic symbolism with Irish Gaels and so the late seventeenth-century Ulster/Scottish heraldic controversy over the legitimate claim to the symbol of the red hand unfolded within a poetic context.[54] This heraldic affinity between Gaelic Scotland and Ireland supported cultural bridges beyond their much-commented sharing of rich poetry and professional orders, but with elements of a distinctive far-northern identity still present.[55]

Heraldic achievements displayed the northern nobility and gentry as part of a wider genteel society.[56] This was perhaps most conspicuous in the depiction of savages as supporters, a common European theme which drew from the codification and extension of the myth of the wild man of ancient traditions that was extant from the twelfth century onwards.[57] While in certain circumstances the crown held Highlanders and Islanders as barbarians, then, a number of clan leaders dissociated themselves from such association and stressed civility over savageness. This represented another marker of their distancing from their fellow clansmen.[58] As heraldic supporters, these savages were protectors of the nobility, thus transformed by heraldic semiotics into 'domesticated guardian[s]' or conventionally perceived attendants.[59]

Clan chiefs projected a personal pride in their own sense of accomplishments and genteel status in much the same manner as warriors on the frontier in early-modern western Hungary. On the carved sandstone overmantel which he erected at Cromarty Castle, Sir Thomas Urquhart extended and crystallised the cryptic genealogy and learned but sometimes whimsical literary style of his written works.[60] More pragmatically, Sir Donald Mackay, first lord Reay, exuded his martial feats in the Thirty Years War by bearing a pikeman and a musketeer as dexter and sinister supporters respectively.[61] The first and second earls of Seaforth gloried in their clan's earlier conquest of Lewis and proudly featured the Macleods of Lewis' characteristic charge of Or (yellow), a rock/mountain azure (blue) in flames proper both as their second and third quarters and/or in their crest.[62] Rather like the two dozen native chieftains who assisted in the Spanish colonisation of Mexico and were granted armorial bearings by the Spanish crown, Seaforth's heraldic achievement, with its reference to the pacification of Lewis, as promoted by the crown, was officialised too.[63] Away from the turbulence associated with the late sixteenth and early seventeenth centuries, Roderick Macleod of Dunvegan (1649–64) cultivated the vision of an educated chief with a unique seal described as bearing 'a classical-looking head of a Roman type'.[64] Commensurate with it was John Mackenzie of Gairloch's visual political statement. In the aftermath of the Union of the Crowns, he displayed a thistle between two roses embossed on his 1606 seal at the top of his shield and, at each side, both a thistle and a rose.[65] This shows that a number of leading chiefs and gentry, besides the Campbell and Seaforth heads, accepted aspects of the British 'civilising' agenda post-1603 and its underlying notion of civility, while underlining also the adaptability and variability of the process.[66]

The phenomenon of a powerful clan heritage is most conspicuous in the case of the Macleods of Lewis. Even after the demise of this Lewis sept, their arms continued to be recorded, retaining a mythic medieval power status, albeit at times with the qualification of being 'sometime of ye Lewis'.[67] The coat of the clan and associated lineage hence survived and developed into either a trophy or an ancestry to be proud of, with all the power and status this entailed.[68]

Painting

In terms of portraiture, as with contemporary clothing, the elite aspired to be paragons of propriety and aesthetic sensibility through a cultural medium invested with its own codification and readability. On the one hand, portraits of the Renaissance sought to be accurate records of a person's features and even physiognomical 'mirrors of the mind'. Nonetheless, they were also constructed works of 'visual poetry' decoded as intangible assets, intellectual, symbolic, and social. Portraits ensured identification and invited interpretation.[69] Indeed, cultivated leaders in the northern Highlands were not necessarily severed from this pictorial culture but, instead, could embrace it as a further sign of their integration into the broader Scottish/British elite.

Women assumed a central position in this culture in which the sumptuousness of their outfits radiated from the canvas. Status combined with elegance. Adopting the usual dress style of widowhood, Isabel Ogilvie, wife of Kenneth Mackenzie of Kintail, wore a garment of black cloth with few trimmings and had her head covered.[70] In her old age, Jane Gordon, countess of Sutherland (died 1629), sat attired in a bonnet and with her deep dark veil of widowhood over her perfectly silvered hair, and her right hand delicately laid on her heart. A faithful Catholic, she wore a rosary suspended in the same hand, with an attached cross on its back.[71] A portrait, probably of her granddaughter, Elizabeth Gordon, by the then leading Scottish portraitist, George Jamesone, also survives. It followed the evolution of feminine fashion, taking a cue from the French-born Queen Henrietta Maria. Elizabeth thereby adopted the trendier pale shades for her dress and sported a wispy fringe of curls on the forehead. Her dress has a square *décolletage* edged with a spreading and particularly rich lace collar. Like the painting of Margaret, countess of Argyll, that of Elizabeth exudes a figure of lightness and restrained elegance.[72] In what is a possible marriage portrait, Isabel, third countess of Seaforth (died 1715), sat for society portrait painter L. Schuneman, who counted other Scottish nobles as clients. She is clothed in a white satin dress and brown robes and is fashionably bejewelled.[73] Amongst all these feminine portraits there appears little by way of a regional identity marker. Instead, the issue revolves around status, social etiquette, and gender and pictorial conventions.

Despite their geographical remoteness from the court, the clan elite of the area participated in its late-Renaissance culture. Those northern Highlanders covered in this article adhered to the dictates of courtly fashion and style and so had their portraits painted. This identification was reinforced by the chiefs' patronage of either leading contemporary artists or painters with a broad-based clientele.[74] Besides, a number of them were actually avid art collectors.[75] This artistic activity introduced another family tradition in the form of the visual recording of a clan/family chief for posterity, as shown by the Mackenzies of Cromarty and the earls of Sutherland.[76] Both Sir Rory Mackenzie of Coigach (died 1626) and Sir John Mackenzie of Tarbat posed with a relatively plain outfit compared to the then *à la mode* sophisticated court dress. Their sober black coats were relieved only by bib-style collars with tasseled band-strings, the last two being decorated in the case of Tarbat. The sobriety of the costume – as with the Presbyterian garments of choice subsequently adopted by Archibald, first marquess of Argyll, during the Covenanting period – points perhaps to a greater anxiety to emphasise their religious affiliation than, restrictively, a display of status. However, this should be qualified to an extent since Cromwellian portraiture embraced a plain-style aesthetic devoid of redolent opulence to depict and match a new mode of piety and power.[77] Throughout the seventeenth century, the portraiture of the Sutherland magnates characterised this admixture of courtly status and contemporary fashion having also politico-religious undertones.[78] However, the Restoration cut loose the stifling of the previous Puritan period as demonstrated in curls, ribbons, puff flounces, and feathers. Men developed a *penchant* for wigs and cravats with a certain stiffness and smart elegance adopted for the canvass. In keeping with these contemporary fashion, status, and conventions of portraiture, Kenneth, third earl of Seaforth (died 1678), sat for the leading Baroque-style painter John Michael Wright wearing robes. His son, Kenneth, fourth earl (died 1701), was painted by the French-born court painter Henri Gascar dressed in a rich red coat and blue cloak and adorned with the blue sash and badge of the Order of the Thistle, with a talbot by his side.[79] The late seventeenth-century portraiture of politicians (George Mackenzie, first earl of Cromarty; Sir George Mackenzie of Rosehaugh) and army commanders (General Hugh Mackay of Scourie) equally follows the contemporary conventions of social class and paintings, dignified and noble poses in rich and sumptuous outfits being essential features.[80]

In his appearance before a gathering of the High Court of Chivalry in Westminster in November 1631, Sir Donald Mackay was apparelled 'in black velvet trimmed with silver buttons, his sword in a silver imbroidered belt, in his order of a Scotish baronet, about his neck'. In other words, his image in front of an audience of British peers and courtiers was one of refined sobriety and martial dignity but with an acknowledgment of the state in the form of his baronet's ribbon. The English commentators at his trial thus did not report on an ethnic or regional appearance.[81] Armour portraits could be set pieces or re-engraved and used as copies. Nonetheless, they were an ostensible sign both of status and wealth and, with the decline of the use of armour on the battlefield, of the glory of ancestral status and timeless heroism, as found in the portrait *à la* Van Dyck of Colin, first earl of Seaforth, or the one of Sir William Gunn. These grounded their identity in military valour, crucially transposing the depiction of honour and status away from ostentatious display of wealth alone.[82] Furthermore, two engravings by George Glover, a leading contemporary engraver, represented Sir Thomas Urquhart accoutred in a sartorial style as flamboyant and sophisticated as his literary *oeuvre*, including his highly allegorical portrait surrounded by the muses.[83] *In fine*, portraiture not only recorded but also crystallised social ascendancy and a sense of belonging.[84]

A rare sketch, possibly of Sir Donald Macdonald of Sleat, has survived, showing him in his full military regalia complete with a helmet. The Skye and North Uist chief sports a doublet richly decorated with Celtic motifs, a plaid worn below the belt like a plaited kilt, a sporran, and a dirk. Sleat proudly displays his claymore with the tip of the blade to the ground. As a result, the Gaelic/Celtic nature of the figure, imposing overall, stands out.[85] Within the context of the Jacobite campaign of 1689, Highland leaders formed a variegated group with their 'tartan garb' woven 'in triple stripe', 'coloured' and 'girded' plaids, 'tartan hose', 'fur bonnets', 'broad belt', and 'ox hide'.[86] In contrast, the portraits of Sir Mungo Murray and of the Irish leader Sir Neil O'Neil by John Michael Wright in the late seventeenth century, and that of the earl of Denbigh in Indian dress by Van Dyck, underscored their decorative and exotic traits. Besides, in Wright's portraits, the personalities of the sitters were subdued as a number of copies were made which betrayed a loss of identity and the prominence of the image over the individual. This shift was a correlate of the flowering of Restoration culture particularly under James, duke of York.[87] Yet, an alternative view has emerged which connects the portrayed figures with new fashions resulting not so much in exotic individuals as cosmopolitan ones. Tartans in red and associated tones were associated with conspicuous consumption and translated as a marker of fashion and wealth.[88] This idea was reinforced in Gaelic praise poetry which dissociated the tartan garb of the Gaels from the black-coloured dress of the Lowlanders, again underscoring the interactions between the different fields of culture (pictorial, textual, etc.).[89] This repositioning should be seen in conjunction with the view of copying not as a 'mania' but as 'a central element of the aesthetic of late Stuart portraiture'.[90] Interestingly, the subsequent pictorial representation of the Highland elite continues to document their 'hybridising' integration into wider Scottish and British noble and gentry society. What stood out was the elegance and refinement of the outfit typical of the higher orders of society, albeit blended with Highland cloths and/or motifs. Unlike the vestiges of the figure of the savage/barbarian present in the said alleged portrait of Sir Donald Macdonald – seen for instance in the fur of his boots and facial hair – the depiction of Iain Breac, chief of the Macleods (died 1693), and John Michael Wright's *Sir Mungo Murray* (c. 1683) present a 'civilised' and gallant Gael.[91] This is a far cry from the group paintings of the Highlanders in the first half of the eighteenth century, presumably outside their personal control, when paintbrushes generally applied colours to perceived traitors and primitive peoples.[92]

Conclusion

Albeit expressed differently, the interplay between the Celtic and the classical continued into the late eighteenth century, in Macpherson's *Ossian* and Runciman's art, and is detectable through to the present day in artworks by Calum Colvin or the twenty-first-century project *An Leabhar Mòr/The Great Book of Gaelic*.[93] The early-modern pictorial discourse needs to be positioned within this historical continuum. Indeed, one could argue that the period from the late Middle Ages to the late eighteenth century set up an interface between political oppression and traditional culture which was fully exploited thenceforth by contemporary artists in a European dimension. In an echo to Saïd's Orientalism, the Celts had to deal with Gaelicism. Yet, this view silences the nuances and mixed visual messages projected by Scottish and British authorities unto their subjects in outlying areas.

Markers of ethnic or regional identity were hardly present at all in the architectural compositions and portraiture of men and women of the clan elite of the northern Highlands except, in the case of the latter, on the western seaboard.[94] These markers were most prominent in heraldic production instead. However pronounced or diluted they were, they coexisted with other markers of status, social etiquette, gender and visual conventions. Culturally speaking, the identity and integration of the northern Highlanders proceeded from these combined markers and aspirations. As a result, and as far as these visual aspects were concerned, these people demonstrated a rather mixed identity and culture that was at times hardly distinguishable from those of Lowlanders.[95] This evolutive socio-cultural process contained variations in terms of people, location, time, and pace, however.

An ongoing process of integration unravelled in the region, driven both from above and below, and the repercussions of which were felt across these clan communities. These cultural elements testified to their openness towards the outside world both in a forced way and through voluntary discovery and curiosity. Besides, women were fully active in this cultural dynamic. This exposition to a pre-existent albeit reinforced multiculturalism made, if not the alienation, at least the distancing between members of the elite and their clansmen even more acute to some degree. Socio-economic, legal, and political conditions further contributed to this phenomenon. This somewhat qualified the extent of the traditional communal culture on the ground. Indeed, the cultural opportunities available to these northern Highlanders fortified their kinship ties and, paradoxically, loosened them at the same time, as they created spaces for individual aspirations.

Notes

1. Gratitude is duly expressed to the late Professor Charles McKean, Mr David Sellar, and Professor Hugh Cheape for commenting on this article.
2. R. H. C. Teske and B. H. Nelson, 'Acculturation and assimilation: a clarification', *American Ethnologist* 1 (1974), 358–65; D. L. Sam, 'Acculturation: conceptual background and core components', in D. L. Sam and J. W. Berry (eds), *The Cambridge Handbook of Acculturation Psychology* (Cambridge, 2006), 17–18. For a logic-based critique of a four-fold paradigm of acculturation consult F. W. Rudmin, 'Critical history of the acculturation psychology of assimilation, separation, integration, and marginalization', *Review of General Psychology* 7 (2003), 3–9, 20–2, 25–9. In terms of definition, as far as assimilation is concerned, it denotes a dynamic process of interpenetration and fusion in which persons and groups are incorporated with other persons and groups in a common cultural life by mental and physical acquisitions and the sharing of experience. In other words, a dominant culture is favoured, in this case, the 'Lowland'/British one. But, because northern Highlanders possessed a number of basic features and cultural elements distinct from those of Lowlanders or other British people, the phenomenon can best be described as integration, i.e. the coexistence of two cultures, also known as partial assimilation. By setting the acculturation process of these communities within a pluralist perspective, it allows for the recognition of a cultural hybridity, namely the retention of one's original culture to some degree and the acquisition of new cultural elements, again to some extent. As a result, one can see a distinction between a rationale of assimilation which underlined crown policy, and the actual integration of a number of northern Highlanders on the ground, but as a process towards assimilation over the *longue durée*.
3. J. E. Wilson, 'Agency, narrative, and resistance', in S. Stockwell (ed.), *The British Empire: Themes and Perspectives* (Oxford, 2008), 245–68. For modern historians, agency represents 'the free capacity people have to do things for themselves'. This statement does not concern other fields, such as language and literature.
4. Admittedly, this is just one view, current at the time and found in the subsequent historiographical literature. This in no way reflects the more composite spectrum of perception/conception of northern Highlanders. Yet, in a sense, the article contributes to the presentation of this composite picture.

5. A. Williamson, 'Scotland and the rise of civic culture, 1550–1650', *History Compass* 4 (2006), 108–14.
6. A. H. Williamson, 'Scots, Indians and Empire: the Scottish politics of civilization, 1519–1609', *Past and Present* 150 (1996), 46–83; J. Leerssen, 'Wildness, Wilderness, and Ireland: medieval and early-modern patterns in the demarcation of civility', *Journal of the History of Ideas* 56 (1995), 30–1, 33–4, 38; S. Pinet, 'Walk on the Wild Side', *Medieval Encounters* 14 (2008), 368–89; E. J Cowan, 'The discovery of the Gàidhealtachd in sixteenth century Scotland', *Transactions of the Gaelic Society of Inverness* [*TGSI*] 60 (1997–8), 259–84; D. Chambre, *La Recerche des Singularitez plvs Remarqvables, Concernant l'Estat d'Escosse* (Paris, 1579), fos 1r-v, 24r-27r, 29v-30r. The origins of the myth of the 'wild man', relevant to that of the 'barbarian', are scintillatingly examined in R. Bartra, *Wild Men in the Looking Glass: The Mythic Origins of European Otherness* (Ann Arbor MI, 1994).
7. T. Brochard, 'The "Civilizing" of the Far North of Scotland. 1560–1640', unpublished PhD thesis (University of Aberdeen, 2011), ch. 6. The 'uncivil' Other was the foundation upon which the Aristotelian vision of society, Whig determinism, and the stadial theory of evolutionism were constructed.
8. J. MacInnes, 'The Gaelic perception of the Lowlands', in W. Gillies (ed.), *Gaelic and Scotland: Alba agus A'Ghàidhlig* (Edinburgh, 1989), 89–100. A fuller exposition of both views, which limited space prevents in this article, can be found in Brochard, 'Civilizing', ch. 6.
9. R. G. Nicholson, 'Domesticated Scots and Wild Scots: the relationship between Lowlanders and Highlanders in medieval Scotland', in *Proceedings of the First Colloquium on Scottish Studies* (s.l., 1968), 3–4; D. G. Adams, 'Some unrecognised depictions of the saffron shirt in Scotland', *Northern Studies* 30 (1993), 63–70.
10. San Marino CA, Huntington Library, William Bowyer, *Heroica Eulogia*, HM160, fo. 141, available at http://dpg.lib.berkeley.edu/webdb/dsheh/heh_brf?Description =&CallNumber=HM+160 (accessed 8 May 2009); G. A. Hayes-McCoy (ed.), *Ulster and Other Irish Maps, c. 1600* (Dublin, 1964), pl. xxiii; Edinburgh, National Library of Scotland [NLS], Robert and James Gordon's Manuscript Maps of Scotland, c.1636–1652, Adv. MS 70.2.10, the draught of Edera Cheules, G11, available at http://www.nls.uk/maps/counties/view/?id=3 (accessed 6 May 2009); S. K. Cohn, 'Highlands and Lowlands in late medieval Tuscany', in D. Broun and M. MacGregor (eds), *Mìorun Mòr nan Gall, 'The Great Ill-Will of the Lowlander'?: Lowland Perceptions of the Highlands, Medieval and Modern* (Glasgow, 2009), 110–12; R. B. Hagen. 'Seventeenth-century images of the true north, Lapland and the Sami', in K. Andersson (ed.), *L'Image du Sápmi* (Örebro, 2009), 143. Professor Hagen is thanked for providing a copy of his article. This beastly model is further present in pro-Union tracts: B. R. Galloway and B. P. Levack (eds), *The Jacobean Union: Six Tracts of 1604* (Edinburgh, 1985), 22.
11. Rome, Archivum Romanum Societatis Iesu [ARSI], Anglia, vol. xlii, fos 5–8; printed in M. J. Yellowlees, '*So Strange a Monster as a Jesuite': The Society of Jesus in Sixteenth-Century Scotland* (Isle of Colonsay, 2003), map between pp. 116 and 117 and transcript at pp. 182–3; M. J. Yellowlees, 'Father William Crichton's estimate of the Scottish nobility, 1595', in J. Goodare and A. A. MacDonald (eds), *Sixteenth-Century Scotland: Essays in Honour of Michael Lynch* (Leiden, 2008), 295–310; D. Shuger, 'Irishmen, aristocrats, and other white barbarians', *Renaissance Quarterly* 50 (1997), 503 n.32. Professor Peter Davidson deserves gratitude for this Jesuit reference.
12. For Professor Davidson, 'barbarorum' seems in some contexts to mean Gaelic-speaking and is not a value judgement. In this particular instance, the term's association with

'semiinermium' appears to be value-loaded. For parallels, see J. D. Selwyn, *A Paradise Inhabited by Devils: The Jesuits' Civilizing Mission in Early Modern Naples* (Aldershot, 2004), introduction and ch. 1. The denigration of people constitutive of the kingdom applied in the Swedish case against the Lapps: P. Burke, *Popular Culture in Early Modern Europe* (1978: Farnham, 2009), 152. MacGregor claims this irreligious strain to be apparently a post-1560 construct: M. MacGregor, 'Gaelic barbarity and Scottish identity in the later middle ages', in Broun and MacGregor, *Perceptions*, 36.

13. M. Lynch, 'Queen Mary's triumph: the baptismal celebrations at Stirling in December 1566', *Scottish Historical Review* 69 (1990), 6–10; T. Dickson et al. (eds), *Accounts of the Lord High Treasurer of Scotland* [*TA*], 13 vols (Edinburgh, 1877–1978), xii, 405–6; M. Wintroub, 'L'Ordre du rituel et l'ordre des choses: l'entrée royale d'Henri II à Rouen (1550)', *Annales: Histoire, Sciences Sociales* 56 (2001/2), 479–505; Williamson, 'Scots', 49–51, 53. The malleability of the model and its multi-polarity is evident in the connection not of Highlanders but of 'Scots and Irishmen ... Turks and Saracens' as the perceived backward and heathen races among European contemporaries: quoted in R. A. Houston, *Literacy in Early Modern Europe: Culture and Education, 1500–1800* (2nd edn, Harlow, 2002), 22.

14. J. Dawson, 'The Gaidhealtachd and the emergence of the Scottish Highlands', in B. Bradshaw and P. Roberts (eds), *British Consciousness and Identity: The Making of Britain, 1533–1707* (Cambridge, 1998), 288–9.

15. J. H. Burton et al. (eds), *The Register of the Privy Council of Scotland* [*RPC*], 38 vols (Edinburgh, 1877–1970), 2nd ser., v, 33, 36–7. Compare with the 1617 royal visit: H. M. Paton et al. (eds), *Accounts of the Masters of Works for Building and Repairing Royal Palaces and Castles*, 2 vols (Edinburgh, 1957–82), ii, xxi, 92.

16. R. Monpays, 'L'image du Languedoc chez les historiens de cette province au XVIIe siècle', *Annales du Midi* 110 (1998), 25–40; D. Newton, 'Borders and Bishopric: regional identities in the pre-modern north east, 1559–1620', in A. Green and A. J. Pollard (eds), *Regional Identities in North-East England, 1300–2000* (Woodbridge, 2007), 57–8.

17. E. Stróbl, 'The figure of the wild man in the entertainments of Elizabeth I', in Z. Almási and M. Pincombe (eds), *Writing the Other: Humanism versus Barbarism in Tudor England* (Newcastle upon Tyne, 2008), 59–78; G. von Bülow, 'Journey through England and Scotland made by Lupold von Wedel in the years 1584 and 1585', *Transactions of the Royal Historical Society*, new ser. 9 (1895), 258.

18. J. Stevenson and P. Davidson, 'Ficino in Aberdeen: the continuing problem of the Scottish Renaissance', *Journal of the Northern Renaissance* 1 (2009), 64–87.

19. *The Book of Record: A Diary Written by Patrick First Earl of Strathmore and Other Documents relating to Glamis Castle, 1684–1689*, ed. A. H. Millar (Edinburgh, 1890), 33. Thanks to Professor Hugh Cheape for this reference.

20. C. McKean, *The Scottish Chateau: The Country House of Renaissance Scotland* (2001: Stroud, 2004); D. Howard, *Scottish Architecture: Reformation to Restoration, 1560–1660* (Edinburgh, 1995); M. Glendinning et al., *A History of Scottish Architecture* (Edinburgh, 1996), chs 1–2. A brief yet balanced overview can be found in A. MacKechnie, 'Renaissance Scotland's martial houses', *History Scotland* 10, no. 5 (Sep./Oct. 2010), 48–54; 10, no. 6 (Nov./Dec. 2010), 36–43. The earlier, late-medieval tradition is illuminated in H. Cheape, 'Caisteal Bharraich, Dun Varrich and the wider tradition', *Northern Studies* 30 (1993), 53–62. Compare Scandinavian architectural composition: M. Davis, 'Some northern European comparisons for Scottish Renaissance tall-houses', *Architectural Heritage* 18 (2007), 2–3, 9–12.

21. McKean, *Chateau*, 17, 22, 81, 104, 122, 127, 195, 240.

22. Edinburgh, National Records of Scotland [NRS], Breadalbane Muniments, GD112/58/3/9; GD112/58/124/1; Howard, *Architecture*, 83–4. The location of other Caithness country seats was already *de facto* defensive: D. MacGibbon and T. Ross, *The Castellated and Domestic Architecture of Scotland from the Twelfth to the Eighteenth Century*, 5 vols (Edinburgh, 1887–92), iv, 297–8; W. Macfarlane (ed.), *Geographical Collections Relating to Scotland*, ed. A. Mitchell, 3 vols (Edinburgh, 1906–8), i, 165. On building contracts see D. Knoop and G. P. Jones, *The Scottish Mason and the Mason Word* (Manchester, 1939), 12–14.
23. NRS, GD112/58/4/1; Royal Commission on the Ancient and Historical Monuments and Constructions of Scotland [RCAHMS], *Third Report and Inventory of Monuments and Constructions in the County of Caithness* (London, 1911), 142; M. H. B. Sanderson, *Mary Stewart's People: Life in Mary Stewart's Scotland* (Tuscaloosa AL, 1987), 48–9; Howard, *Architecture*, 49–50, 55, 110. The viewing platform that capped the octagonal six-storey tower at Foulis can be dated, almost undoubtedly, to the late seventeenth century. On the fifth storey was the library with an admirable view: McKean, *Chateau*, 37, 74. It is rather telling that the contract was entered by both the earl and countess of Caithness and that only her signature was adhibited to the document.
24. Howard, *Architecture*, 58–60; NLS, Adv. MS 70.2.10, part of Rcs, G18; Rosse, G20; online at http://www.nls.uk/maps/counties/view/?id=4 and http://www.nls.uk/pont/specialist/gordon20.html (accessed 5 May 2009). Building works on the hall at Milntown are on record for 1627: Floors Castle, National Register of Archives for Scotland [NRAS] 1100/1353, the account of the rents of Milton, 1627. A sense of verticality is conveyed at Fairburn Tower and Ardvreck Castle: M. Salter, *The Castles of Western and Northern Scotland* (Malvern, 1995), 11, 75, 94; NLS, Pont Manuscript Maps of Scotland, c.1583–1614, Adv. MS 70.2.9, Pont 4v [Loch Assynt], online at http://maps.nls.uk/pont/specialist/pont04v.html (accessed 6 May 2009). Ordnance Survey makes a distinction between 'Milntown' for the country seat and 'Milton' for the area.
25. McKean, *Chateau*, 10. The old Cromarty Castle greeted the visitors with a monumental entrance with an overhead heraldic tablet and with the munificence of a broad balustraded flight of stairs: H. Miller, *Scenes and Legends of the North of Scotland or the Traditional History of Cromarty*, ed. J. Robertson (Edinburgh, 1994), 77.
26. Howard, *Architecture*, 49–50.
27. H. M. Meldrum, *Kilmuir Easter: The History of a Highland Parish* (Inverness, 1935), 12, 106; J. Gifford, *The Buildings of Scotland: Highland and Islands* (London, 1992), 430; G. Stell, 'Architecture and society in Easter Ross before 1707', in J. R. Baldwin (ed.), *Firthlands of Ross and Sutherland* (Edinburgh, 1986), 109. Architectural crossovers were also evident in the techniques of composition, such as was manifested for the renovations at Portmahomack church in the seventeenth century: M. Carver. *Portmahomack: Monastery of the Picts* (Edinburgh, 2008), 43–5.
28. H. G. Slade, 'Craigston Castle, Aberdeenshire', *Proceedings of the Society of Antiquaries of Scotland* [PSAS] 108 (1977), 274–5; H. G. Slade, 'The Gordons and the North-East, 1452–1640', in R. D. Oram and G. P. Stell (eds), *Lordship and Architecture in Medieval and Renaissance Scotland* (Edinburgh, 2005), 269–70; Edinburgh, RCAHMS, Grampian, Banff and Buchan, Craigston Castle, e.g. AB/562-3, AB/565-6; M. Bath, *Renaissance Decorative Painting in Scotland* (Edinburgh, 2003), 7, 17, 21–3, 147, 151–3, 155, 166, 185–90, 198–200. According to Professor Davidson, these panels could possibly represent *ars memorativa* and relate to Urquhart's 'studie hous': personal communication, 17 April 2010; NRS, Commissariot of Edinburgh, Register of Testaments, CC8/8/20, p. 400.

29. R. Miket and D. L. Roberts, *The Mediaeval Castles of Skye and Lochalsh* (1990: Edinburgh, 2007), xxvii–viii; Dunvegan Castle, Dunvegan Muniments, 3/4/25, 28, 47; R. C. MacLeod (ed.), *The Book of Dunvegan*, 2 vols (Aberdeen, 1938–9), i, xxxi, xxxiv. The Urquhart laird of Cromarty indulged in this roof-top *bon-ton* with handsomely carved pediments as a statement of wealth and prestige as did the cadet Angus Mackay of Bighouse at his newly-built residence, probably a small country-seat, at Kirkton in 1630: Howard, *Architecture*, 53–7; Slade, 'Craigston Castle', 275; E. Beaton, 'Bighouse and Strath Halladale, Sutherland', in J. R. Baldwin (ed.), *The Province of Strathnaver* (Edinburgh, 2000), 149–51, 169. There was a long tradition of west Highland carving that mixed Celtic elements and style with various non-Celtic art styles and designs and which continued well into the seventeenth century if not later: K. A. Steer and J. W. M. Bannerman, *Late Medieval Monumental Sculpture in the West Highlands* (Edinburgh, 1977), 4–5, 81; I. F. Grant, *The MacLeods: The History of a Clan* (1959: Edinburgh, 1981), 628.

30. RCAHMS, *Ninth Report with Inventory of Monuments and Constructions in the Outer Hebrides, Skye and the Small Isles* (Edinburgh, 1928), xlv, 100, 108, 126–7, 129, 187–8; RCAHMS, Canmore Database, available at http://canmore.rcahms.gov.uk/en/advanced/, Eilean Donan Castle (accessed 14 and 26 May 2009); J. Dunbar, 'The medieval architecture of the Scottish Highlands', in L. Maclean (ed.), *The Middle Ages in the Highlands* (Inverness, 1981), 53.

31. RCAHMS, Inverness-shire, Kisimul Castle, IND/82/5/P; G95690 PO; RCAHMS, Canmore Database, available at http://canmore.rcahms.gov.uk/en/advanced/, Castle Tioram and Dounreay (accessed 14 and 26 May 2009); *Discovery and Excavation in Scotland* (1998), 59; J. MacLeod, *Official Guide, Dunvegan Castle, Isle of Skye, Scotland* (2003: Dunvegan Castle, [2009?]), 11; D. H. Caldwell and N. A. Ruckley, 'Domestic architecture in the lordship of the Isles', in Oram and Stell, *Lordship*, 116. Samson argues against the mutual exclusiveness of strength and comfort: R. Samson, 'Tower-Houses in the Sixteenth Century', in S. Foster et al. (eds), *Scottish Power Centres from the Early Middle Ages to the Twentieth Century* (Glasgow, 1998), 135–6.

32. A. I. Macinnes, 'Scottish Gaeldom from clanship to commercial landlordism, c.1600–c.1850', in Foster, *Power Centres*, 165–6, 168–9; M. Bangor-Jones, *Historic Assynt* (Dundee, 2000), 4; G. Stell, 'Castle Tioram: a statement of cultural significance', unpublished statement prepared for Historic Scotland (2006), 52–3, 77. In 1573, within the master of Caithness' Braal country seat were superimposed (from the bottom up) a 'nedder hous', a 'lytill hall', a 'chalmer', and a 'galrie': NRS, Sinclair of Mey Papers, GD96/124.

33. Edinburgh, University Library [EUL], Carmichael-Watson Collection, CW132A, fos 33v-34v. The 'castle' tag probably only referred to a martial parapet required for reasons of nobility. The late Professor McKean provided the author with a water-colour reconstruction of Ormacleit.

34. Shuger, 'Irishmen', 503, 511.

35. Howard, *Architecture*, 110; Paton et al. (eds), *Accounts*, i, 188 (slates, 1535), 201, 232–4 (timber, 1538), 333 (slates, 1611); ii, 388 (slates, 1633); L. B. Taylor (ed.), *Aberdeen Shore Work Accounts, 1596–1670* (Aberdeen, 1972), 113, 115, 569–70, 572; A. Fenton, *The Northern Isles: Orkney and Shetland* (Edinburgh, 1978), 111–2, 160. The Balnagown Rosses commercially exploited their timber for the crown, perhaps on an occasional basis yet over a long period of time, especially in terms of providing masts for the English navy from the 1650s and as regards buildings projects in the 1660s and 1670s: T. C. Smout et al., *A History of the Native Woodlands of Scotland, 1500–1920* (Edinburgh, 2007), ch.

12; K. Newland, 'James Baine, His Majesty's master wright, c. 1630–1704: 'an honest and ingenuous spirit...', *Review of Scottish Culture* 24 (2012), 52–3.
36. *West Highland Notes & Queries* [*WHN&Q*] (Isle of Coll, 1988–), ser. 3, vol. 1 (Aug. 2000), 10–11; H. Cheape, 'Woodlands on the Clanranald estates: a case study', in T. C. Smout (ed.), *Scotland since Prehistory: Natural Change and Human Impact* (Aberdeen, 1993), 56, 58; Stell, 'Castle Tioram', 47. From the late seventeenth century, the Coigach estate would initiate the development of its coniferous assets, these becoming fully commercially exploited from the early eighteenth century: M. Clough, 'Early fishery and forestry developments on the Cromartie estate of Coigach, 1660–1745', in J. R. Baldwin (ed.), *Peoples and Settlement in North-West Ross* (Edinburgh, 1994), 235–42.
37. In October 1630, George Seaton, third earl of Winton, imported 9,000 slates to roof his seat near Haddington (East Lothian) at the cost of £200: Historical Manuscripts Commission [HMC] *Second Report of the Royal Commission on Historical Manuscript* (London, 1871), App. 199.
38. Paton et al. (eds), *Accounts*, ii, 313, 318; P. J. M. McEwan (ed.) *Dictionary of Scottish Art & Architecture* (Woodbridge, 1994), 476. Huntly's very tall and imposing great villa in Inverness would have been a fashion template for the region. His Fortrose pendant possibly appears in Slezer's view of the Chanonry (on the left): http://maps.nls.uk/slezer/view/?sl=43 (accessed 25 June 2013). The late Professor McKean provided these points and the reference.
39. For instance, the most impressive formula of staircases, that of the scale and platt stair, a Renaissance novelty with straight flight and landing, fashionable from the 1580s, can be found at Dounreay, Castle Leod (c. 1616), Redcastle (1640s), and at a 1679 house in Thurso: McKean, *Château*, 74; RCAHMS, *Third Report*, 116; Salter, *Castle*, 13, 85, 91, 108. Visual records do not seem to have survived for another Renaissance characteristic of interior decoration, namely lavish painted ceilings, as commissioned by David Ross of Balnagown (1644–1711) and his wife, Anne Stewart: RCAHMS, Ross and Cromarty, Balnagown Castle, RC/70, RC/71; M. R. Apted, *The Painted Ceilings of Scotland, 1550–1650* (Edinburgh, 1966), chs 4–5; Bath, *Decorative Painting*.
40. Howard, *Architecture*, 3–4, 106–7.
41. The last kings of Man and the Isles in the mid-thirteenth century were armigerous as, it would seem, were Ranald, son of Somerled (fl. c. 1200), ancestor of the Macdonalds and other families. The arms of Macleod of Dunvegan and of Macleod of Lewis, both of whom recognised the supremacy of the Macdonald lords of the Isles, appear in the fifteenth-century Armorial de Berry: David Sellar, personal communication, 4 July 2013.
42. A. W. Johnston and A. Johnston (eds), *Old Lore Miscellany of Orkney, Shetland, Caithness and Sutherland*, 10 vols (London, 1907–46), vii, 27.
43. NLS, Scottish Heraldry, Blazons of Scottish Arms by Sir James Balfour of Denmilne, 1630, Adv. MS 15.1.11, fo 34v; *Scottish Genealogist* 26, no. 1 (1979), 20. Even during periods of dissent with the Sutherland House, the Mackays' idiosyncratic heraldic displays could likewise be interpreted as an emancipation from the comital family.
44. A. M. Findlater, *Scots Armorials from Earliest Times to the Start of the Eighteenth Century or Aspilogia Scoticana* (s.l., 2006), 18–19, 21, 23, 41, 45, 51–3, 64. With similar rolls, like the so-called Hamilton Armorials, a number of heraldic achievements were replicated more or less faithfully within these interconnected works.
45. In 1571 Thomas Dingwall of Kildun had the Mackenzies' stag's head cabossed which, *inter alia*, ornamented his seal. Indeed, a 1546 seal was probably identical: W. R. Macdonald (ed.), *Scottish Armorial Seals* (Edinburgh, 1904), p. 73 no. 647; J. H. Stevenson and M.

Wood (eds), *Scottish Heraldic Seals: Royal, Official, Ecclesiastical, Collegiate, Burghal, Personal*, 3 vols (Glasgow, 1940), ii, 316; J. M. Munro and R. W. Munro, 'The Dingwalls of Kildun: a genealogy', *Clan Munro Magazine*, 11 (1969), 36–7.

46. Edinburgh, Lyon Office [LO], Porteus' Manuscript, MS33, p. 41, nos 33–4; Fraser's Funeral Escutcheons, MS6, fo. 79v, no. 1. The official register, begun in 1672, contained the coats of many cadet or minor families and individuals prior to 1700: R. Gayre and R. Gayre (eds), *Roll of Scottish Arms*, 2 vols (Edinburgh, 1964–9), i, 32–3, 53, 150, 216, 260–4, 290–1, 300, 302, 347–8, 366–9, 404.

47. In practice, individuals further down the social scale adopted the clan/family arms as recorded on carved tomb-slabs: NRS, Caithness Commissary Court Records, CC4/2/1, bundle '1628', testament of Margaret Crawford, 25 April 1628; A. Mackay, *The Book of Mackay* (Edinburgh, 1906), 279–82; W. R. Macdonald, 'The heraldry in some of the old churchyards between Tain and Inverness', *PSAS* 36 (1902), 689–90, 694, 702–6, 709–12. The graveyard of Kincardine parish possesses a number of flatstones incised with the heraldic Ross lion and the Munro eagle: A. S. Cowper et al. (eds), *Some Sutherland Burial Grounds, Pre-1855 Tombstone Inscriptions*, 15 vols (Edinburgh, 1979–87), xiii, nos 31, 45–6, 122, 149, and p. 22; xiv, nos 56, 191; xv, p. 2; A. S. Cowper et al. (eds), *Some Caithness Burial Grounds, Pre-1855 Tombstone Inscriptions*, 15 vols (Edinburgh, 1981–9), vii, 6 no. 2, 7 no. 4; viii, nos 153, 344; x, no. 65.

48. J. A. Goodall, 'An Illyrian armorial in the society's collection', *Antiquaries Journal* 75 (1995), 265–6; I. G. Tóth, *Literacy and Written Culture in Early Modern Central Europe* (Budapest, 2000), 158–9. In the 1630s, some forty native Irish families registered their pedigrees in the office of Ulster King at Arms, which underlined the accommodations between the central government's aspirations for social stability and the needs of the local elite for social recognition: R. Gillespie, 'Negotiating order in early seventeenth-century Ireland', in J. M. Braddick and J. Walter (eds), *Negotiating Power in Early Modern Society: Order, Hierarchy and Subordination in Britain and Ireland* (Cambridge, 2001), 195–6.

49. F. Gillespie, 'Heraldry in Ireland: an introduction', *Double Tressure* 23 (2000), 9, 13–15.

50. The misidentification of the Macneil coat dates from at least the early eighteenth century. Their armorial bearings are wrongly recorded prior to 1720 in relation to an event of the second half of the sixteenth century. The quartering given was First, Azure a lion rampant argent; Second, a right hand or fesse-ways couped gules holding a cross-crosslet fitchy azure in pale; Third, Or a lymphad sable; Fourth, parted per fesse argent and azure 'that represent the sea' out of which issueth a rock gules; supporters, two fishes 'like Salmons'. Interestingly, these arms do not have the nine fetterlocks which refer to the claimed descent from Niall Noígiallach ('of the nine hostages'). Several printed works of the eighteenth and nineteenth centuries replicated this error in that – unlike Sir David Lindsay's 1601 armorial and James Esplin's book of blazons of 1630 in which the (similar) achievement appears as 'Mackoneil Laird of Dunnivege & Glennes' and 'Lard of kentayre mak onil' – they mistook the arms of Macdonald of Dunivaig for those of Barra. Whereas this was a normal way to spell Macdonald at the time, this was not so for Macneil: London, British Library [BL], Histories of the Clan Mackenzie, Add. MS 40720(1), p. 341; LO, Seton Armorial, MS4A, no. 80; A. M. Findlater (ed.), *Lord Crawford's Armorial Formerly Known as the Armorial of Sir David Lyndsay of the Mount Secundus* (s.l., 2008), 230–1; L. Hodgson (ed.), *The Dublin Armorial of Scottish Nobility* (s.l., 2006), 140–1; A. Nisbet, *A System of Heraldry*, 2 vols (new edn, Edinburgh, 1816), i, 415–16; *Scottish Genealogist* 6, no. 1 (1959), 14–15; 36, no. 4 (1989), 125–6.

51. Similarly, flags used in the Dalmatian cities bore the image of their patron saint: Goodall, 'Armorial', 268.
52. For instance, two of the charges found in the heraldic achievement of the captain of Clanranald, the lion and the lymphad, were picked up by clan poets and singers and used, for example, as signature device in a waulking song in which *Le sìol Ailein nan long leòmhainn*, 'Ship and lion rule Clanranald' (literally, the seed of Alan of the ships and lions): J. L. Campbell and F. Collinson (eds), *Hebridean Folksongs*, 3 vols (Oxford, 1969–81), i, 62–3; R. W. Mitchell (ed.), *The Hague Roll* (Peebles, 1984), HR678; also A. Matheson, 'Poems from a manuscript of Cathal Mac Muireadhaigh', *Éigse* 11 (1964–6), 4, 6.
53. Goodall, 'Armorial', 267.
54. G. Ó Riain, 'Quatrains relating to the controversy of the Red Hand', *Ériu* 61 (2011), 171–8; R. F. Pye, 'The armory of the western Highlands', *Coat of Arms* 11 (1970), 3–8, 51–8; A. Campbell, 'A closer look at west Highland heraldry' *Double Tressure* 19 (1997), 46–67. For instance, the dexter hand appaumé gules found in the arms of the captain of Clanranald in the Hague Roll of 1592 ornamented the armorial achievements of the Lord of the Isles, Ulster families, and families across the northern half of Ireland: LO, MS33, p. 31; R. W. Mitchell (ed.), *Hector le Breton's Armorial* (Peebles, 1984), HBA70; A. Maxwell (ed.), *The Slains Roll: A Photographic Facsimile of a 16th Century Scots Armorial Roll* (Edinburgh, 2006), fo. 97; Gillespie, 'Heraldry', 11–12. It would be worth investigating the heraldry and seals of the period of the civil wars, since the clan chiefs on the western seaboard initially shunned the recruitment of Irish troops, as Macinnes has highlighted: A. I. Macinnes, *Clanship, Commerce and the House of Stuart, 1603–1788* (East Linton, 1996), 99–100.
55. W. McLeod, *Divided Gaels: Gaelic Cultural Identities in Scotland and Ireland, c. 1200–c.1650* (Oxford, 2004); D. S. Thomson, 'Gaelic learned orders and literati in medieval Scotland', *Scottish Studies* 12 (1968), 57–78.
56. The actual mechanics of the registration of these coats of arms are not known, whether it originated from the Lord Lyon and/or the heralds or from the persons who wanted these to be officially recognised: W. David H. Sellar, Lord Lyon King of Arms, personal communication, 7 April 2009. Nevertheless, the latter most probably were the originators of their heraldic achievements, if only for their choice of charges: NLS, Sutherland Papers, Dep. 313/491, no. 1778. The presence is evident of Lyon officials, such as James Law, Snawdoun herald, who is recorded in Cromarty in 1618: NRS, Particular Register of Sasines for Inverness, Ross, Sutherland and Cromarty, 1st ser., 1617–1660, RS37/1, fo. 66r.
57. Bartra, *Wild Men*, 2–3, 53–6, 63. For instance, the 1638 armorial known as Kings and Nobilities Arms II is the repository of 111 coats, twenty of which bore at least one savage (either as one or two supporters or in crest or both): LO, Kings and Nobilities Arms II, MS21. The heraldic use of savages is known in Scotland as early as the mid-fourteenth century in the seals of the earls of Dunbar: David Sellar, personal communication, 4 July 2013.
58. Brochard, 'Civilizing', ch. 6. This acerbic rhetoric varied in intensity, in its application, and with time.
59. LO, Pont's Manuscript, MS1, p. 4 no. 6, p. 14 no. 34; G. Mackenzie, *The Families of Scotland*, eds J. Irvine and J. Munroe (Edinburgh, 2008), 79; Bartra, *Wild Men*, 104–6, 138–40, 179–82, 192, and fig. 3 p. 5. The display of two demi-savages as supporters on the arms of the Lord of Lewis in 1566 is noticeable in this respect: LO, Forman-Workman's Roll, MS17, vol. 1, p. 37; vol. 5, p. 248; Kings and Nobilities Arms I, MS20, p. 67; J.

Malden and E. Malden (eds), *The Dunvegan Armorial* (s.l., 2006), 132–3; Findlater, *Lord Crawford's Armorial*, 222–3.

60. Tóth, *Literacy*, 158; H. G. Slade, *Old Cromarty Castle* (Cromarty, 1993), 21; http://www.scran.ac.uk/database/record.php?usi=000-100-000-368-C&scache=6a7 qpedkwv&searchdb=scran (accessed 12 August 2009); H. Tayler, *History of the Family of Urquhart* (Aberdeen, 1946), 54. Urquhart had three bears' heads for his shield but his arms on the panel were actually three boars' heads erased with two collared greyhounds as supporters: LO, MS1, p. 165.

61. NRS, Reay Papers, GD84/2/246, frontispiece. It is significant that, prior to Reay's time, the Mackay hand was displayed appaumé rather than associated with these sharp weapons: A. Mackay, 'An account of the Aberach-Mackay banner', *PSAS* 38 (1903–4), 527–32. On his 1623 targe, the hand does not grasp the sword: University of Glasgow, The Hunterian Museum, GLAHM C.72, online at http://www.huntsearch.gla.ac.uk/cgi-bin/foxweb/huntsearch/DetailedResults.fwx?collection=all&SearchTerm=C.72&mdaCode =GLAHM&reqMethod=Link (accessed 30 April 2010). Aonghas MacCoinnich is duly thanked for this reference.

62. NLS, James Workman's Armorial, Adv. MS 31.3.5, fo. 86r; and generally R. MacLeod, 'The Heraldry of Clan Macleod', *Double Tressure* 4 (1982), 22–3; *Clan Macleod Magazine* 9, no. 54 (1952), 6–10; NRS, Seaforth Muniments, GD46/14/22; W. D. H. Sellar and A. Maclean, *The Highland Clan MacNeacail (MacNicol)* (Lochbay, 1999), 8–11. David Sellar deserves gratitude for this last reference.

63. S. A. Nelson, '16th century Spanish grants of arms to Aztec and Tlaxcalan natives', *Double Tressure* 31 (2008), 2–6; Gayre and Gayre, *Roll of Scottish Arms*, i, 361. Seaforth used the Macleods of Lewis' mountain in flames in the crest and, as supporters, two savages whose batons and hair were also burning. Furthermore, the motto, *Luceo Non Uro*, 'I shine but do not burn', was reminiscent of the Macleods' 'I Burn While I See'.

64. Armadale, Clan Donald Centre Library, Lord Mcdonald Papers, GD221/5330/6/1; L. Macdonald, 'Gleanings from lord Macdonald's charter chest', *TGSI* 14 (1887–8), 78, and facsimile between pp. 74 and 75.

65. London, British Library, Seal of John Mackenzie of Gairloch, 1606, Seal, Detached, xlvii. 2317. The use of the thistle as a decorative architectural ornament is illustrated in Miller, *Scenes*, 77; Miket and Roberts, *Castles*, frontispiece. After 1603 the Tudor rose was another patriotic motif which further applied to architectural ornamentation. The emblems of the rose and the thistle manifested support for the Union and loyalty to the crown: Glendinning et al., *Architecture*, 30, 37, 40, 59.

66. The acceptance of the British 'civilising' agenda by some leading Highland chiefs can be found in A. I. Macinnes, *The British Revolution, 1629–1660* (Basingstoke, 2005), 49, 60–1; M. MacGregor, 'The Statutes of Iona: text and context', *Innes Review* 57 (2006), 159–61.

67. LO, MS1, p. 115; Gentlemen's Arms, MS22, fo. 72r, displays the arms of the Lewis Macleods according to the caption but actually bore the charge of the Harris clan, a castle argent.

68. The fact that Roderick Mackenzie of Coigach erected Castle Leod rather than Castle Kenneth is significant in the celebration of the Macleod ancestral heritage when compared to the Mackenzie one: MacLeod, 'Heraldry', 23. Oral tradition of the Sleat Macdonalds shared in that glorification of the ancestry of the Lewis Macleods: W. McLeod and M. Bateman (eds), *Duanaire na Sracaire Songbook of the Pillagers: Anthology of Scotland's Gaelic Verse to 1600* (Edinburgh, 2007), 456–7.

69. J. Woods-Marsden, 'The meaning of the European painted portrait, 1400–1650', in B. Bohn and J. M. Saslow (eds), *A Companion to Renaissance and Baroque Art* (Chichester, 2013), 442–62; L. Syson, 'Introduction', in N. Mann and L. Syson (eds), *The Image of the Individual: Portraits in the Renaissance* (London, 1998), 9–14 P. Bourdieu, 'The Forms of Capital', in J. G. Richardson (ed.), *Handbook of Theory and Research for the Sociology of Education* (New York, 1986), 241–58; R. Strong, *The English Icon: Elizabethan & Jacobean Portraiture* (London, 1969); M. Glozier, 'Clothing and the fashion system in early modern Scotland', *Journal of the Sydney Society for Scottish History* 3 (1995), 39–44. Beyond the depiction of the self, it is important to bear in mind that the individual is set within the collective as there was no distinction between the particular self and that person's societal role.

70. The portrait can be seen at Bunchrew House Hotel: R. K. Marshall, *Women in Scotland, 1660–1780* (Edinburgh, 1979), 58–9. Lady Frances Herbert, fourth countess of Seaforth, is depicted in mourning before Brahan Castle: Seaforth portraits in Fortrose Town Hall. Thanks to Aonghas MacCoinnich and Andrew McKenzie, personal communication, 26 June 2013.

71. J. L. Caw, *Scottish Portraits*, 2 vols (Edinburgh, 1903), i, 64–5, and pl. xxiv; attributed to George Jamesone in J. Bulloch, *George Jamesone: The Scottish Vandyck* (Edinburgh, 1885), 180–1; A. Pearson, 'Portraiture's Selves', in A. Pearson (ed.), *Women and Portraits in Early Modern Europe: Gender, Agency, Identity* (Aldershot, 2008), 1–13. As the countess of Bothwell, her apparel resembled, though in a less elaborate style, that worn at the time by Agnes, countess of Moray: Edinburgh, Scottish National Portrait Gallery [SNPG], Lady Jean Gordon, Countess of Bothwell, PG 870; R. K. Marshall, *Costume in Scottish Portraits, 1560–1830* ([Edinburgh], 1986), 8, 32.

72. Aberdeen University Library [AUL], Academic Portraits, undated, MS U591/2/1/16; D. Thomson, *The Life and Art of George Jamesone* (Oxford, 1974), 118. Jamesone's inflated reputation has been revised: D. Macmillan, *Scottish Art, 1460–2000* (Edinburgh, 2000), 58, 60–7. A pencil sketch of Elizabeth Gordon can be found in AUL, Papers of John Bulloch, MS 690, p. 49 inverted with p. 35. A portrait of Anna Mackenzie, daughter of Colin, first earl of Seaforth, and countess of Balcarres, shows her with curly hair, a pearl necklace and brooches, and a floral headband: private collection, courtesy of Andrew McKenzie; *Catalogue of the Inverness Exhibition of Art and Industry, Held in the Music Hall, September 1867* (Inverness, [1867]), p. 7, no. 10; NRS, GD46/15/6/38-9, transcript in GD46/15/6/40-3.

73. Seaforth portraits in Fortrose Town Hall. Andrew McKenzie, personal communication, 26 June 2013.

74. In October 1674, Sir George Mackenzie of Tarbat recruited the service of the Aberdeen portraitist and heraldic painter Patrick Alexander, for eight months and for 200 merks Scots: NRS, Cromartie Muniments, GD305/1/147/16; M. R. Apted and E. Hannabuss (eds), *Painters in Scotland, 1301–1700: A Biographical Dictionary* (Edinburgh, 1978), 22. The 'earle of cathnes', presumably George, sixth earl (ruled 1643–1676), commissioned the portraitist Isaac Visitella for four portraits worth £15 sterling and which were still with Visitella at the drawing up of his inventory in June 1657, prior to his death later that year. It suggests that these paintings were recently completed. The 'lord of mey', presumably Sir James Sinclair (died 1662), contracted him for one portrait worth £2 10s sterling: NRS, CC8/8/69, p. 163; Apted and Hannabuss, *Painters*, p. 99.

75. At the time of his death in 1651, George, second earl of Seaforth, possessed a collection of at least 64 portraits. But with a collective value of £64, the rationale behind such a collection could not have been financial but rather of a familial, social, and/or artistic

nature: NRS, Smythe of Methven Papers, GD190/2/212. In December 1622, Sir John Sinclair of Greenland left in his will to his son Thomas 'certane broades of emperioures pictoures': NRS, CC4/8/1, fo. 4r.

76. NRS, GD305/1/147/16; W. Fraser (ed.), *The Earls of Cromartie*, 2 vols (Edinburgh, 1876), ii, 434; W. Fraser (ed.), *The Sutherland Book*, 3 vols (Edinburgh, 1892), i, v. Well-bred ladies bequeathed pictures in their will as heirlooms for the family: Fraser, *Sutherland Book*, i, 203, 278.

77. Fraser, *Earls of Cromartie*, i, facing p. xlviii and facing p. liv; J. Holloway, *Patrons and Painters: Art in Scotland, 1650–1760* (Edinburgh, 1989), 14–15; D. Bentley-Cranch, 'Effigy and portrait in sixteenth-century Scotland', *Review of Scottish Culture [ROSC]* 4 (1988), 16–19; SNPG, Archibald Campbell, first marquess of Argyll, PG 1408; L. L. Knoppers, 'The Politics of Portraiture: Oliver Cromwell and the plain style', *Renaissance Quarterly*, 51 (1998), 1283–1319.

78. Fraser, *Sutherland Book*, i, facing p. 171; facing p. 209; http://www.scran.ac.uk/database/record.php?usi=000-000-057-500&searchdb=scran (accessed 27 August 2009); S. Maxwell and R. Hutchison, *Scottish Costume, 1550–1850* (London, 1958), 46-7. One can compare the costume of the thirteenth earl (died 1615) with those worn in the portraits of Sir Nathaniel Bacon and Sir Robert Bruce Cotton in London, National Portrait Gallery [NPG], NPG 2142; NPG 534. The thirteenth earl's brother, Sir Robert Gordon, was painted in 1621, prior to his renewed appointment at court, by an unknown artist: SNPG, Sir Robert Gordon, PG 1513; and compare with the portrait of Henry de Vere, eighteenth earl of Oxford, in NPG, NPG 950.

79. Portraits in Fortrose Town Hall; Andrew McKenzie, personal communication, 26 June 2013; E. Waterhouse, *Painting in Britain, 1530 to 1790* (New Haven CT, 1994), ch. 6. Art sales websites further record Seaforth portraits by Nathaniel Hone the younger and Thomas van der Wilt as well as a portrait of Sir Robert Munro, sixth baronet (died 1746), by William Aikman: e.g. http://artsalesindex.artinfo.com/asi/search.action (accessed 18 June 2013). This highlights the greater prevalence of portraiture in the area.

80. SNPG, George Mackenzie, first earl of Cromarty, PG 304; Sir George Mackenzie of Rosehaugh, PG 834; London, National Army Museum [NAM], NAM 1961-06-9-1.

81. T. B. Howell and T. J. Howell (eds), *Cobbett's Complete Collection of State Trials and Proceedings for High Treason and Other Crimes and Misdemeanors from the Earliest Period to the Present Time*, 34 vols (London, 1809–28), iii, col. 486.

82. Portrait in Fortrose Town Hall; D. G. Thompson, 'In the Footsteps of Sir William Gunn', *Gunn Herald* (Mar. 1999), 12; S. Stevenson, 'Armour in seventeenth-century portraits', in D. H. Caldwell (ed.), *Scottish Weapons and Fortifications, 1100–1800* (Edinburgh, 1981), 345–76. Andrew McKenzie is thanked for his suggestion that the portrait was possibly intended to represent George, second earl of Seaforth.

83. NPG, Sir Thomas Urquhart, D27904; T. Maitland (ed.), *The Works of Sir Thomas Urquhart of Cromarty, Knight* (Edinburgh, 1834), xxiv, 297b.

84. An engraving of Sir William Gunn, of humble origin and later imperial baron, has been recently traced to Germany: Thompson, 'William Gunn', 12–18.

85. A. Macdonald and A. Macdonald, *The Clan Donald*, 3 vols (Inverness, 1900–4), iii, facing p. 54. The same martial ethos was present in monumental sculpture: R. A. Dodgshon, *From Chiefs to Landlords: Social and Economic Change in the Western Highlands and Islands, c.1493–1820* (Edinburgh, 1998), 92.

86. J. Philip, *The Grameid: An Heroic Poem Descriptive of the Campaign of Viscount Dundee in 1689 and Other Pieces*, ed. A. D. Murdoch (Edinburgh, 1888), 122–57.

87. SNPG, Lord Mungo Murray, PG 997; NPG, William Feilding, first earl of Denbigh, D28209; London, Tate Gallery, Sir Neil O'Neill, T00132; J. Fenlon, 'John Michael Wright's "Highland laird" identified', *The Burlington Magazine* 130, no. 1027 (Oct. 1988), 767–9; S. Stevenson et al., *John Michael Wright, the King's Painter* ([Edinburgh], 1982), ch. 2. An exotic Indian parallel directly modelled on Wright's is found in K. R. Muller, 'From palace to longhouse: portraits of the four Indian kings in a transatlantic context', *American Art* 22, no. 3 (Fall 2008), 26–49.
88. H. Cheape, '*A' lasadh le càrnaid*: rhyme and reason in perceptions of tartan', *Journal of the Scottish Society for Art History* [*JSSAH*] 13 (2008–9), 33–8.
89. MacInnes, 'Gaelic perception', 94–5.
90. R. Nicholson, 'Patronage and portraiture of the exiled Stuarts', *JSSAH* 3 (1998), 2–7. Illustrative of this are the Mackenzie prints found in the Fitzwilliam Museum: http://www.fitzmuseum.cam.ac.uk/ (accessed 24 June 2013).
91. SNPG, PG 997; T. McCaughey, 'Bards, Beasts and Men', in D. Ó Corráin et al. (eds), *Sages, Saints and Storytellers* (Maynooth, 1989), 105–6. In the same vein is the painting of Charles Campbell of the Glenorchy branch (died 1632/3) accoutred in the latest cosmopolitan fashion with no visible Highland element, his coat of arms notwithstanding: Skoklosters slott, Skokloster, inventarienummer 2263, online at http://emuseumplus.lsh.se/eMuseumPlus, s.v. 'Karl Kammel' (accessed 7 June 2013). Steve Murdoch is thanked for this reference. See also Marshall, *Costume*, 12.
92. The pictorial rehabilitation of the Highlanders came in the late eighteenth and early nineteenth centuries: M. Amblard, 'Du rebelle au héros: les highlanders vus par les portraitistes des Lowlands entre 1680 et 1827', *Études Écossaises* 11 (2008), 193–205.
93. M. Macdonald, 'Art as an expression of northernness: the Highlands of Scotland', *Visual Culture in Britain* 11 (2010), 355–71; http://www.leabharmor.net/ (accessed 3 June 2013).
94. A larger body of portraiture from the area is necessary to establish firmer claims either way.
95. That commonality of culture can be found across many aspects of life, such as everyday clothing comparable in style and fashioning: M. Kane, 'Covered with such a cappe: the archaeology of Seneca clothing, 1615–1820', *Ethnohistory* 61 (2014), 1–25; A. S. Henshall and W. A. Seaby, 'The Dungiven Costume', *Ulster Journal of Archaeology*, 3rd ser., 24–25 (1961–2), 119–42.

NORTHERN MAPS: RE-NEGOTIATING SPACE AND PLACE IN THE NORTHERN ISLES AND NORWAY IN THE EIGHTEENTH CENTURY[1]

SILKE REEPLOEG

Introduction

In a 2010 public lecture, 'Loss and Gain: The Social History of Knowledge, 1750–2000',[2] Peter Burke pointed out just some of the significant social processes that have taken place since the mid-eighteenth century in Europe and the world. Reform, quantification, secularisation, professionalisation, democratisation, nationalisation, globalisation and technologisation have all played an important part in the way knowledge has been constructed.[3] This statement relates very well to what happened to maps and mapping in Northern Europe during the eighteenth century. The relationship between representations and descriptions of place changed, influenced by the images and activities of map-making as a cultural and historical practice, and the political and social context of the period, particularly the European Enlightenment.[4] Landscapes were quantified and re-arranged visually, via the map and chart. Nature and landscape, no longer seen solely as God's creation and subject to his will, became secular spaces and human territory, providing resources and wealth for humanity, and the basis for the creation of individual and communal identities.[5]

This article argues that cartography and topographical description played a significant role in the way in which areas of the Scottish Northern Isles were represented and visualised, as a regional space, after the political union of England and Scotland in 1707, and, alongside that, the development of the concept of a British state and nation.[6] Not only did topographical literature become more professionalised and commercially-oriented during the eighteenth century, but the visual representations of territories created in maps and charts became part of a network of cultural practices that both linked and divided historical regions across the British Isles. On the one hand, map-making re-negotiated national spaces in order to contribute to the formation the United Kingdom or Great Britain (itself a complex national entity) and, on the other hand, it provided an opportunity to re-create a sense of place or Northern regional identity, continuing to be part of an intercultural Northern European maritime region linked by the North Sea.[7] As can be seen in the following case studies from the Shetland Islands and Western Norway, at 'image level',[8] the change in perceptions about a region's identity (or one's own, within that region), often follows a long process, 'since shifts in the attitudes of mental mapping tend to slowly follow changes in political and social conditions, mixing with philosophical and aesthetic conventions of the time'.[9]

Re-negotiating Space and Place

The histories of the Northern European regions, which became absorbed into national and imperial territories during the eighteenth and nineteenth centuries,[10] and the internal and external colonisation processes that took place during that time, have their beginnings in previous European aristocratic regimes. By examining the complex beginnings of national histories, we can see what it meant to become part of zones and territories on a larger scale, part of a realignment of Northern European boundaries and geo-political spaces.[11]

As part of this dynamic, there are many differences, but also important parallels, that can be found between Norwegian and Scottish national histories. Both countries, for example, share the experience of becoming part of a larger geo-political entity in this period, respectively, the Dano-Norwegian Kingdom and the British Empire.[12] Regarding the latter, Scotland became part of the governance zone of the United Kingdom of Great Britain from 1707, prior to which three separate kingdoms and parliamentary systems had functioned: in England, Scotland and Ireland.[13] In England, political representation was also expressed in a number of 'important local assemblies, in the City of London, in Cornwall, in Wales, in the Isle of Man, and in the Channel Islands'.[14] Norway, equally, had been an independent kingdom from 900–1030 AD, after which it became, first, part of the Kalmar Union (1396–1523), then experienced union with Denmark (1523–1814), and Sweden (1814–1905), emerging as an independent nation-state only in the twentieth century.[15] From a Danish perspective, the integrating state or *helstat* aimed towards the Oldenburg state-model, which meant consolidating smaller administrative districts or territories into one 'whole'.[16] From a Norwegian viewpoint, this meant a political programme of centralising power in Denmark, rather than Norway. Dano-Norwegian integration or homogenisation strategies also coincided with a global period of mercantilism, which saw economic gain increasingly 'professionalised', as a way to wealth and power (rather than passed on through aristocratic inheritance).[17] Both within and outwith Europe, regions became primarily a source of economic resources for centralised governments, with political interests complicit in growing internal and external colonialism.[18]

In Scotland, this makes for a complex historical and political background, with its incorporation as the region of 'North Britain' in the growing British Empire between the eighteenth and early twentieth centuries, and with Scots taking up important positions, both at home and, abroad, as imperial colonisers.[19] The eighteenth century is therefore a period in which perceptions about Northern European territories were transformed from them being viewed as peripheral and under-explored areas to them becoming spaces allowing for commercial and political expansion. This was both a scientific and cultural process that incorporated peripheries into a new, national 'mental map' which, in turn, shaped ideas and concepts about both places and the people inhabiting them.[20] Map-making and cartography, then, clearly form part of a series of cultural and political negotiations that organised landscapes and peoples into their respective national and regional territories. However, the history of eighteenth-century mapping begins with two diverging ideas about the role of landscape and place: the pictorial and human. Both had a significant impact on map-making in Britain and the Nordic countries, with different polities created around the concepts of 'land' and 'landscape'.

The History of the Map and the Landscape Polity

Human geographer Kenneth Olwig has traced the fundamental differences that developed between continental and British landscape geography, on one hand, and its Nordic equivalent, on the other, in terms of their related 'landscape polities'.[21] Using the work of two prominent nineteenth-century geographers, Frederik Schouw (1789–1852) and Henrik Steffens (1773–1845), Olwig illustrates the way in which two very different polities 'perceive and conceptualise landscape'.[22] Whereas Steffens supported the idea that societies or nations were determined by nature (and the continental 'blood-and-soil' nationalisms that grew out of this environmental determinism), for Schouw the Nordic landscapes 'have more in common between them, culturally and socially, than the nation-states that divide them'.[23] Inspired by the German Romantic movement, Steffens brought these ideas back to Denmark, and 'gave expression to an emerging concept of landscape as pictorial scenery, built up in layers, as on a stage, in which nature is the foundation of culture.'[24] For Steffens, nature provided the foundation and platform on which human existence was played out, a 'scenic space' where 'nature and culture were bound into a single national unity'.[25] Two different modes of representations of landscape had developed from the Renaissance onwards, and with it the emerging differentiation between the *Land* (regent plus people) and the *Landschaft* or landscape (represented by the state). As Olwig states: 'The scenic/pictorial representation of landscape emerged from the need of the state of the monarch/prince to represent its legitimacy in a way that could compete with the representative polity of the "*Landschaft*"/landscape.'[26]

The pictorial approach was supported by the emerging science of geology, but was also transmitted and reinforced by cultural production such as cartography. Mapping technology, such as the surveying and construction of pictorial representations of the map, chart and atlas, 'further contributed to the impression of godlike rule cultivated by Renaissance rulers through the use of such "landscape" representations as the backdrop for theatrical productions'.[27] Pictorial approaches used landscape scenery to 'represent and legitimate state power'.[28] Olwig sees the development of surveying and mapping techniques as part of the processes that map and regulate the 'land' under the regent's domain into regions. For him, this 'facilitated a transition in the meaning of *land* and *landscape* from designations for a polity, to the designation of a geometric area of territory or property (as in six acres of *land*) owned by the individual regent or one of his minions'.[29] According to Olwig, the geometric mapping of territory set the scene for a monolithic nation-state, while Steffens' reconfiguration of the conception of landscape is itself an imagined pictorial unity of citizens and nation, which was also used 'to visualise Britain as a physical geographical body, equivalent to the body politic of the regent, under him as its head of state'.[30] As noted by Olwig, this particular conceptualisation of landscape as a national territory gained further influence, particularly in the English-speaking world, through Carl Sauer. Subsequent writers such as George Perkins Marsh, Yi-Fu Tuan and David Lowenthal, on the other hand, argued for an emphasis on human agency, rather than environmental determinism.[31]

Following Schouw, the Nordic conceptualisation resisted such a drive for a monolithic landscape or national territory, arguing instead for a unity of natural landscapes across national borders. The 'Nordic' approach to geography, which Olwig identifies with Schouw, 'is characterised by a concern with history, custom/law, and language and culture as they work together in forming a landscape polity and its geographic place'.[32] This means that there is no foundational environment that determines national territories or societies. Instead, landscapes and cultural spaces are created and continuously re-negotiated by human activities and (social and economic) policies. The 'Nordic' historical approach to landscape is concerned with settlement patterns, administrative divisions and legal traditions, which can cross national state boundaries, and consciously engage with the ideological constructions of landscapes over time. Embedded within this perspective of landscape is the view that 'the history of Norden precedes that of the modern Nordic states, and transcends the boundaries of those states'.[33]

It is important to keep these two models of constructing and perceiving landscape in mind when comparing examples of national and regional maps in Northern Europe during the eighteenth century. Both an impetus towards presenting a unitary nation-state through pictorial landscape mapping and the counter-hegemonic practice of detailed topographical description are evident. As types of knowledge, maps are then examples of what Peter Burke calls systems of 'countervailing trends – the coexistence and interaction of trends in opposite directions', which often occur during periods of social and political change.[34] The re-negotiation of space and place is thus not merely geographical, but also

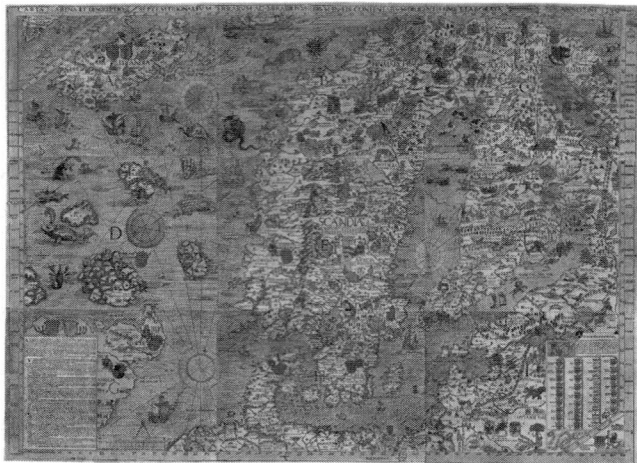

Figure 1. The 1539 Carta Marina by Olaus Magnus. James Ford Bell Library, University of Minnesota (available at: http://bell.lib.umn.edu/map/OLAUS/indexo.html).

has a political and ideological function. Jouni Häkli refers to this process as the production of 'discursive structures of territoriality'[35] which function as features of modern state government, where 'territoriality has become the privileged form of organisation, and geographical imagination'.[36] This process can be evidenced using historical maps and charts which, over time, have constructed, altered and re-contextualised territories, in order to accommodate social, political and cultural changes.

Northern Maps in Nordic History: A Case Study

An interesting example of how historical maps shape our ideas about cultural and historical territories is the *Carta Marina* by Olaus Magnus published in Rome in 1539.[37] It is one of the earliest maps of the Nordic region, and shows the Scottish Northern Isles of Orkney and Shetland (*Vesterhavsoyene*) as part of a Nordic geography (implying continuing historical and political links). It is a geographical statement, then, a piece of the world reduced to a flat depiction, but it is also a work of the imagination. The map records the 'marvels of the North' (including folklore, ethnographic information and history) as a piece of geographical art, designed to hang on the wall for display of ownership and control of space. However, as a visual (and perhaps also patriotic) record of the North, it also provides a particular discursive perspective on Nordic territory and boundaries, with parts of mainland Northern Scotland only just making it on to the map's bottom left-hand corner. As an example of a particular geographical imagination, the *Carta Marina* contains a mixture of fact and fiction, with topographical and territorial features neatly combined with a variety of religious, political and cultural information. Trading links and sites are shown via the presence of Hanseatic vessels navigating the Baltic, North Sea and North Atlantic oceans, while mythological and folkloric creatures are also added to enhance a visual seascape and landscape that are both real and imaginary.[38]

As an 'imagined evocation of space', the *Carta Marina* provides a visual narrative of Northern places, merging history, art and geography.[39] This multi-layered approach informs the (southern) audience about Northern spaces that are not empty wastelands, but full of people and unique regional cultures.[40] As an example of a macro-regional map, the *Carta Marina* depicts the Orkney and Shetland Islands as large island groups, perhaps of greater importance than the Scottish mainland, which is hidden behind a descriptive panel. And, although not containing any great topographical detail, the archipelagos' main harbours and some ecclesiastical buildings are shown. The islands are clearly still part of a Nordic cultural space, as imagined by Magnus, expressing a mental map that has not yet adjusted to a change in the geo-political situation, with both Shetland and Orkney becoming part of Scotland in the late fifteenth century.

Indeed, affinities and links with Nordic places have continued since, particularly during and since revivals of Scandinavian cultural identity in the islands during the late nineteenth and early twentieth centuries.[41] However, many historians have argued that, for example, Shetland's cultural links with Norway, together with its Nordic identity, rapidly diminished after the islands' transfer from the Norwegian to the Scottish kingdom or, in line with an increased acculturation or 'Scottification', even before then.[42] This view corresponds to Steffen's conception of landscape and geography as an imagined, pictorial unity, which visualises nation states as physical, geographical bodies, with determined cultural and political boundaries.

With the rise of nation-state government administration during the eighteenth and nineteenth centuries and national interests polarising research into neat, state-set borders, it became an accepted practice to isolate cultural and historical studies within static national or regional borders. Subsequent social, political and cultural historians have generally respected established political or linguistic boundaries, with cultural identity often hinged upon 'belonging' to one or the other homogenous nation-state, ethnic group or language area. This means a corresponding strengthening or weakening of perceived cultural connections to and from a homogenous centre or 'mother country' over time. In terms of belonging to a British national territory, and as noted by Hance Smith in a 1984 book, *Shetland Life and Trade 1550–1914*, this approach has 'led some authors to believe that Shetland – and indeed Scotland – did not emerge from the Middle Ages until [the Act of Union] 1707!'.[43] A national-historical perspective on the Northern Isles is, of course, by no means restricted to Britain. Norwegian history books mention Orkney and Shetland in a medieval context, or during 'the migration of the Northmen', but then cease to refer to non-Scandinavian links at all due to what is referred to as post-medieval 'territorial consolidation'.[44]

Both regions and islands are thereby subsumed under separate national polities (and historiographies) – and with them an intercultural history that connects both landscapes and people. However, by comparing eighteenth century topographical and cartographic vocabularies on both sides of the North Sea, it is possible to trace how, through co-existing, countervailing trends of geography and chorography, Scotland and Norway become two very different places.[45]

Countervailing Trends: The Role of Chorography

Chorography, or the writing about place (from the Greek *khoros* = place, *graphein* = writing), is the geographical description of regions. The geographer, Ptolemy, for example, could be considered a chorographer.[46] Chorographical practice and vision were revived during the fifteenth century, referring both to the descriptions of particular regions and visual representations of place through mapping.[47] Chorography, as a description of place, therefore remained separate to chronology, which is the description of time. In the English-speaking world, chorography came to be associated with antiquarian descriptions and reports, but also county or provincial maps. Maps and illustrations of landscapes often accompanied antiquarian and topographical descriptions as visual representations of place. Embedded in a descriptive practice, rather than documents by themselves, maps often accompanied a more detailed report or description of a particular place. They added a visual narrative to the topographical text, even if many maps were also separated from the description and appeared in published map collections such as atlases. During the seventeenth and eighteenth centuries, the term chorography was slowly superseded by terms such as topography or cartography, although its 'characteristic approach remained current and relevant'.[48] So, for example, Samuel Johnson's 1755 dictionary already makes a distinction between geography, chorography and topography, defining chorography as 'the art or practice of describing particular regions, or laying down the limits or boundaries of particular provinces' stating that it 'is less in its object than geography, and greater than topography'.[49] Darrel Rohl argues that 'chorographic thinking' continued.[50] Although the term eventually disappeared, chorographic practices and ideas were retained, especially in the activities of eighteenth-century naturalists and antiquarians, who produced maps as part of a series of chorographical activities, such as the publications of travel accounts and journals of tours. Rohl argues that:

> As the definition adopted here states, chorography is at its most basic level about the *representation of space/place*. This fundamental focus on 'representation' suggests and leads to an inherently *multi-media* approach, including written description, multiple modes of visualization, and performance.[51]

The history of different modes of mapping is worth returning to when comparing Dano-Norwegian and Scottish examples of what look like, but are not always defined as, chorographical motivations and practices. So, for example, when chorographic ideas are applied to coastal regions such as the Northern Isles, it becomes apparent that there are two types of coastal landscapes: the land-based topographical description or *Beskrivelse* of the landscape, and the coastal report or *Beretning* of the seascape or 'sailscape' of the ocean.[52] Both arrange spatial information in different ways, but are similar in their objectives, which is to provide detailed descriptions of place. During the eighteenth century this, increasingly, became carried out as part of a professionalised system of state governance, and in line with the consolidation of national territories. In addition, advances in printing technology meant that maps previously only accessible to a few people such as monarchs became increasingly visible to larger, professional groups of people (both administrative and military) tasked with the establishment and defence of territories.[53] The development of both land-based maps and nautical charts therefore relates to the development of a standardised, scientific practice, but is also motivated by political interests.

Arranging the Sea: The Nautical Chart

Mapping is not restricted to land-based territories, of course. By definition, maritime maps or charts play a significant role in the re-negotiation of coastal spaces and places too.[54] Nautical charts, during the eighteenth century, were often accompanied by a narrative or description, usually sailing directions, which contain information on water depth and places to anchor. In terms of arranging and re-negotiating space and landscape, from the eighteenth century regional charts, like maps, feature an interesting mixture of cultural, topographical and antiquarian information. The eighteenth century navigational chart (Figure 2) is already the result of semi-professional, usually state-sponsored, scientific investigations and measurements. Significantly, sea-charts are very much seen as international documents, which are constantly subject to corrections from a variety of international sources. So, for example, this official chart gives an overview of the North Sea and the Kattegat, the sea channel between Denmark's Jutland peninsula and Sweden's coastal provinces of Västergötland, Scania, Halland and Bohuslän.

The chart draws on information from a French chart published in 1777, and in London in 1796, showing the area from the Straits of Dover to the Shetland Islands and North Bergen in Norway, and east through the Kattegat to Copenhagen.[55] It is in a modern Portolan style, also known as a harbour-finding chart, compass chart, or rhumb chart, meaning a navigational chart characterized by rhumb lines, or lines that radiate from the centre in the direction of wind or compass points. These were used by pilots to lay courses from one harbour to another, which means that instead of an empty sea, the ocean contained descriptions of the sea base, some fishing grounds and, of course, coastal placenames including harbours. Following an international approach, the chart shown includes an example of

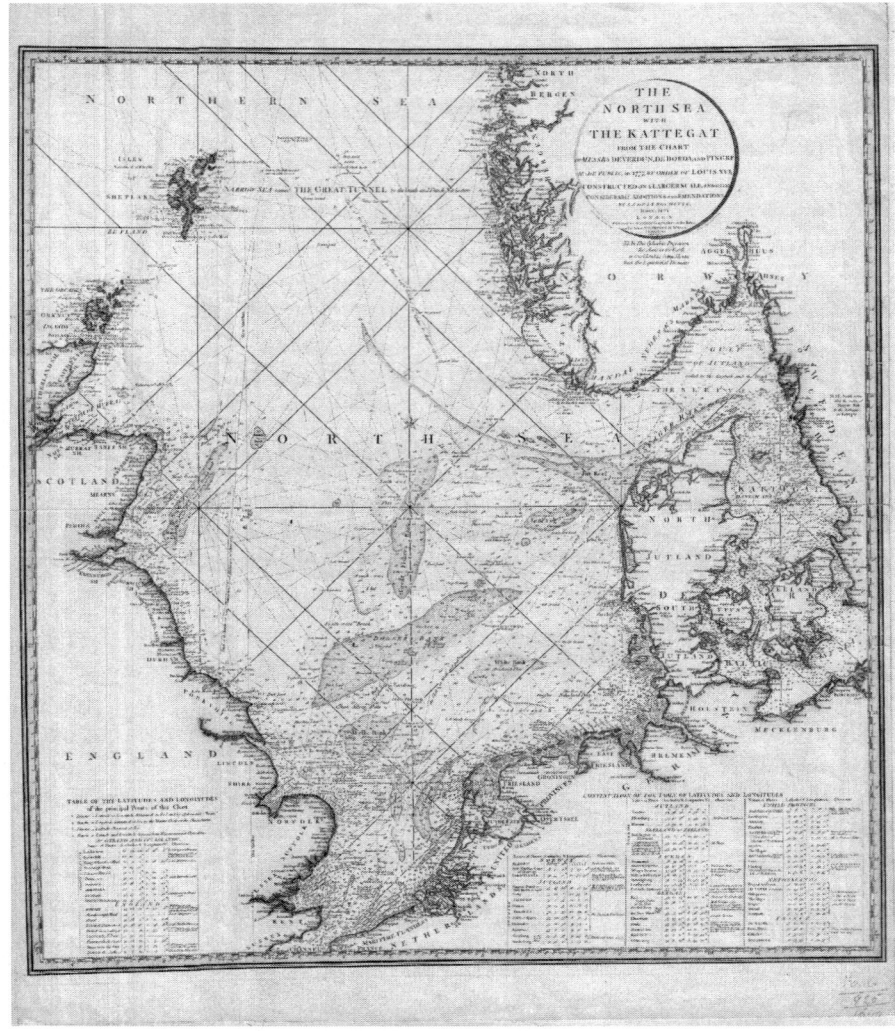

Figure 2. T. Foot, *Sjøkart over Nordsjøen og Kattegat, fra 1796* (map). Stavanger, Statens kartverk Sjø. (available at: http://commons.wikimedia.org/wiki/File:Sj%C3% B8kart_over_Nordsj%C3%B8en_og_Kattegat,_fra_1796.png).

multiple placenames for the same landscape feature, with the landmass projecting out from Mandal in the south-western corner of Norway named 'Lindesness' being 'called by the Dutch and French THE NAZE' (Figure 2). It also contains extensive tables and annotations, and shows soundings, banks, shoals, towns, islands, harbours, bays and other sailing details. So, what, to a land-based map maker, would be a boundary to the land, to the North Sea navigator is arranged into defined spaces and places, that are named with all the information currently available to seafarers. Just as with regional maps, regional coastal charts arrange the sea around the land, providing a visual seascape, as well as practical instructions and visual clues such as sailing directions and coastal profiles. These accompany the chart separately, or are incorporated into a multi-layered visual statement such as the example below of a detailed regional chart of the Shetland Islands.

The marine chart of the Shetland Islands shown in Figure 3 combines several views and types of charts and maps, offering more information about the sea and navigation, but also about landscape features and areas of interest for fishing. It was produced by Captain Thomas Preston, a professional navigator and surveyor, as *A New Hydrographical Survey of the Islands of Shetland* (1781). In contrast to our Dano-Norwegian example (Figure 4), it was sponsored by private chart publishers Robert Sayer and John Bennett, rather than the state or crown. The rich content of the chart includes an interesting feature no longer displayed on charts: the coastal profile. Added to the sides of the chart, coastal profiles show prominent landscape features as seen when approaching by sea, which were also added to our next example, the *Beretning om et Forbedret Kaart over de Hetlandske Öer, tilligemed trende blade med landtoninger og et speciel kaart over Valey-Sund paa Hetland* published by the Royal Naval Charts Archive or Kongelige Sjø-kaarte Archiv in Copenhagen in 1787 (Figure 4).

Landtoninger: Coastal Profiles

Coastal profiles on charts were often copied from one chart to another. So, for example, the coastal profiles of the islands of Shetland seen on Preston's map (Figure 3) were transferred (as separate pages) to the Danish chart and coastal description, the *Beretning om et Forbedret Kaart over de Hetlandske Öer* (Figure 4). This *Beretning* or report was compiled by Captain-Lieutenant Poul de Löwenörn (1751–1826) for the Danish king in 1787, checking and correcting what he refers to as an *Engelske Kaart* (English Chart), presumably Preston's chart, and demonstrating the transnational and professionalised nature of maritime mapmaking during the eighteenth century.

Paul de Löwenörn joined the Danish Navy as a cadet in 1765 and became a lieutenant in 1770. He was promoted to Captain Lieutenant in 1781, later becoming the head of the first Royal Danish Sea Chart Office. As was the case with his British counterpart, Preston, Löwenörn was employed as a Naval Captain (in the British and Danish Navy respectively), and was an experienced navigator, who was able to access information from a variety of international sources. Löwenörn used notes by a French hydrographer, Bellin, the *Essai Geographique sur les Isles Britanniques* published in 1757, and his coastal views and landmarks of the region are taken both from previous English (that is Greenville Collins' *Great Britains Coasting Pilot*) and French sources, as well as from new drawings made by the Danish surveyors that accompanied him. The printed description is

Figure 3. T. A. Preston, *New Hydrographical Survey of the Islands of Shetland* (map). Edinburgh, National Library of Scotland, 1781.

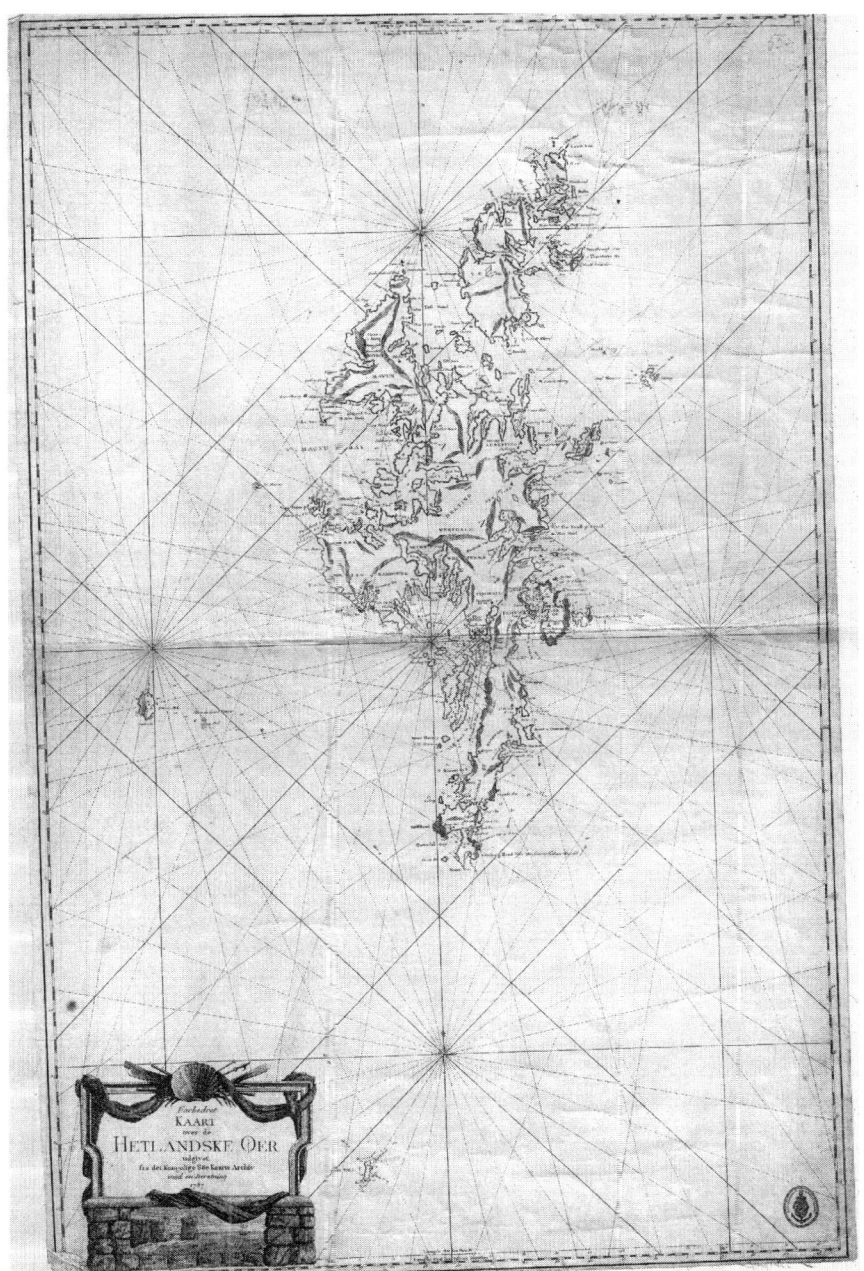

Figure 4. Forbedret Kaart over de Hetlandske Öer, in *Beretning om et Forbedret Kaart over de Hetlandske Öer, tilligemed trende blade med landtoninger og et speciel kaart over Va'ey-Sund paa Hetland* (Copenhagen, 1787).

accompanied by the sea chart shown in Figure 4, which was issued as an appendix to the report.

A short inscription to the Danish version of the account states the intention of providing 'Nordic seafarers' (*nordiske Söemænd*) with an accurate chart of the islands. Interestingly, as with Preston's chart, it then gives detailed sailing directions and a special regional chart to the island of Vaila.[56] This small island on the western coast of the Shetland archipelago had been owned by a Norwegian family from near Ålesund until 1576.[57] Its presence (and prominence) within the report highlights the conservative nature of map- and chart-making, as seen in the previous example of the *Carta Marina* (Figure 1). Chorographical detail is included by noting an important landscape feature near the harbour entrance, the 'Pictish Castle', as well as explaining the local names for coastal features such as cliffs, stacks and bays (Figure 5) to Danish readers:

> To explain some names that you will find on the chart, I add the following. *Voe* means entrance, or incoming bay from the sea. *Holm* is a little island. *Skerry* is a cliff. *Stack* is a high, peak or sharp cliff, which stands out of the sea. *Muckle* or *Stour* means big.[58]

Finally, Löwenörn adds a decorative drawing which shows the catching of seabirds on Nosshead from Pennant's *Artic Zoology* (1784), to the bottom left-hand corner of the chart, pointing out regional customs: 'I have finally added a small vignette underneath the chart, which shows the catching of birds on Nosshead, taken from Pennant's *Arctic Zoology*.'[59]

Coastal Mapping of Intercultural Spaces: Shetland

As was seen from Olaus Magnus' *Carta Marina* (Figure 1), the Scottish Northern Isles of Orkney and Shetland were very well known to Dano-Norwegian, and also Dutch and German traders and fishermen, throughout the sixteenth and seventeenth centuries.[60] However, up until the introduction of a regular steamship service from the Scottish mainland in the mid-nineteenth century, the Shetland Islands, in particular, were almost unknown to Scottish and English visitors, including cartographers. One of the first Scottish descriptions and a map (Figure 6) of the islands was provided by Thomas Gifford, a landowner and merchant from Busta, Shetland. He compiled a *Historical Description of the Zetland Islands in the Year 1733,* published in 1789, which was accompanied by a map showing the divisions of local parishes and some coastal placenames.[61]

Although the map lacks topographical detail, particularly when compared with other regional maps of Scotland of the period, it provides an interesting perspective on a Scottish landowner's relation to space and place during the eighteenth century. Gifford is clearly interested in administrative matters, including local governance and taxation. Rather than cataloguing placenames or landscape features, his focus is therefore on parish divisions and

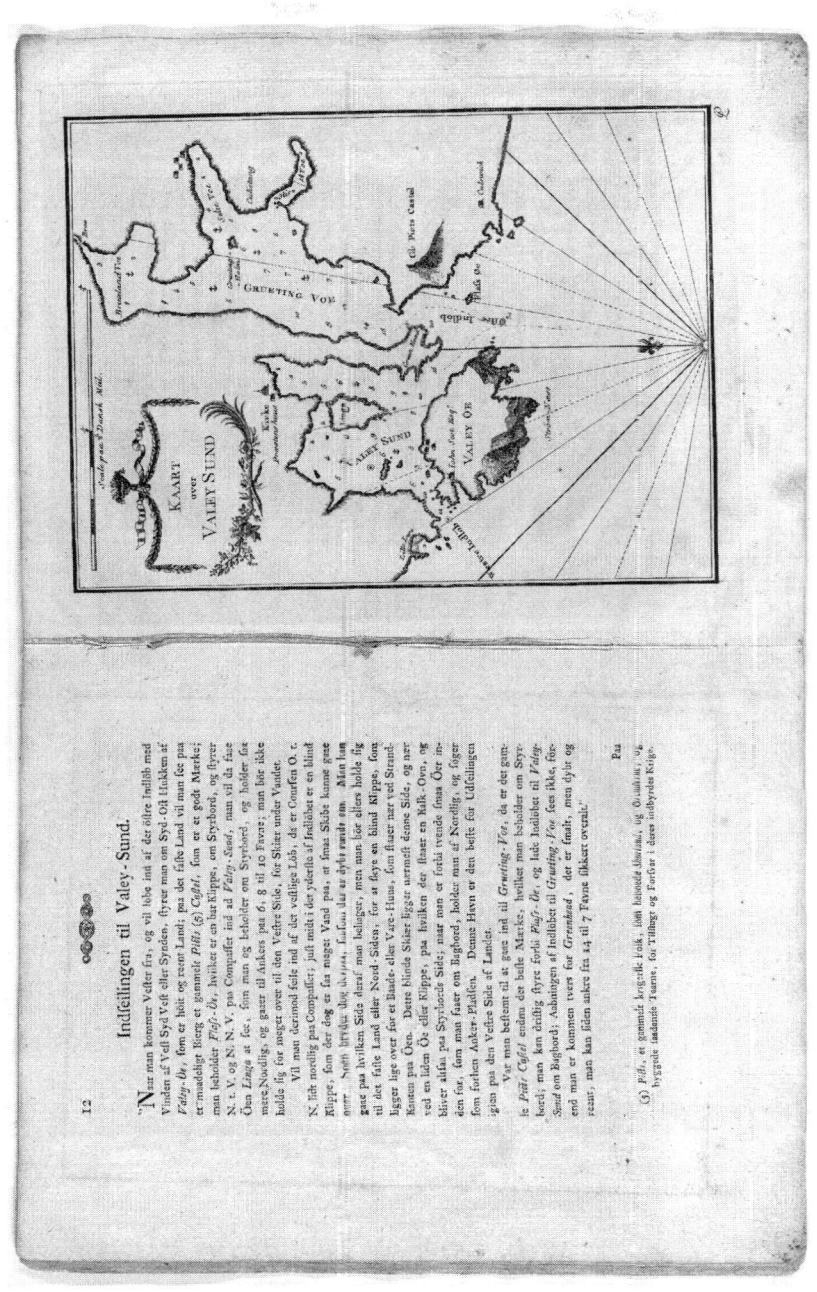

Figure 5. Sailing directions and map of Vaila Sound (Indseilingen til Valey-Sund, Kaart over Valey Sund), in *Beretning om et Forbedret Kaart over de Hetlandske Öer, tilligemed trende blade med landtoninger og et speciel kaart over Valey-Sund paa Hetland* (Copenhagen, 1787).

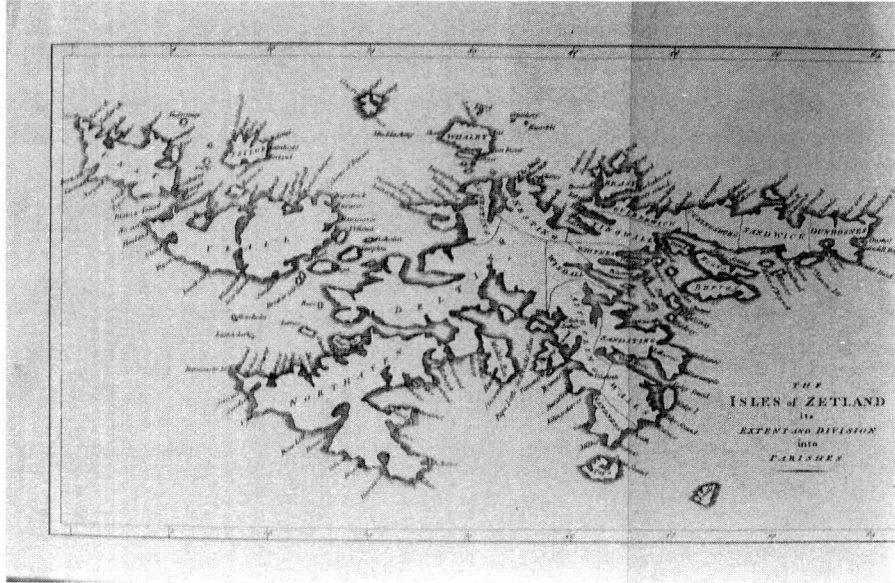

Figure 6. T. Gifford, *The Isles of Zetland, it's Extent and Division into Parishes* (map), 1733. Lerwick, Shetland Museum and Archives, P00191.

territorial boundaries, demonstrating the crown-representative and landowning perspective.[62] To find chorographical detail, we need to look to other sources.

Gifford's historical description of the Shetland Islands was accompanied by a range of eighteenth- and nineteenth-century travel descriptions written by visitors to the islands, such as that by the Scottish cleric and naturalist, the Rev. George Low.[63] Low was born in Edzell, Angus, in 1747 and educated at Marischal College, Aberdeen, and at St Andrews University. After moving to Stromness, Orkney, as a tutor in 1768 (in 1771 becoming licensed Minister of the Presbytery of Cairston), Low took up the study of the natural history of the Northern Isles. He catalogued birds, flora and fauna, and marine life, as well as constructing his own microscope. Crucially for his career, in 1772, after a visit to Iceland, the explorer and naturalist Sir Joseph Banks visited Orkney in the company of the Swedish botanist Dr Daniel Solander, and physician Dr James Lind. Through them Low was able to widen his scientific network and correspondence and, in 1774, he began a tour of the south islands of Orkney and the whole of the Shetland Islands resulting in *A tour through the islands of Orkney and Schetland: containing hints relative to their ancient modern and natural history collected in 1774.*[64] Low's account was not published until 1813, although some content was used in Pennant's 1784 publication of *Arctic Zoology*, which had a wider distribution.

As with other naturalist-antiquarians of the period, Low provides a humanist approach that combines regional descriptions with scientific and spiritual enquiry.

As such, he is clearly motivated by the eighteenth-century intellectual milieu of political and economic progress through exploration and discovery, an approach which finds parallels in other authors from Shetland such as Arthur Edmonston[65] who saw his chorographical description as part of a:

> wish to rouse, by candid enquiry, those who possess influence in this country, to a just sense of their relative situation, and to the study of their true interests, by embracing more enlarged and liberal views of political economy than have yet existed generally among them.[66]

As is the case in the examples of map- and chart-making discussed previously, the emphasis on 'improving' the national and local political economy by providing information is clearly aimed at a free market and at increased production within a defined political landscape-entity, the British nation-state. This perspective conceives of regional landscape and people primarily as an economic unit, with the regional and cultural aspects documented by Low and Hibbert seemingly occupying a separate sphere. As part of this re-negotiation of space and place, two different landscape polities therefore constitute the maps of Northern Scotland: the natural and cultural landscape, and the economic and physical resource. These separate perspectives are very much intertwined in the Nordic regional landscape, which is constructed according to a polity closer to Schouw's conceptions of the human, cultural landscape.[67]

The Nordic Coastal Region: Søndmør

A good example of Nordic chorographical practice is Hans Strøm's *Physisk og Oeconomisk Beskrivelse over Fogderiet Søndmør I-II* ('Description of the district of Søndmør') in Western Norway.[68] Strøm supplies an extensive descriptive text of more than 780 pages collected in two volumes published in 1762 and 1766. Volume One consists of a catalogue, of both the people and natural environment of the region, and includes a detailed regional map (Figure 7). He describes physical characteristics such as topography, plants and animals, as well as regional aspects of material culture, commercial activities (especially what type of fisheries or farming activities are prevalent, what kind of boats people use, even what kind of wind to expect in the fjords). Strøm gathers statistical information, region-specific names and details, as well as topographical descriptions and cartographic information. Volume One of the *Beskrivelse*, for example, begins with the detailed regional map, which features coastal landscape enriched with cultural information, such as placenames; the division between land and sea (*Vesterhavet*, the Western Sea, visible as empty space northwest of the land); placenames of islands and fjords reaching into the sea; distances, and *Alfar Vey* or public pathways in the area; location of churches, larger farms and commercial centres.[69]

In his introduction to a new edition of Strøm's works published in 2001, Stein Ugelvik Larsen comments that Strøm divides his work between nature (including

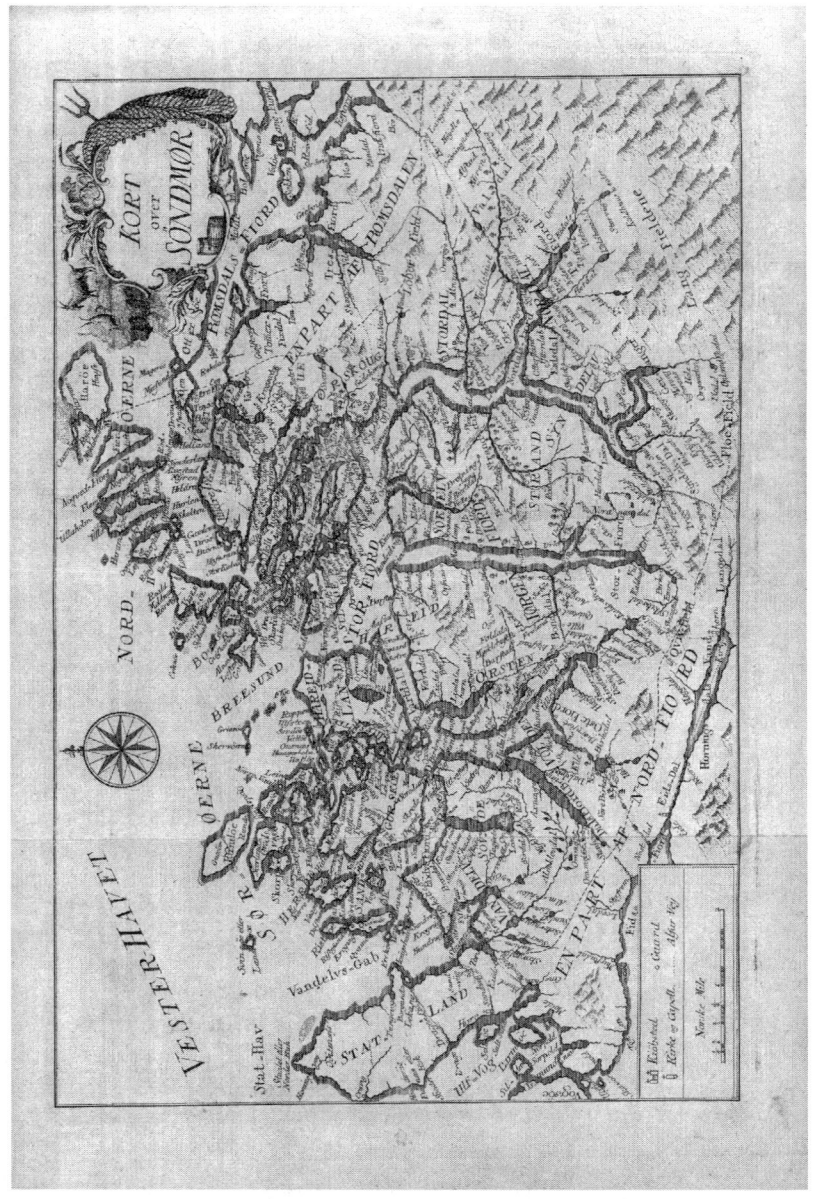

Figure 7. Hans Strøm, Kort over Søndmør, 1762. Courtesy of the National Library of Norway.[70]

topography and a map) (Volume I) and the *besønderlige* (what is culturally unique to this region), which is the focus of Volume II. So, Strøm can be said to move from mapping and observations of natural phenomena towards people and cultural aspects, integrating the culturally unique into a natural order.[71] At the top right hand corner of the map (Figure 7) we find a pictorial representation of the economic activities of fishing and farming in the region, with a vignette depicting two sheep, two barrels, a fishing net and two fish.

Hans Strøm is one of four significant historical figures in the Sunnmøre region on the Norwegian west coast, who were all active in collecting, preserving and transmitting antiquarian, linguistic and cultural information during the eighteenth and nineteenth centuries.[72] Strøm was born in 1726 in Borgund Sunnmøre, taking a degree in theology in 1745. He lived at home in Borgund from 1745 to 1750, teaching pietistic and philosophical literature from his father's library. This was followed by a period as chaplain at Meldahl, elsewhere in Borgund, for fourteen years (1750 to 1764), and then vicar in Volda (1764–1779).

In 1750, Strøm discovered Erik Pontoppidan's natural history and Linnaeus's botanical work. Pontoppidan was a Danish author, historian and antiquary, who wrote on the natural history of Denmark and Norway, whereas the Swedish physician Carl Linnaeus became well known for his scientific classification of the natural world. Both travelled widely, and their work inspired Strøm to start a series of his own travels and investigations of the nature and environment around the Sunnmøre area. The results were published in his *Physisk og Oeconomisk Beskrivelse over Fogderiet Søndmør I-II*, a work that established him as a scientific authority in the field of natural history. Typically for the period, Strøm's work spans several disciplines (natural sciences, theology, social sciences) and includes another description, the *Physisk-oeconomisk Beskrivelse over Eger-Præstegiæld i Aggershuus Stift* (1784) and a large volume of sermons for Aggershuus Stift (1792).[73]

The most remarkable element of Strøm's map is the regional detail, particularly in terms of placenames. These are arranged in a visual catalogue that documents and transmits the places in the coastal landscape, as well as the topographical landscape features of islands, mountains and fjords. Through this chorographic practice, Strøm demonstrates the interplay between nature and human activities, as well as giving his readers a visual representation of a regional, unitary area, where the interaction between nature, industry and culture was in a particularly dense interplay.[74]

As a geographical description of a region between two major trading centres, Bergen and Trondheim, the motivation behind both the description and the map is easy to see: to show a region with political and economic potential, supported by Strøm's detailed lists of natural and human resources. However, the method of listing and cataloguing regionally unique landscapes and natural phenomena also shows an intention for it to be used both as a reference or lexicon, and as a guide to the area.[75] Similar to the examples from Scotland mentioned above, it is significant that Strøm's intended readership is not only both the king and representatives of the Dano-Norwegian state, but also a professional, international, scientific readership independent from the state, which he addresses in a separate introduction. The act of map-making thus becomes part of a whole range of cultural and political practices that are not merely documentary, but part of a new 'graphic language'.[76] This re-negotiates space and place according to changing political and economic contexts, producing both a physical and mental map of the North.[77]

Mental Maps: Regionalisation and Regionalism Reimagined

This article has discussed two types of mapping that illustrate different processes of re-negotiating space and place through either: regionalisation (the process by which smaller spaces are joined together to form larger territories), or regionalism (a way in which very specific places are described and represented in detail through chorographic practice). As has been shown in the examples discussed, these two activities are sometimes complementary, but can also exist in tension with each other, in systems of 'countervailing trends', as defined by Burke.[78]

Map- and chart-making in Northern Europe provided both source material and context for regional Scottish and Norwegian charts and maps during the eighteenth century. Cartography, as an established profession, continued to be a politically motivated activity in connection with the creation and re-organisation of national and international territories and spaces.[79] However, map makers also engaged in detailed descriptions of place and region, and continued the practice of 'chorographical thinking' in their production of micro-regional maps and charts.[80] In this, Northern map makers participated in three important changes that took place during the European Enlightenment, concerning the production, distribution and use of maps and charts.

Firstly, there was a clear integration of the work of newly created, state-sponsored scientific and scholarly institutions such as the Royal Society (est. 1660), the *Académie royale des sciences* (Paris, 1666), the Royal Society of Edinburgh (est. 1783), and the *Det Kongelige Norske Videnskabers Selskab* (Royal Norwegian Society of Sciences and Letters, est. 1760). This organised knowledge creation took place on a transnational level, with chart makers such as Thomas Preston or Paul de Löwenörn routinely sharing, reinterpreting and finessing existing navigational charts within their professional maritime networks. However, mapping also became increasingly a national, and patriotic, effort, and an integral part of the work done within individual national scientific societies, such as is seen in Preston's letters to Joseph Ames, a Fellow of the Royal Society, where he offers to survey the 'Islands of Zetland' for the society.[81]

Secondly, intersections between maps and scientific inquiry played an increasingly important role in terms of the integration of the work of new scientific foundations, such as the royal societies, within governmental and administrative institutions. This meant that national institutions were now able to commission and undertake surveys in order to provide civil and military authorities at home and in colonial settings with geo-political and topographical information. Until 1800, and in contrast to the Dano-Norwegian chart by Löwenörn, which was commissioned by the Danish Navy, this remained very much an *ad hoc* process within Scotland and the rest of the United Kingdom, with many surveys being sponsored privately as in the case of London chart publishers Robert Sayer and John Bennett.

Finally, the influence of increasing economic and political stability and growth after 1650 within Northern Europe cannot be underestimated.[82] With increased literacy and opportunity to access and participate in the construction of new knowledge, the eighteenth century saw a rising interest in map consumption – both as a scientific and cultural phenomenon. Changes in printing technology resulted in both maps and charts becoming available, if not to the general population, at least to a widening social group. This meant that cartographic imagery was added to the developing national and regional cultural vocabularies and discourses which defined landscape, place and space.

Maps and map-making thus acted as 'representations of belief and ideology – rooted in particular cultures and institutions – as well as 'factual' images of scientific knowledge.'[83] Significantly, in terms of the element of knowledge construction embedded in Northern maps, chorographical practices can be seen to continue, although more research is required to investigate the impact, motivations and complex patterns of use of regional maps and charts, both from the perspectives of the user, as well as that of the producer, and to assess their impact in terms of establishing regional identities within historical and cultural regions during this period and beyond.[84]

In conclusion, the practice of mapping demonstrates the re-negotiation of complex sets of perceptions of space and place. When comparing the examples of maps from the Northern Isles and Norway's coastal regions, the close link between chorography and historiography becomes apparent, with different landscape polities constructed and applied. This article has demonstrated that map making, as a cultural practice, is historically located, and, just as with other narratives, be they visual or literary, maps tell a story from a particular point of view, and are complicit in the development of specific landscape polities. Northern maps and charts ultimately create a series of cartographic statements that utilise a vocabulary of images and discourses in order to communicate both the social and political changes and countervailing trends of a given historical period. Using the aesthetic conventions of the time, the transnational, national and regional map and chart can thus be defined as a visual narrative produced via selective cultural and historical processes.[85] The eighteenth century Northern map thus not only re-negotiated space and place within a specific historical period, but helps us understand the complex, multi-layered nature of our regional, national and international geographical imagination today.

Notes

1. Research for this article was made possible through mobility funding from the Norwegian Research Council (Norges Forskningsråd). I wish to thank the participants of 'Negotiating Space, Arranging Land: A Workshop on Mapping in the Nordic Countries, 1720 until today' (Oslo, 7–9 December 2012) for their comments and suggestions, and am grateful to two anonymous reviewers who made valuable further recommendations.
2. P. Burke, 'Loss and Gain: the social history of knowledge, 1750–2000', text of public lecture, Birkbeck College, University of London, 9 November 2010, available at: http://theoryculturesociety.org/peter-burke-on-the-social-history-of-knowledge-1750-2000 (accessed 23 December 2013).
3. P. Burke, 'Theory, Culture and Society', available at: http://theoryculturesociety.blogspot.com/2010/12/peter-burke-on-social-history-of.html (accessed 23 December 2013).
4. J. B. Harley, 'The Map and the development of the History of Cartography', in *The History of Cartography* (Chicago IL, 1987), 1–42; Angela Byrne, *Geographies of the Romantic North: Science, Antiquarianism, and Travel, 1790–1830* (London, 2013).
5. H. K. Bhabha, *Nation and Narration* (London, 1990).
6. L. M. Cullen, 'Scotland and Ireland, 1600–1800: their role in the evolution of British society', in Robert Allen Houston and Ian D. White (eds), *Scottish Society 1500–1800* (Cambridge, 1989).
7. Hanno Brand (ed.), *Trade, Diplomacy and Cultural Exchange: Continuity and Change in the North Sea Area and the Baltic, c.1350–1750* (Hilversum, 2005); Steve Murdoch, *Network North: Scottish Kin, Commercial and Covert Associations in Northern Europe, 1603–1746* (Leiden, 2006); David J. Starkey and Morten Hahn-Pedersen (eds), *Concentration and Dependency. The Role of Maritime Activities in North Sea Communities, 1299–1999* (Esbjerg, 2002); Juliette Roding and Lex Heerma van Voss (eds), *The North Sea and Culture (1550–1800): Proceedings of the International Conference Held at Leiden 21–22 April 1995* (Hilversum, 1996); S. Reeploeg, 'The Uttermost Part of the Earth: islands on the edge ... and in the centre of the North Atlantic', in Jodie Matthews and Daniel Travers (eds), *Islands and Britishness: A Global Perspective* (Newcastle upon Tyne, 2012); 'Reading Material Culture in the North Atlantic: traditional wooden boxes as intercultural objects', in *Across the Sólundarhaf: Connections between Scotland and the Nordic World, Journal of the North Atlantic (JONA)* Special Volume 4 (2013), 52–60; 'Nordic Regions of Culture: Norway and Shetland – intercultural links, regionalization and communities of narrative after 1770', *Scandinavica* 49(2) (2010), 74–6; Arne Bang Andersen, Basil Greenhill and Egil Harald Grude (eds), *The North Sea. A Highway of Economic and Cultural Exchange: Character – History* (Stavanger, 1985).
8. P. Stadius, 'The North in European Mental Mapping', in Maria Lahteenmaki and Päivi Pihlaja (eds), *The North Calotte: Perspectives on the Histories and Cultures of Northernmost Europe* (Helsinki, 2005).
9. Ibid., 25.
10. Harald Baldersheim and Krister Stahlberg (eds), *Nordic Region-Building in a European Perspective* (Aldershot, 1999); Stephen Conway, *Britain, Ireland and Continental Europe: Similarities, Connections, Identities* (Oxford, 2011).
11. Sven Tägil, Gunnar Törnqvist and Christer Jönsson, *Organising European Space* (London, 2007).
12. M. Lynch, *Scotland: A New History* (London, 1992), 41–55.

13. Ibid., 45; C. W. J. Withers, *Geography, Science, and National Identity: Scotland since 1520* (Cambridge, 2001).
14. Norman Davies, *The Isles: A History* (London, 1999), 448.
15. Rolf Danielsen, et al. (eds), tr. Michael Drake, *Norway: A History from the Vikings to Our Own Times* (Oslo, 1998).
16. S. Dyrvik, *Norsk Historie 1625–1814*, 6 vols (Oslo, 1999), iii.
17. Ibid.
18. Laura Benton, 'The British Atlantic in Global Context', in David Armitage and Michael J. Braddick (eds), *The British Atlantic World, 1500–1800*, (Basingstoke, 2009).
19. Colin Kidd, *Subverting Scotland's Past* (Cambridge, 2003), 340; Alexander Murdoch (ed.), *The Scottish Nation, Identity and History* (Edinburgh, 2007); Linda Colley, *Britons: Forging the Nation 1707–1837* (London, 2009).
20. Harley, 'History of Cartography'; Stadius, 'The North in European Mental Mapping', 14–25.
21. Kenneth R. Olwig, *Landscape, Nature and the Body Politic: From Britain's Renaissance to America's New World* (Madison WI, 2002).
22. Ibid., 219.
23. Ibid., 220.
24. Ibid., 220.
25. Ibid., 220.
26. Kenneth R. Olwig, 'In Search of the Nordic Landscape: a personal view', in Jan Öhman and Kirsten Simonsen (eds), *Voices from the North: New Trends in Nordic Human Geography* (Aldershot, 2003).
27. Olwig, 'In Search of the Nordic Landscape', 224.
28. Ibid., 224.
29. Ibid., 223.
30. Ibid., 224.
31. Carl O. Sauer, 'The Morphology of Landscape', in John Leighly (ed.), *Land and Life: A Selection from the Writings of Carl Ortwin Sauer* (Berkeley CA, 1982), 315–50.
32. Olwig, 'In Search of the Nordic Landscape', 226.
33. Ibid. 227. The local term 'Norden' literally means 'Northern Countries'. It is used in Northern Germanic languages such as Danish, Norwegian and Swedish, with 'Norden' generally referring to a transnational region in Northern Europe and the North Atlantic that consists of Denmark, Norway, Sweden, Finland, and Iceland, including their associated territories (Greenland, the Faroe Islands, and the Åland Islands) according to the Nordic Council. The region's five nation-states and three autonomous regions share much common history as well as common traits in their respective societies, such as political systems and what is referred to as the 'Nordic model' of society.
34. Burke, 'Theory, Culture and Society'.
35. Jouni Häkli, 'Borders in the Political Geography of Knowledge', in Lars-Folke Landgren and Maunu Häyrynen (eds), *The Dividing Line: Borders and National Peripheries* (Helsinki, 1997).
36. Ibid., 9.
37. The full title is *Carta marina et Descriptio septemtrionalium terrarum ac mirabilium rerum in eis contentarum, diligentissime elaborata Anno Domini 1539 Veneciis liberalitate Reverendissimi Domini Ieronimi Quirini*. (it translates as 'A marine map and description of the Northern Lands and of their marvels, most carefully drawn up at Venice in the year 1539 through the generous assistance of the most honourable lord and patriarch Hieronymo Quirin').

38. Gordon Donaldson, *A Northern Commonwealth: Scotland and Norway* (Edinburgh, 1990); Natascha Mehler and Mark Gardiner, 'On the Verge of Colonialism: English and Hanseatic trade in the North Atlantic islands', in Peter Pope and Sharon Lewis-Simpson (eds), *Exploring Atlantic Transitions* (Woodbridge 2013), 1–14.
39. Harley, 'History of Cartography', 30.
40. P. Stadius, *Southern Perspectives on the North: Legends, Stereotypes, Images and Models* (Gdańsk, 2001).
41. Toril Øien, 'The Northern Isles – between two nations', *Northern Studies* 39 (2005), 80–104; M. Lange, *The Norwegian Scots: An Anthropological Interpretation of Viking-Scottish Identity in the Orkney Islands* (Lewiston NY, 2007); J.R. Baldwin (ed.), *Scandinavian Shetland, an ongoing Tradition?* (Edinburgh, 1978); S. Seibert, *Reception and Construction of the Norse Past in Orkney* (Frankfurt, 2008); B. Cohen, 'Norse Imagery in Shetland', unpublished PhD thesis (University of Manchester, 1983).
42. D. Waugh (ed.), *Shetland's Northern Links, Language and History* (Lerwick, 1996); E. Marwick, *The Folklore of Orkney and Shetland* (Lonodn, 1975/2000), 15.
43. H. Smith, *Shetland Life and Trade 1550–1914* (Edinburgh, 2003), 289.
44. R. Danielsen et al. (eds), *Norway: A History from the Vikings to Our Own Times* (Oslo, 1998), 21.
45. Burke, 'Loss and Gain'.
46. In his text of the *Geographia* from the second century, Ptolemy defines geography as the study of the entire world, meaning both its quantitative and qualitative features. Chorography is the study of its smaller parts, that is, provinces, regions, cities, or ports, using the same method. See D.J. Rohl, 'The chorographic tradition and seventeenth- and eighteenth-century Scottish antiquaries', *The Journal of Art Historiography*, 5 (2011), 15–18.
47. R. Helgerson, 'The Land Speaks: cartography, chorography, and subversion in Renaissance England,' *Representations*, 16 (1986), 51–85.
48. Rohl, 'The chorographic tradition', 15–18.
49. Samuel Johnson, *A Dictionary of the English Language: In Which the Words Are Deduced from Their Originals, and Illustrated in Their Different Significations by Examples from the Best Writers: To Which Are Prefixed, a History of the Language, and an English Grammar* (London, 1785), 379.
50. Rohl, 'The chorographic tradition', 6.
51. Ibid.
52. J. Garcia Redondo, 'Sailscapes. La Construcción Del Paisaje Del Océano Pacífico En El Giro Del Mondo De Gemelli Carreri', *Anuario de Estudios Americanos*, 69:1 (2012), 253–75.
53. Harley, 'History of Cartography', 32.
54. Peter Whitfield, *The Charting of the Oceans: Ten Centuries of Maritime Maps* (London, 1996).
55. With longitude only recently available as a measurement (the publication of the Nautical Almanac starting in 1767), we can see on the lower left hand side that its determination is still a work in progress.
56. Vaila island – originally owned by Gorvel Fadersdatter of Giske (an island near Alesund) who had inherited the estate in 1490 – was granted to Robert Cheyne in 1576 by James VI, eventually passing to James Mitchell of Girlsta, a Scalloway merchant, who built the 'Old Haa' in 1696. See John Ballantyne and Brian Smith (eds), *Shetland Documents 1195–1579* (Lerwick, 1999), 170–1. Passing by descent to the Scotts of Melby, Vaila was sold in 1893 to Yorkshire mill owner Herbert Anderton, who had been brought to Shetland through wool-buying. With his brother, Anderton developed Vaila as a farm and a place

to shoot and fish during summer visits. See: http://www.britishlistedbuildings.co.uk/sc-45305-vaila-cloudin-farmhouse-including-outbuil (accessed on 23 December 2013).
57. Ballantyne and Smith (eds), *Shetland Documents*, 170–1.
58. Paul Löwenörn, 'Beretning om et Forbedret Kaart over de Hetlandske Öer, tilligemed trende blade med landtoninger og et speciel kaart over Valey-Sund paa Hetland' (Copenhagen, 1787), 16, University of Aberdeen Special Collections Centre, SB 591: 'Til Forklaring paa nogle Navne, som findes paa Kaartet, tiener fölgende. *Voe* betyder en Indgang, eller Indlöb fra Söen. *Holm* en lille Öe. *Skerry* en Klippe. *Stack* en höi, spids eller skarp Klippe, som staaer op av Vandet. *Muckle* eller *Stour* betyder Stor.'
59. Ibid.: 'Endelig har jeg under Cartouchen paa Kaartet anbragt en liden Vignette, som forestiller Fugle-Fangsten ved Nosshead, af *Pennants* Arctic Zoology, fee Europ. Magaz. Maii 1780, eller Historiske Portefeuille December 1785.'
60. Kathrin Zickermann, 'Shetland's Trade with Northwest German Territories in the Seventeenth and Eighteenth Century', in *Across the Sólundarhaf: Connections between Scotland and the Nordic World, Journal of the North Atlantic*, Special Volume, 4 (2013), 43–51; Alexander Fenton, *The Northern Isles: Orkney and Shetland* (Edinburgh, 1978/1997); Donald J. Withrington (ed.), *Shetland and the Outside World 1469–1969* (Aberdeen, 1983); C. W. J. D. Turnock, *The Historical Geography of Scotland since 1707* (Cambridge, 2003); C. W. J. Withers, *Geography, Science, and National Identity: Scotland since 1520* (Cambridge, 2001); Richard Smith, 'Developments in Shetland's Economy 1770–1820', unpublished PhD thesis (University of Edinburgh, 1986).
61. Thomas Gifford, *An Historical Description of the Zetland Islands of 1733* (London, 1879).
62. Gifford was a local steward and justiciar-depute.
63. Thomas Seccombe, 'Low, George (1747–1795)', *Oxford Dictionary of National Biography*, (Oxford, 2004).
64. George Low, *Orkney and Schetland 1771* (Inverness, 1978).
65. Arthur Edmonston, *A View of the Ancient and Present State of the Zetland Islands*, 2 vols (London, 1809).
66. Ibid., i, ix.
67. Michael Jones and Kenneth R. Olwig, *Nordic Landscapes: Region and Belonging on the Northern Edge of Europe* (Minneapolis MN, 2008).
68. Hans Strøm, *Physisk Og Oeconomisk Beskrivelse over Fogderiet Søndmør, Beliggende I Bergens Stift, I Norge* (Copenhagen, 1762).
69. *Allfarvei* is a general term for a road available for general use by the public. The word is a combination of the old-Danish word *adel-farvei og alfaren* (vei) or public path, or *algaden* the name for a main street in Danish: http://snl.no/allfarvei (accessed 23 December 2013). My translation.
70. H. Strøm, *Physisk og Oeconomisk Beskrivelse over Fogderiet Søndmør, beliggende i Bergens Stift, i Norge* (Copenhagen, 1762), National Library of Norway, at http://urn.nb.no/URN:NBN:no-nb_digibok_2009100713001 (accessed 23 December 2013).
71. Marie Louise Brekke, 'Merkverdige Ting I Naturleg Orden. Ein Presentasjon Av Hans Strøms Physisk Og Oeconomisk Beskrivelse Av Fogderiet Søndmør, 1762–1766', unpublished PhD thesis (Nordisk Institut Bergen, 1996).
72. The others are Ivar Aasen, Peder Fylling and Olaus Johannes Fjørtoft.
73. A. Apelseth and Arne, *Hans Strøm (1726–1797): Ein Kommentert Bibliografi* (Volda, 1995).
74. H. Strøm, *Physisk og Oeconomisk Beskrivelse over Fogderiet Søndmør, beliggende i Bergens Stift, i Norge* (Volda 2002), 'Introduction', xvii. My translation.
75. Brekke, 'Merkverdige ting', 25.

76. Harley, 'History of Cartography', 2.
77. Stadius, 'The North in European Mental Mapping', 28.
78. Burke, 'Loss and Gain'.
79. Reeploeg, 'Nordic Regions of Culture', 74–6.
80. Rohl, 'The chorographic tradition', 8.
81. T. Thomas Preston, 'Two Letters from Mr. Thomas Preston to Mr. Joseph Ames, F. R. S. Concerning the Island of Zetland,' *Philosophical Transactions* 43 (1744), 472–7.
82. Michael Lynch, *Scotland: A New History* (London, 1992); Stephen Conway, *Britain, Ireland and Continental Europe: Similarities, Connections, Identities* (Oxford, 2011).
83. Harley, 'History of Cartography', 3.
84. Christer Jönsson, *Organising European Space* (London, 2000/2007).
85. Joep Leerssen, *National Thought in Europe: A Cultural History* (Amsterdam, 2006).

A FORGOTTEN DIASPORA: THE CHILDREN OF ENSLAVED AND 'FREE COLOURED' WOMEN AND HIGHLAND SCOTS IN GUYANA BEFORE EMANCIPATION

DAVID ALSTON

The job of the historian is to make it clear that a certain event happened. We do this as effectively as we can, for the purpose of conveying what is was like for something to have happened to those people when it did, where it did and with what consequences ... It's our job to get it right, again and again and again.

Tony Judt[1]

The colonies of Demerara, Essequibo and Berbice, on the Caribbean coast of South America, united to create British Guiana in 1831 and now form the Republic of Guyana. They have recently been described – along with Grenada and Trinidad – as the 'last frontier' of British colonial expansion in the West Indies and indeed, at the end of the eighteenth century, they were the most undeveloped colonies in the region, on the margins of empire, populated not only by enslaved Africans and their descendants but also by 'free coloured' people, many of whom were mobile, and by often transient speculators and adventurers from Europe, North America, and other parts of the Caribbean.[2] Scots were prominent among these adventurers in Demerara and Essequibo, both under Dutch rule and after the colonies were seized from the Dutch in 1796, and there were also new opportunities in Berbice, which had traditionally been 'suspicious of outsiders' but from about 1790 opened itself to settlement.[3] By the mid-1790s, these colonies had come to hold a particular allure for many Highlanders, as a result of the success of a few early adventurers from the north of Scotland and the importance to prospective emigrants of kin-based networks.[4]

The white population of these colonies was small and, even by 1820, when the number of enslaved people in Guyana peaked at over 100,000, there were less than 600 'whites' in Berbice and at most 3,500 in Demerara–Essequibo. In proportion to the number of enslaved, this was markedly lower than in other colonies.[5] The Demerara-born historian of British Guiana, Henry Dalton (1818–74), writing in the 1850s, had the impression that a large proportion of the white Europeans had come from Scotland and were 'for the most part of humble extraction, uneducated, and glad to accept any opening that presented itself'. Dalton believed there had been many examples of both dramatic success and of abject failure among these Scots and that many had exhibited what he called 'the characteristic recklessness of the Gaelic race' in their behaviour.[6] It would be more reasonable to describe them as risk takers, venturing their capital, their health, friendships, and family life on the prospect of what one Highland clan chief, Lord Seaforth, described as 'very rapid and splendid fortunes'.[7]

Young men who arrived from Britain, often in their late teens, saw themselves as isolated, especially from the companionship of European women. In 1806, Edward Fraser (1786–1813) of Reelig (Inverness-shire), admitted in a letter to his mother that the young wife of his employer 'being the only woman almost I ever see she will run in my head'.[8] And in 1830 a young doctor of Highland descent, Pierre Antoine Munro, wrote to his mother in Montreal saying, 'We are living here like hermits, being so few Whites in the place. You will probably not believe that I have not seen the face of a white lady for three months.'[9] Some tried to maintain the standards in which they had been brought up. Edward Fraser told his mother that they were 'almost entirely without the society of women which acts as a check on the liberties men would otherwise take' and, in another letter, explained that 'this country has great attractions for some people but they are people I hope I never will resemble'. He stayed for ten years despite becoming 'more disgusted and sick than ever with the country and manners and everything in it', but a few found it intolerable.[10] Dr George Bethune (1760–1803) from Dingwall, and his younger brother Divie (1771–1824), settled in Demerara about 1790 but Divie found 'the pestilential moral atmosphere was so thoroughly distasteful ... that at the risk of forfeiting his brother's affection he left him, and in 1791 came to New York City'.[11] However, Dalton believed that most Scots in Guyana had lost what he considered their characteristic 'reserve, temperance, and zeal for religion' and 'separated from the austere influence of domestic examples at home ... [had] plunged as readily as others into the vortex of dissipation'.[12]

Sexual abuse and 'sexual leverage'

One aspect of this 'vortex of dissipation' was the sexual abuse of enslaved women and of enslaved female children.[13] For example, the enslaved girl Susannah (1796/7–c.1851) was no more than twelve years old when, in 1808, she gave birth to her first child, fathered by George Munro (1766/7–1824) from Easter Ross, the owner of *Alness* in Berbice, a plantation notorious for its harsh discipline. She bore him two more children before she was sixteen.[14] In a letter from Hugh Munro Robertson (1787–1819), the son of the parish minister of Kiltearn (Ross-shire), written in 1806 to his close friend Dr Thomas Traill (1781–1862) in Liverpool, we see the common assumption that, having been purchased, enslaved females were therefore sexually available. After describing the prevalence of venereal disease among the enslaved population, Robertson commented that 'a person runs a greater risque in this Country than among the fair nymphs at home', a reference to prostitutes.[15] Evidence from slave plantations in Brazil and Jamaica suggests that, given the power of masters over slaves, homosexual abuse of enslaved men and boys will also have occurred.[16]

These are difficult and sensitive topics. From the mid-1980s studies of enslaved and free women of colour in the Caribbean, and of sexual exploitation within colonies of the British Empire, led to polarised views and much heated debate. Ronald Hyam argued, often in unnecessarily provocative terms, that in providing 'sexual services' many women made choices which were not wholly determined by their social and economic circumstances, a view strongly rejected by others, such as Barbara Bush and Mark Berger, who stressed the deep inequalities of power in these interactions.[17] Since then, studies by Hilary Beckles, Pedro Welch and, most recently, Kit Candlin, have detailed the high degree of agency, and often ingenuity, which could be exercised in at least some relationships by 'free black' and 'free coloured' women and, within greater constraints, enslaved women, in order to advance themselves and their wider families.[18] A balanced interpretation must recognise not only the extent of these women's control of their own lives, but also the dangers to which they were exposed, the boundaries to their control, and the limited choices open to them.

While sexual abuse was common, some men sought what they, at least, could persuade themselves were more consensual, intimate and semi-permanent relationships. There were also the practical advantages of having someone to remove 'jiggers', a parasite which burrowed into the skin, and to nurse them through the almost inevitable bouts of fever, to which those of African descent had greater immunity.[19] The perspective of such men was expressed by Henry Bolinbroke, a young clerk in Demerara:

> When an European arrives in the West Indies ... he finds it necessary to provide himself with a housekeeper, or mistress. The choice he has an opportunity of making is various, a black, a tawney, a mulatto, or a mestee ... When once an attachment takes place it is inviolable ... They embrace all the duties of a wife, except presiding at table; so far decorum is maintained, and a distinction made ... Their usefulness in preserving the arts and diffusing the habits of cleanliness is felt and allowed by all, there being a lack of civilized European women.[20]

It is questionable if women commonly shared this perspective and Candlin concludes that, although they entered into relationships with white men, many 'lived largely outside of men and marriage in transient, enterprising and independent ways' with 'a high degree of self reliance and agency'.[21] In line with this we can see that, although many women were regarded as sexually available, there were fewer women in the new colonies of the southern Caribbean who could fulfil the role described by Bolinbroke, and for a time, before more European women settled in Guyana, this gave some 'free coloured' women an opportunity to advance themselves through what can be called 'sexual leverage'. I have taken this term from Gaiutra Bahadur's study of indentured women in Guyana after emancipation.[22] Bahadur describes a situation where 'men enormously outnumbered women' but it should be noted that even small differences in the gender balance will, in principle, result in significant changes in the 'bargaining position' of one sex or the other.[23]

This is against the background, noted by Gad Heuman, that across the Caribbean, from the early nineteenth century, free people of colour had become 'a significant element in their respective societies ... [and] were determined to improve their condition'.[24] Rawle Farley argued that, as a result of the population structure in Guyana in the early nineteenth century and the economic necessity of running the plantations, 'free coloured' people in Berbice came to 'enjoy rights far greater than the coloured free in the rest of the British Caribbean'. This enhanced status was, Farley concludes, a consequence of the small number of white settlers and the large number of enslaved and, although granting of these rights was resisted, the final outcome demonstrated the bargaining power of free people of colour in the colony.[25] We should, for similar reasons, expect that 'free coloured' women in Guyana were in a particularly strong position in negotiating advantages through their sexual relationships. Enslaved women had fewer choices but, notwithstanding the power of European males and the prevalence of sexual abuse, the possibility of a relatively stable sexual relationship with an owner, manager, clerk, or overseer gave similar 'leverage' to a few domestic slaves, who could, if they bore children, create for themselves a route to freedom.

Free coloured women and their children

Many of the 'free coloured' women who entered into relationships with Europeans in Guyana came from other Caribbean colonies. One of the most remarkable was Dorothy Kirwan, known as Doll Thomas, who was described by one traveller as 'The Queen of Demerara' and by another as 'the richest woman in the colony'. Candlin devotes a chapter to her in *The Last Caribbean Frontier* and Cassandra Pybus has written an account of both Doll Thomas and her daughters.[26] Although born a slave, through her own relationships and those of her daughters she created a network of influence which spread across a number of colonies and into major merchant families in Britain. She was reputed to have danced in Grenada with the future William IV, when he was a young sailor in the Royal Navy, and in 1837 she arrived in London, dressed flamboyantly, with diamonds in her hair, a necklace of gold doubloons, ostrich feathers, and a skirt made of five-pound notes sewn together. She sought and was granted an audience with the Colonial Secretary, perhaps having given the impression that she was a foreign princess.

Doll Thomas is an important reminder of the power which such women could acquire. One of her daughters, Eliza, formed a relationship with Gilbert Robertson (1774–1839) who, although he ultimately had limited success, was part of an extended network of Highland, Glasgow and Liverpool-based families, which included some of the wealthiest merchants operating in the Caribbean. Gilbert was the second son of Anne Forbes and Harry Robertson, parish minister of Kiltearn. Three of his mother's brothers had gone to the West Indies and, by the time Gilbert was sixteen, the Robertson family were developing their own interests there. His older brother William (1773–1837) was in Demerara, his uncle John (1751–98) was in Tobago, while his uncle George (1756–99) was a merchant in Grenada. Two other brothers would follow him to Guyana and later four nephews, the sons of his sister Christian.[27]

In 1789, George Robertson in Grenada took as an apprentice, Charles Parker (1771–1828), from a Scots family in Virginia, and in 1790 the two men, along with Samuel Sandbach (1769–1851), joined with the Demerara merchant James McInroy (1759–1825), from Highland Perthshire, to create the company McInroy, Sandbach & Co. The business was described in the early 1820s as 'the Rothschilds of Demerara' and, under various names, it would remain one of the most successful trading companies in the Caribbean.[28] Gilbert Robertson's sister Elizabeth (1782–1859) married Sandbach in 1803 and the network was further strengthened when his cousin, Margaret Rainy (1774–1844), a daughter of the parish minister of Creich (Sutherland), married Gilbert's partner, Charles Parker. Two of Margaret's brothers had also gone to Guyana, Gilbert Rainy to Berbice, where he died in 1808, and George Rainy (1790–1864) to Demerara, from where he rose to become a partner, in Liverpool, in Sandbach, Tinne & Co, which had subsumed McInroy, Sandbach & Co.

Gilbert Robertson had probably been sent first to Grenada to work with his uncle George and then to Trinidad when McInroy, Sandbach & Co expanded their operations. Here, in 1794, he had a son, also named Gilbert, with an enslaved woman.[29] He moved to Demerara about 1797, after his younger brother Harry (1779–95) drowned in the colony,[30] and with Charles Parker purchased a cotton estate, *L'Amitie*. From 1806 until about 1818 he also owned plantation *Kiltearn* in Berbice, managed by another brother, Hugh Munro Robertson.[31] Gilbert formed a relationship in Demerara with Eliza Thomas, one of the six daughters of Doll Thomas, and a son Henry (1807–81) was born in 1807. Gilbert had lost an infant child, Ann, in August 1806 and Eliza may also have been her mother.[32] Along with a number of Doll Thomas's other grandchildren, Henry was sent to school in Scotland, possibly to Dollar Academy. In a letter written to his wife in 1810, Charles Parker caustically remarked, 'Who do you think is in Glasgow but Gilbert Robertson's Mother in Law Doll Thomas with about 19 other children &

grandchildren come home for education?'³³ Doll Thomas's will, written in 1846, included the following legacy:

> I give and bequeath to my grandson Henry Robertson son of my daughter Eliza the sum of two thousand two hundred guilders considering what I have already advanced for his education and maintenance equal to any claim his mother could have on my estate.³⁴

There is a tone of discontent in the phrasing of this bequest suggesting she was disappointed in her grandson. Henry was licensed by the Society of Apothecaries of London in 1828, a qualification which required a five-year apprenticeship and which was the standard route to becoming a general medical practitioner. However, he had only passed the Society's examinations at the second attempt, seven years after he had been first indentured.³⁵ He joined his father in Demerara in February 1832 and was well liked by the colonists, although his father regretted '... that the bent of his mind is decidedly against following the profession for which he very nearly qualified himself. If he would only agree to follow the medical profession he might ere now live respectably settled in this colony.'³⁶ In fact, Henry had qualified but his business as a 'surgeon and apothecary, dealer and chapman' in London had failed and bankruptcy proceedings had followed.³⁷ He subsequently returned to Britain and was in practice again by 1841, ending his life in modest circumstances.

Like Eliza Thomas, the 'free coloured' woman Elizabeth Swain Bannister, with her partner William Fraser, made great efforts to secure a future for their children but with less success than she might have hoped. Fraser (1787–1830) was the son of a house-carpenter in Cromarty and arrived in Berbice in 1803, aged sixteen.³⁸ Bannister (d.1828) was born as a slave in Barbados and her freedom was secured in 1806 by a Susannah Ostrehan. Bannister was in a sexual relationship with Fraser, in Berbice, by 1809 and they had four children: John (b.1810), George (b.1815), Elizabeth (d. before 1822) and Jane (c.1821–c.50).³⁹ Fraser also had a daughter, Anna Maria (c.1810–93), with a Mary Stuart in Barbados, probably a 'free coloured' woman.

By 1821, Fraser had a successful business at *Goldstone Hall*, with 330 slaves and a modern steam-powered sugar mill, 'assets' which were valued at almost 2.2m florins (about £183,000).⁴⁰ Elizabeth Bannister meanwhile had advanced her own position. In 1817, Fraser had made returns for twenty-six slaves he held in his own name and, as their father, for sixteen slaves belonging to his children.⁴¹ But, by 1822, Fraser had only fourteen slaves of his own, while Bannister and her children had sixty-three, transferred by sale from Fraser and his former partner, Richard Clark Downer. She had also ensured a good education for her children. In 1823, John and George were attending Paisley Grammar School, where in 1827 John would be among the prize-winners, and Jane was at school in Liverpool. Bannister died in Berbice in 1828 leaving property to her four children, including £3,000 'to be applied to the maintenance, education and support of my daughter Jane Frazer who is at present at school in Glasgow'.[42]

William Fraser had visited Britain in 1823 and successfully petitioned the Privy Council for 'letters of legitimation' which would enable his children to inherit his property. He made his own will in Berbice in January 1830, after a protracted illness, and then returned to Scotland where he married nineteen-year-old Elizabeth Munro (b.1811), from Munlochy (Ross-shire). His young wife and his daughter Anna Maria, who was living with the Munros, were the same age.[43] Fraser, who was by then seriously ill, died in August 1830 and his hasty marriage seems to have been intended to provide for his children, particularly his daughters, by giving them the security of a family in Scotland. He had sold *Goldstone Hall* and then made an unsuccessful offer of £10,000 for the estate and elegant mansion house of Braelangwell, near Cromarty, with the intention that his new wife and his daughters, Anna Maria and Jane, should live there together.[44] It took many years for Fraser's estate to be settled, its value being insufficient to meet the demands of his creditors and pay the legacies, and a compromise agreement was not reached until 1846.[45] In this process the claims of Elizabeth Munro, including her entitlement under an ante-nuptial contract, were in competition with the claims of Fraser's children and it is clear that his desire that his wife and daughters live together harmoniously as a family was never realised.

Elizabeth Bannister had sought to provide for her children by ensuring their education, particularly that of her daughter Jane. What, then, became of her children and of William Fraser's daughter by Mary Stuart? In 1829, before leaving Berbice, Fraser had bought *L'Esperance*, a sugar plantation in the neighbouring Dutch colony of Surinam, where slavery would not be abolished until 1863. His son George returned to South America, managed this on behalf of Fraser's executor, later purchased the plantation, and was the owner until at least 1859.[46] In 1832, 'John Fraser of Berbice' was indentured as an apprentice surgeon in Cromarty but he became mentally incapacitated and died sometime before 1845.[47] In 1838, Jane married Giles Dixon, a 'merchant and manufacturer', and in 1841 she was living in Rothesay, with her husband and a daughter Maria.[48] They moved to Devon the following year, a son John was born about 1850, Jane subsequently died, and her husband emigrated with their children to Chicago where he worked as a carriage painter.[49] In 1834 their half-sister, Anna Maria, had written to the Colonial Secretary in London stating that 'the only money I possessed I laid out in the purchase of a negro slave' and seeking advice on claiming compensation following emancipation. She received £35 9s 10d. Anna Maria lived with her half-sister Jane in Rothesay and Devon, before returning to Inverness where she died, unmarried, in 1893.[50] Thus the only child to prosper was George, who had returned to South America where there was a recognised role for 'free coloureds'.

The four 'coloured' children of George Inglis (1764–1847) and Susanne Kerr (d.1814) also came to Scotland for education but, unlike the Fraser children, they lived in Inverness in the shadow of their father's legitimate offspring. George Inglis was the youngest son of an Inverness merchant, Hugh Inglis (1711–82), and went to the Caribbean island of St Vincent about 1780 as a clerk for the Highland-born slave trader George Baillie (1755–1810). The Inglis family had already spread themselves across the Atlantic. His father's half-brother was in Carolina, where he had been joined by two of George's older brothers. Of his other brothers, Hugh (d.1796) captained one of Baillie's slaving ships and William (1747–1801), who remained in Inverness, had already become a successful merchant and a senior member of the burgh council.[51]

By 1790, George Inglis had progressed from a clerkship to a partnership with Baillie and the brothers Archibald Alves (1765–1839) and William Alves (1780–1835), who had strong Inverness connections. He then acquired a plantation in Demerara and in 1792 returned to St Vincent to dissolve the partnership there. A letter from his brother Hugh to William, now Dean of Guild in Inverness, vividly illustrates the allure of Demerara:

> George ... reckons himself worth £6000. This is a handsome sum for a young man and acquired very speedily for George had not much to reckon on when he took it into his head to become a Demerary planter and inconsiderately and inadvisedly threw himself out of one of the most eligible and profitable situations in the West Indies.[52]

George had formed a relationship in St Vincent with Susanne Kerr, a 'free mulatto woman', who through this alliance linked herself, like Eliza Thomas, to a transatlantic merchant network. After moving to Demerara, she and George Inglis had four children, named William, Hugh, George and Helen. They were all born before 1798, when Inglis returned to Inverness to marry sixteen-year-old Helen Alves (1782–1876), the sister of his former partners in St Vincent. He brought his four 'natural' children with him and they were all educated at Inverness Academy, leaving Susanne Kerr in Demerara, where she maintained a relatively prosperous position in society. At her death in 1814, she was the owner of fourteen slaves and among her possessions was a silver nutmeg grater, the gift of Mrs Wilson, whose husband was the agent for John Gladstone of Liverpool. She also owned table silver and an impressive range of personal jewellery – ten pairs of ear-rings, two garnet necklaces, five finger rings, two pairs of bracelets, a gold head ornament, a gold thimble and a silver watch.

In 1801, William Inglis, who had risen to be provost of Inverness, committed suicide and this devastated George, who in a letter to his former partner, George Baillie, confided: 'I have serious thoughts of removing with my wife and our little ones to some country Town in England where we can live a life of seclusion best suited to my melancholy & dejected mind.' George and his family moved to Clifton (Bristol) but 'his little ones' did not include Kerr's four children, who remained at school in Inverness.[53] In 1813, faced with increasing financial problems, Inglis felt obliged to return to the Demerara and take control of his affairs. He kept a notebook, entitled a 'Memorandum for General Conduct in Demerary',[54] which reveals pious attitudes probably very different to those of the young merchant who had formed a relationship with Susanne Kerr. He was also determined to 'observe rigidly temperance in my living ... [and] the utmost economy in my expenses'. On 1 March 1814, among notes about keeping hogs and sheep, deepening drainage canals, and reducing the number of 'house Negroes', is the entry: 'Keep in view the future disposal of the House in Georgetown & the disposal of —— effects for her Daughter.' This, a blank in a notebook, is his only reference to Susanne Kerr, who drew up her will on 14 April 1814. She died shortly afterwards.

What, then, of Susanne's children? Her oldest son, William, had become a lieutenant of infantry in the East India Company's army; George was apprenticed to a cooper in Liverpool; and nothing is known of Hugh. During her father's absence in Demerara, Helen had eloped with George Hepburn (1791–1840), a 'master in the Royal Navy'. Inglis concluded a marriage settlement with Hepburn, who left the navy and became a merchant captain in the Demerara trade, based in Greenock and Port Glasgow, where the couple had six children. When the settlement of Otago, New Zealand, was established in March 1848, with strong connections to the recently formed Free Church of Scotland, the early arrivals included three daughters of Helen Inglis – grandchildren of Susanne Kerr – two of whom had married in Inverness.[55] Were their darker skins more accepted in the new colony than they had been in Scotland? Their grandfather, George Inglis, had returned to Kingsmills House, in Inverness, and his legitimate children, their spouses and grandchildren were part of the town's social elite. It is unlikely that the parallel Inglis households co-existed easily. Perhaps, for Kerr's grandchildren, their grandfather's death in 1847 ended any lasting attachment to the town.

Kerr had left the bulk of her own estate to her daughter Helen because her sons were 'in such situations in the world as to enable them to support themselves comfortably'. It was the daughters of such relationships who generally faced a more uncertain future. Some, such as Henrietta Fraser and Eliza Williams (see below), trained as teachers or governesses. A few, perhaps aided by the prospect of an inheritance, were able to marry. These included Helen Inglis, Jane Fraser (below), Minny Iver (below), and Mary Fraser (1815–94). Mary was one of the four surviving children of the 'free coloured' woman Elizabeth Brotherson and Thomas Fraser (1784–1835) from Artigan, near Beauly, who had come to Demerara sometime before 1813, with his brother William (1787–1856). They rose from running a task gang of slaves to be among the most respected planters in the colony.[56] Thomas Fraser died in 1835, leaving annuities of £100 to each of his children, and in 1851 Mary married James Nichol, a prominent Edinburgh bookseller and publisher, while her sister Eliza remained single.[57]

Some couples made little or no attempt to settle their children in Britain, recognising that their best opportunities lay among the 'free coloured' population of Guyana or elsewhere in the expanding British empire. Joan Cameron

(1782–1862) of Glen Nevis went to Berbice sometime after 1797[58] and prospered in a partnership with Donald Charles Cameron, also from Lochaber, trading as D C & J Cameron from 1816 to 1840.[59] In 1835, the partners received compensation of almost £30,000 for the emancipation of 571 enslaved people[60] and John Cameron returned to Britain before 1846.[61]

From about 1809, Cameron was in a relationship with Elizabeth Sharpe, a 'free coloured' woman, with whom he had seven children.[62] There is no evidence that Cameron and Sharpe married but one of their sons, and possibly their other children, were baptised in the colony church in New Amsterdam, suggesting considerable social acceptance of their relationship.[63] Their three older sons married in Guyana, at least two of them to 'free coloured' women.[64] The two unmarried younger brothers returned to Britain, perhaps with their father, and then sailed from London to Australia, arriving in 1845 to become graziers on the Darling Downs.[65] John Cameron sold his property in Scotland about 1850 and moved to St Helier (Jersey) with his two daughters.[66] Between 1850 and 1854, the three older sons and their families also left Guyana and emigrated to Australia,[67] leaving their unmarried sisters to care for their ageing father, who died in London in 1862.

In Scotland, the Camerons of Glen Nevis simply faded from memory. In 1899, a correspondence on their fate began in the *Celtic Monthly*, a 'magazine for Highlanders'.[68] All were agreed that the last of the family to live in Lochaber was John Cameron and that he had become a planter in Berbice. One writer believed that 'he ended his days in the Channel Islands' but added that 'if he left male off-spring I never heard of them'. None were aware of his numerous descendants in Australia, who celebrated their connection to Glen Nevis but they were of 'mixed race'.

Only very rarely did 'free coloured' women accompany their partners to Scotland and this writer has discovered only one case of a woman coming from Guyana to the Highlands. The brothers John (d.1818) and Alexander Fraser (d.1808), from the Inverness area, began their careers about 1766 as clerks in the merchant house of Smith & Baillies in St Kitts and soon after 1804 acquired a share in plantation *Good Intent* in Demerara.[69] When John died at Findhorn, Moray, he was living with a 'free mulatto woman' Henrietta Fraser, formerly a slave on the island of Nevis. Henrietta was presumably the servant who is recorded as leaving Demerara with him the previous year.[70] Their son, James, was a 'a teacher in the County of Middlesex or Essex' and Elizabeth Fraser, a 'free coloured girl' who was the daughter of an enslaved woman, Rose, on the same estate in Nevis, was living in Alnwick, Northumberland.[71]

Enslaved women and their children

As already noted, sexual abuse was endemic on plantations and many of the 'mixed race' children consequently born to enslaved women lived out their own lives in a state of slavery. Their number, recorded after 1817 in the slave registers, is an indication of the extent of sexual abuse – but only an indication, partly because of high rates of infant mortality. Of the 23,768 slaves registered in Berbice in 1819, 355 (1.5%) were 'mulattos', that is the children of white fathers and enslaved black women. These ranged in age from infants to adults who had lived as slaves for decades. A further 123 enslaved people were the descendants of enslaved 'mulatto' women, fathered by white men or fellow slaves. In total, about 480 (c.2%) of the enslaved people in Berbice would have been regarded by their owners as of 'mixed race'.[72] In the following year, 1820, there were 77,373 slaves registered in Demerara–Essequibo, suggesting a total 'mixed race' slave population in Guyana of at least 2,000 in 1819/20, the year in which the enslaved population peaked. Although behind almost all of these 2,000 or so individuals is a now lost account of sexual exploitation, these enslaved 'coloured' children were nevertheless born with higher status, seldom worked in the field, and were more likely to have domestic roles if female or train in some skilled trade if male.[73] They were also better dressed and might receive some education.[74]

Despite the origin of these relationships, bonds of genuine affection could be established while such ties, or a sense of responsibility by fathers to their children, might lead to the costly legal process of manumission by which both the enslaved woman and the couple's children were freed. Stephen Foster's *A Private Empire*,[75] a cross-generational study of the Macpherson family of Blairgowrie, gives an account of William Macpherson (1784–1866), whose relationship with an enslaved woman in Berbice, and the birth of three children, led to years of tension within his family. For the woman, given the name Countess while enslaved and Harriet at manumission, it brought freedom but also abandonment and a parting from her children, Eliza (1807–37), Matilda (1809–?) and Allan (1810–96), who were taken to Britain by their father. The children were given the surname Williams, rather than Fraser, and lived life in the shadows, referred to by Macpherson's mother as 'the little moonlight shades' and only slowly gaining some limited acceptance within the family. This is probably the fullest and most intimate account of such a relationship that can be recovered from the history of slavery in these colonies and Foster believes that Macpherson 'loved [Countess] with emotions similar to those any young lover might feel for his more conventional mistress or bride.' Macpherson's father had encouraged both William, and his brother Allan, to enter into some form of stable relationship in Berbice, counselling them to avoid 'loose women' who would be 'certain destruction to your health, character, money & happiness in this world & ruin to your Soul in the world to come'. This was followed by the pragmatic concession, 'I by all means recommend you to keep a decent Native woman of the Country where you may be as your constant concubine.' Yet this made William's attempt to integrate Countess's children into his Scottish family no easier.[76]

A similar mixture of tacit acceptance of a relationship coupled with unease about the birth of 'coloured' children can be seen in the case of Andrew

Rose (1783–1832). He came from Banff-shire to Demerara in 1800 as a land surveyor, followed in 1806 by his sister, Anna (1778–1827), who married a Dutch merchant. In June 1807, Anna, who had just given birth to her own son, wrote to her mother saying, 'I told you in my last letter that Andrew had lost his little Mary. On the whole it is a fortunate circumstance as 'tis next to impossible to bring up a girl of that colour virtuously'. Despite his sister's disapproval, Andrew's relationship continued and four years later he manumitted 'a negro woman named Minkie, and her mulatto child Anna'.[77]

Some family members in Guyana could be supportive of the children born to enslaved women. When Andrew Cuming died in Demerara in 1810, it was a wealthy relation, Thomas Cuming (1739/40–1813), originally from Moray and by this time regarded as the 'patriarch' of the colony, who petitioned for the manumission of his 'two coloured Children named Andrew and William'.[78] Similarly, when Alexander Munro, from Cromarty, died in Demerara in 1823 and his executors offered for sale 'the woman Eve and her five mulatto children',[79] it was Alexander's brother John who appears to have intervened. As a result the children were free when John, in his own will of 1833, divided his estate between his mother and sister in Scotland, and Alexander's five daughters in Demerara.[80]

A father might make provision for manumission in his will, with the cost met from the sale of his assets. James Fraser, a carpenter from Inverness, went to Demerara, worked for several years at plantation *Dochfour*, and built up his own gang of enslaved carpenters. He was prosperous enough in 1798 to subscribe ten guineas to the Northern Infirmary, in Inverness, and when he died of fever in July 1801, his will instructed the manumission of a young enslaved woman and their child.[81]

Provision for children could be generous as in the case of Hector Mackenzie, from the parish of Clyne in Sutherland, who established plantation *Dunrobin* on the east sea-coast of Berbice. He died in July 1804 leaving instructions to free his slave Nancy, the mother of his 'mulatto daughter Rose', to whom he left £1000.[82] Hugh, Baron Fraser (1784–1824), from Inverness, also left £1,000 to each of his two 'mulatto' children, Mary and James, with instructions that they be manumitted. They were also to receive six slaves but this was significantly less than the £4,000 each and nine slaves bequeathed to his two children born to the 'free coloured' woman Elizabeth le Blair.[83]

The three children of the enslaved African woman Charmion (b. c.1790) and Peter Fairbairn (1762–1822) were similarly freed under his will and in this case we have more knowledge of the intertwining lives of his 'parallel' families in Scotland and Guyana. Charmion became a domestic slave on one of the plantations owned by Lord Seaforth, chief of Clan Mackenzie, who had bought land in Berbice in 1800. Peter Fairbairn, who had been Seaforth's secretary from about 1794,[84] arrived in Berbice to manage the properties in 1801, when he was almost forty, and remained in Guyana until his death in 1822.[85] Fairbairn had a wife and eight children in Scotland and had never intended to remain overseas. In 1808 he was hoping 'to return next year after 8 years abroad' and felt that he had stayed for the previous two years 'to the injury' of his family and children.[86] Seaforth had now begun to query Fairbairn's competence because he believed he had not been provided with adequate accounts of what was happening in Berbice and at the same time Fairbairn had become deeply concerned about his family because his wife had not paid the rent on their farm, on Seaforth's estate, and payments of her annuity had consequently been withheld.[87] In Fairbairn's words, 'Our West India speculation does in this instance sicken me to the heart. It would seem that I am suspected here and that my family must starve at home.'[88]

By 1811, there was a sexual relationship between Fairbairn, now almost fifty, and twenty-two-year old Charmion, who he later described as 'stout and good looking', and they had five children over the next ten years, although two died of fever. Fairbairn now appeared reconciled to life in the colony and was resident at plantation *Kintail*, his 'favourite place', neatly laid out 'like a European farm'. James Baillie Fraser (1783–1856) of Reelig, who visited him in 1814, judged him to have neglected his family in Scotland and could only offer a limited explanation: 'I hardly know how to account for it—but when the general laxity of manners prevalent in these colonies is considered ... we may find the shadow of a reason.'[89] Fairbairn had the power to liberate Charmion and their children but this 'gift' of freedom was withheld until his death, after which his executors followed his instructions and manumitted his family.[90]

Before his death, Fairbairn's two families had come into some kind of contact in Guyana. Three of his legitimate sons had joined him there, although they died in an epidemic of yellow fever in 1823, the year after their father's death. They had been educated at Inverness Academy, alongside the 'coloured' children of other Highland Scots, and in Guyana would have known of, and may well have met, their own 'mulatto' half-brothers and half-sisters. The attitude of one son, Dr James Fairbairn (1791–1823), towards 'coloureds' is revealed in the diary of the missionary John Smith.[91] Dr Fairbairn presented himself as a free thinker 'half inclined to deny the divine authority of Scripture' but he was as conventionally prejudiced as others in the colony. According to Smith he seemed 'desirous of marrying; but will not marry a coloured'. Later Mrs Smith observed that:

> Doctor Fairbairn was about to take Mary-Ann Hamar, a mulatto girl, into keeping; adding at the same time, that she thought it very improper, & that it would have been much more to the girl's credit to have been legally married to Wm Chisholm as they had been attach'd to each other. Mr K[elly] replied that the information was correct, & intimated that Dr F endeavoured to justify his conduct, by saying that colour'd men were cruel to females. Dr F will not marry her.

William Chisholm was almost certainly a 'free coloured' man and may already have been known to Dr Fairbairn, since one of his class-mates at Inverness

Academy had been 'William Chisholm of Demerary'.[92] Either way, Dr Fairbairn is unlikely to have warmed to his own 'coloured' half-brothers and sisters.

The voices of enslaved women, such as Charmion, are elusive and nothing is known of her, or her children, after she regained her freedom at the age of thirty-two. Formerly enslaved women were, however, capable of pursuing their rights using whatever means were open to them. Susannah, on plantation *Alness*, who bore children to George Munro, later gained her own freedom and saw her children become the heirs to their father's estate, along with his nephews and nieces in Scotland. However, the children appear not to have received their inheritance and Susannah, although illiterate, in her own will of 1850 instructed her executors, in London and Guyana, to pursue her family's claims against Munro's estate.[93]

Education in Scotland

A number of children born to enslaved and 'free coloured' women were raised in the Highlands, sometimes from a very young age. In 1804, the Bethune family 'got home two little Foreigners, children of their Brother the late Doctor George Bethune'. The youngest was only a year old. Mrs Robertson, the wife of the parish minister, whose own sons were in Guyana, noted that 'They are yellow, ugly things. I think it would be best to leave them in their own country.' She was, perhaps, unaware of the existence of her own 'coloured' grandchildren. Fortunately, the children were cared for by their aunt and one of them, Agnes Bethune (1803–after 1851), lived with her in Dingwall until the aunt's death forty-five years later.[94] Elizabeth Bannister's daughter, Jane Fraser, can have been little more than two when her father brought her from Berbice to Liverpool in 1823.[95]

'Coloured' children were enrolled in many schools in the Highlands in the early nineteenth century and, in addition to the evidence of school registers, there are two more detailed accounts. Rev. Donald Sage described his friendship with three brothers named Hay, 'the offspring of a negro woman', at school in Dornoch between 1801 and 1803, and Hugh Miller recorded that, about 1815:

> There was a mulatto lad, a native of the West Indies, who sat at the same form with me. He was older and stouter than I, and much dreaded by the other boys for a wild, savage disposition which is, I believe, natural to most of his countryfolks.[96]

Two of the Hay brothers spend part of their holidays with Sage's family in Kildonan, while, in contrast, Miller's relationship with his school fellow led to a knife fight. I have found no examples of black pupils at Highland schools after the 1820s and conclude that by 1830 this had become much less common.

Children from Guyana attended schools in the Highlands at Inverness, Fortrose, Tain and Dornoch, and 'coloured' Guyanese children of Highland fathers were educated in Dollar, Paisley, Glasgow, Liverpool, London and, no doubt, elsewhere. In some cases the connection with the Highlands was indirect. Minny Iver (c.1809–80), who attended Tain Academy from 1816, was the illegitimate, Demerara-born daughter of Archibald Iver (d.1845), a merchant in Georgetown. He had returned with her to Edinburgh, where he married Mitchell Shaw, the daughter of an Inverness merchant, and it may have been his new wife's origins which led to the choice of school.[97]

Some returned to Guyana after their schooling. John Noble (d.1826) from Inverness was manager of *La Bonne Intention* in Demerara where he had two children, John and Mary Ann, with Susan Ross, a 'free coloured' woman. In 1811 his son left Demerara with Noble's friend Lewis Corbet and Noble later wrote to James Grant, provost of Inverness, saying: 'I hope in God they are both safe at Inverness long ere this'. He asked that his son 'be placed at the Inverness Academy as a boarder with one of the Masters or at any other Genteel Boarding House'.[98] When John Noble senior died at Plymouth in November 1826 his two children inherited his property and both were back in Guyana by 1832, if not before.[99] Some regarded education of this kind as a mistake. After the death of a cousin in St Vincent, a Thomas Fraser wrote from the colony to relations in Inverness:

> There is a Mulatto boy of his in Glasgow on whose account there is now due to the woman at whose house he boards at least one hundred pounds sterling, it was a piece of foolish extravagance to have him sent home for I never saw one of the colour sent home that came to any good.[100]

Eliza (Elizabeth) Junor (1804–61) is the only child I have identified who was born to an enslaved or 'free coloured' woman in Guyana, was educated in the Highlands, and lived there until her death, albeit after a troubled absence in London. Eliza and her brother William (1810–73) were baptised in the parish church at Rosemarkie in August 1816.[101] Their father Hugh Junor (d.1823), who was probably a carpenter, had prospered in Guyana where he had bought a half-share in the timber estate *Industry*, in Essequibo, with its sixty-six slaves.[102] They had all left Guyana in June and nothing is known of their mother.[103]

In the same church, in September 1817, Hugh, despite his relatively humble origins, married Martha Matheson, daughter of Colin Matheson of Bennetsfield, chief of Clan Matheson. The Matheson family had extensive interests in Guyana and Martha's sister and three brothers all, at various times, lived in Berbice.[104] Hugh and his wife returned to Guyana, where a son Colin was born. Eliza and William attended Fortrose Academy, where Eliza was awarded the prize for 'proficiency in penmanship'.[105] When he died in 1823, Hugh's property in Guyana passed to his legitimate infant son and his wife.[106]

In 1837 Eliza had an illegitimate child in London, a daughter Emma, whose father was recorded as 'Thomas McGregor, gentleman'. In 1841 Eliza was living with Emma in Lambeth but by 1851 she had returned to the north, working as a dress-maker in Fortrose, where she died on 20 April 1861. The 1861 census, which had been taken twelve days before, shows that she had been visited by her daughter, who described herself to the census enumerator not as a family member but as a 'visitor', employed as a governess in England. But Emma was with her mother when she died and reported the death to the registrar, now identifying herself as Eliza's daughter.[107] There appears to be no further trace of Emma. Eliza's brother, William, became a cabinet maker and emigrated, before 1835, to Buenos Aires, Argentina, where he opened a shop, married a fellow Scot, and in addition to following his trade became a 'devoted Bible agent' of the Methodist Episcopal Church, until his death in 1873.[108]

Conclusions

Sexual abuse was endemic in the plantations of Guyana, as elsewhere in the Caribbean, and almost all of the details of this are now irrecoverable. However, given the small number of European women in these colonies, a few enslaved women and more 'free coloured' women were able to turn the situation to their advantage, securing their freedom if enslaved and acquiring property through their relationships, often with Highland Scots. They also sought, by whatever means were open to them, to secure a future for their children, often parting with them so that they might have the benefit of an education in Britain. But, by the 1830s, the enrolment of 'coloured' children in Highland schools had all but ended and their prospects in Britain had narrowed.

In the examples given, an attempt has been made to capture something of the intertwining of the families of Highland Scots and their related families of African descent in Guyana, both enslaved and free. This created blood relationships of surprising closeness to prominent figures in British society. The children of the enslaved woman Charmion and Peter Fairbairn were first cousins to two prominent Victorian engineers, Sir William Fairbairn, appointed president of the British Association in 1861, and Sir Peter Fairbairn, lord mayor of Leeds.[109] The 'two little Foreigners', children of Dr George Bethune, were within three degrees of consanguinity to the future prime minister, William Ewart Gladstone – Dr Bethune and Gladstone's mother were first cousins. And marriages brought others into close, though probably unacknowledged, proximity, as with Minny Iver who became a 'niece' of the essayist William Hazlitt through his second wife, Isabella Shaw, a sister of Minny's step-mother.[110] Just the same was true in all social classes, including the many Highland Scots 'of humble extraction'. But in all cases consanguinity was a currency which was quickly devalued. The examples considered here suggest that these children struggled to find a place in society in Scotland, certainly not in the Highlands, and many returned to Guyana or emigrated to other colonies.

Note

Further information on most of the individuals in this study can be found on my website at www.spanglefish.com/slavesandhighlanders

Notes

1. Tony Judt with Timothy Snyder, *Thinking the Twentieth Century* (London, 2013), 268.
2. Kit Candlin, *The Last Caribbean Frontier, 1795–1815* (Basingstoke, 2012), xii.
3. Johannes Postma, *The Dutch in the Atlantic Slave Trade, 1600–1815* (Cambridge, 1990), 216; *Naamlyst der bestierders, officieren en bediendens &c. op de Colonie der Berbice, 1794*, transcribed by Paul Koulen at www.rootsweb.ancestry.com/ nyggbs/Transcriptions.htm (accessed 20 July 2013).
4. Douglas Hamilton, *Scotland, The Caribbean and the Atlantic World, 1750–1820* (Manchester, 2005); David Alston, '"Very rapid and splendid fortunes"? Highland Scots in Berbice (Guyana) in the early nineteenth century', *Transactions of the Gaelic Society of Inverness* 63 (2004), 208–36.
5. Henry Gibbs Dalton, *The History of British Guiana*, 2 vols (London, 1855), ii, 538–9; B. W. Higman, *Slave Populations of the British Caribbean, 1807–1834* (Kingston, 1995).
6. Dalton, *British Guiana*, i, 306–8.
7. Alston, 'Very rapid and splendid fortunes'.
8. Edinburgh, National Archives of Scotland [NAS], GD46/17/26, Peter Fairbairn to Lord Seaforth, 10 Oct 1804; National Register of Archives of Scotland [NRAS] 2696, Edward Fraser to his mother, from No. 28, West Coast Berbice, 7 April 1805 and 13 January 1806.
9. Clan Munro exhibition, Foulis Castle (2007), Pierre Antoine Conefroy Munro to Mrs M. J(osephet) Ser(indac) Munro at Montreal, from Berbice, Foulis Plantation 12 December 1830.
10. NRAS 2696, Edward Fraser to his mother, 30 May 1805, 13 December 1807 and 15 January 1808.
11. George Duffield, *Record of the Golden Wedding of Rev. George Duffield, D D. and Isabella Graham Bethune Duffield* (Philadelphia, 1867), 37.
12. Dalton, *British Guiana*, ii, 306.
13. Alvin O. Thompson, 'Enslaved children in Berbice', in Alvin O. Thompson (ed.), *In the Shadow of the Plantation* (Kingston, 2002), 183–5.
14. London, The National Archives [TNA], Records of the Prerogative Court of Canterbury [PROB] 11/1712, fo. 474, will of George Munro; PROB 11/2176, fo. 30, will of Susannah Munro; TNA T71, Office of Registry of Colonial Slaves and Slave Compensation Commission, Slave Registers, Berbice, 1818/19 and 1822; Eirene O'Jon, *Slave Society in Early Nineteenth Century Berbice* (Guyana, 1992).
15. Edinburgh, National Library of Scotland [NLS], GB233/MS 9332, fo. 69, Hugh Munro Robertson to Thomas Traill, 9 September 1806.
16. James H. Sweet, *Recreating Africa: Culture, Kinship and Religion in the African–Portuguese World, 1441–1770* (North Carolina, 2003), 73–4; Trevor Burnard, *Mastery, Tyranny, and Desire: Thomas Thistlewood and His Slaves in the Anglo-Jamaican World* (North Carolina, 2004), 207.
17. Barbara Bush, *Slave Women in Caribbean Society, 1650–1838* (Indiana, 1990); Ronald Hyman, *Empire and Sexuality. The British Experience* (Manchester, 1990) Mark Berger,

'Imperialism and Sexual Exploitation', *Journal of Imperial and Commonwealth History*, 17 (1) (1988), 84.
18. Hilary Beckles, *Natural Rebels: A History of Enslaved Black Women in Barbados* (New Brunswick, 1989); Pedro Welch, *Slave Society in the City: Bridgetown, Barbados 1680–1834* (Kingston, 2003); Candlin, *The Last Caribbean Frontier*.
19. Thomas Staunton St Clair, *A Residence in the West Indies*, 2 vols (1834), i, 110–12.
20. Henry Bolinbroke, *A Voyage to the Demerary* (London, 1807), 43.
21. Candlin, *The Last Caribbean Frontier*, 161.
22. Gaiutra Bahadur, *Coolie Woman: The Odyssey of Indenture* (London, 2013), 26.
23. Tom Hartford, *The Logic of Life* (London, 2009), 73–7.
24. Gad Heuman, *The Caribbean: A Brief History* (London, 2014), 97.
25. Rawle Farley, 'The Shadow and the Substance', *Caribbean Quarterly* (December, 1955), 132–53.
26. Candlin, *The Last Caribbean Frontier*, 25; Cassandra Pybus, 'Tense and Tender Ties', in Paul Longley Arthur (ed.), *International Life Writing: Memory and Identity in a Global Context* (Abingdon, 2013), 5–17.
27. George Sherwood (ed.), *The Pedigree Register* (London, 1910–1914), ii, 185; *Gentleman's Magazine*, 1787; NLS, GB233 Papers of Thomas Stewart Traill, in particular MSS 19330–19334.
28. University of London, SOAS Library, Journal of J. C. Cheveley, ii, 124.
29. *Australian Dictionary of Biography* (1967), ii; NAS, CS96/1526; Cassandra Pybus, 'The Colourful Life of Gilbert Robertson', at http://launcestonhistory.org.au/wp-content/uploads/2012/03/CassandraPybus20112.pdf (accessed on 2 June 2014).
30. NLS, GB233/MS19332, fo. 86, Hugh Munro Robertson, Berbice, to Dr Traill, 4 June 1809.
31. NLS, GB233/MS19332, fo. 69, Robertson to Traill, 9 September 1806; TNA, T71, Slave Registers.
32. NLS, GB233/MS19332, fo. 67, Robertson to Traill, 17 August 1806.
33. Liverpool Record Office, Parker Family Papers, 920 PAR 1/53, 11 August 1810.
34. PROB 11/2007/434, will of Dorothy Thomas born Kirwan, 26 February 1842.
35. London, Society of Apothecaries, Court of Examiners Candidates' Qualification Entry Book 1826–29, 558 and 619.
36. NLS, GB233/MS19332, fo. 21, Gilbert Robertson to Doctor Traill, Liverpool, 23 October 1832.
37. *London Gazette*, 15 January 1833.
38. General Register Office of Scotland [GROS] Old Parish Registers [OPR] 061/00 0010 0156; TNA, CO 111/96, Petition from William Fraser, formerly of Berbice, then residing in the city of London, 19 October 1823.
39. PROB 11/1780/160, will of William Fraser; Pedro L. V. Welch, 'What's in a name?: from slavery to freedom in Barbados', Barbados Association of Retired Person's Lecture, 23 September 2003 at www.h-net.org/ slavery under Discussion logs, March 2005 (accessed on 2 June 2014). Dates of birth from TNA, CO 111/96 and, for Jane, from census returns. For Elizabeth, see TNA, T71, Slave Registers, Berbice.
40. NAS, CS96/2131, William Fraser, plantation owner, Berbice, journal 1819–29.
41. NAS, CS96/2131; TNA, T71, Slave Registers, Berbice.
42. Robert Brown, *The History of Paisley Grammar School* (1875), 523; will of Elizabeth Swayne Bannister cited in Pedro L. V. Welch, 'Madams and Mariners', Annual Conference of the Association of Caribbean Historians, April 7–12, 1997 at www.reocities.com/Athens/Ithaca/1834/document3.htm (accessed on 2 June 2014).

43. PROB 11/1780/160, will of William Fraser of Berbice.
44. NAS, CS96/2131; OPR 073/00 0020 0195, Parish of Suddie and Kilmuir Wester, 25 May 1830; *Inverness Journal* 13 August 1830.
45. NAS, CS238/C20/10, John Cameron v Fraser's Legatees; NAS, CS238/M15/11, Colin Munro v Aeneas Barkly.
46. NAS, CS238/C20/10 and CS238/M15/11; NAS, CS96/2131; *Accounts and Papers of the House of Commons* (1860), 81.
47. Documents in possession of M. G. Smith, London; NAS, CS238/C20/10 and CS238/M15/11.
48. OPR 622/00 0170 0551; Census return 1841.
49. NAS, CS238/C20/10 and CS238/M15/11; US Federal Census: 1860, 1870 and 1880.
50. TNA, T71/1610, 26 June 1834 from Anna Maria Fraser; GROS 098/00 0406.
51. Inverness Museum, Inglis Papers.
52. Inglis Papers.
53. NAS, GD46/17/20, Edward Satchwell Fraser to Lord Seaforth, February 1801; Inglis Papers.
54. Inglis Papers.
55. Passenger arrivals at Port Chalmers, New Zealand, March 1848–January 1851 at www.ngaiopress.com/drhocken.htm (accessed on 2 June 2014).
56. Walter Rodney, *Guyanese Sugar Plantations in the Late Nineteenth Century* (1979), reprinted from *The Argosy* (1883).
57. PROB 11/1856, fo. 333, will of Thomas Fraser, 1836; OPR 685/02 0470 0274; SC70/4/107, contract of marriage.
58. *The New Statistical Account of Scotland* (Edinburgh, 1845), ix, Parish of Kilmallie (May 1835), 121.
59. NAS, CS96/972–981, papers of D. C. Cameron and Company and D. C. and J. Cameron and Company, both of Berbice.
60. TNA, T71/885, British Guiana claim nos 291, 292 and 422.
61. NAS, CS238/C20/10, John Cameron Esq. v Fraser's Legatees.
62. The identity of Elizabeth Sharpe as their mother is confirmed in the Australian death records of the five sons. TNA, T71, Slave Registers, Berbice, 167 and 929 describe Sharpe as a 'free coloured woman'.
63. Baptismal certificate extracted from church records, at http://trees.ancestry.co.uk/tree/54521931/person/13677317165 (accessed on 2 June 2014). See comments of Governor Beard in House of Commons, *Command Papers* (1825), xxvi, 227.
64. The sons were Alexander (1812–81), Evan (1817–72), John (1821–1904), Charles Matheson (1825–1907) and Donald Charles (1828–1914); the daughters were Helen (1809–84) and Isabella (1826–65).
65. Elizabeth Tarnawski, *The Camerons of Southeast Queensland* (1984).
66. TNA, Census Returns for England and Wales, 1851, Channel Islands, Jersey, St Helier, District 18.
67. For Evan Cameron see New South Wales, Australia, Unassisted Immigrant Passenger Lists, 1826–1922 at www.records.nsw.gov.au/state-archives/research-topics/immigration/immigration (accessed on 2 June 2014); for Alexander Cameron see State Records Authority of New South Wales, Passengers Arriving 1855–1922, NRS13278 [X91], reel 400.
68. *The Celtic Monthly* VII (1899)
69. NAS, SC29/55/11/331; John Campbell, *Reports of Cases Determined at Nisi Prius* (London, 1809), 149; *Essequebo and Demerara Royal Gazette*, 23 April 1808.

70. *The Royal Gazette* (Demerara), 22 February 1817.
71. NAS, SC70/1/25, will of John Fraser, died Findhorn, May 1818.
72. TNA, T71, Slave Registers, Berbice.
73. Heumann, *The Caribbean*, 36.
74. Quoted in Alvin O. Thompson, 'Enslaved Children in Berbice', in Alvin O. Thomson (ed.), *In the Shadow of the Plantation* (Kingston, 2002), 169.
75. Stephen Foster, *A Private Empire* (New South Wales, 2010).
76. Foster, *A Private Empire*, 161.
77. Alistair and Henrietta Tayler, *Domestic Papers of the Rose Family* (London, 1926), 157; *Essequebo and Demerara Royal Gazette*, 12 October 1811.
78. *Essequebo and Demerara Royal Gazette*, 8 May 1810.
79. Folarin Shylion, 'Slave Advertisements in the British West Indies', *Caribbean Studies* 18 (1978/9), 175–99.
80. NAS, SC25/44/3.
81. Highland Council Archive [HCA], D122/2/3, Donald Mackay, Abary Coast, Demerary to Alexander Fraser, Inverness, 20 March 1802.
82. PROB 11/1440, fo. 259, will of Hector MacKenzee.
83. PROB 11/1697, fo. 784, will of Hugh B. Fraser.
84. Finlay McKichan, 'Lord Seaforth and Highland estate management in the first phase of Clearance (1783–1815)', *Scottish Historical Review* 221 (2007), and 'Lord Seaforth: Highland proprietor, Caribbean governor and slave owner', *Scottish Historical Review* 230 (2011).
85. *Guiana Chronicle and Demerara Gazette* (Georgetown, Guyana), 8 July 1822.
86. NAS, GD46/17/31, Fairbairn to Lord Seaforth, 7 April 1808.
87. NAS, GD46/17/36, James Baillie Fraser to Lord Seaforth, 14 February 1814.
88. NAS, GD46/17/31, Fairbairn to Lord Seaforth, 7 April 1808.
89. NAS, GD46/17/36, James Baillie Fraser to Lord Seaforth, 14 February 1814.
90. *Papers Relating to the Manumission, Government and Population of Slaves in the West Indies, 1822–1824* (London, 1825), 9.
91. School of Oriental and African Studies, University of London, CWM/LMS/West Indies and British Guiana/Journals/Box 1, Journal of John Smith.
92. Inverness Royal Academy, Student Registers.
93. TNA, CO 111/84, Beard to Bathurst, 12 Aug 1816; PROB 11/2176, fo. 30, will of Susannah Munro, written in 1850.
94. NLS, GB233/MS19331, fo. 83, Anne Robertson, Kiltearn, to her daughter Christian (Mrs Watson), Crantit, Orkney, 20 April 1804; Census returns 1841.
95. TNA, CO111/96 and Census return 1841, Rothesay.
96. Donald Sage, *Memorabilia Domestica* (Wick, 1889), 157; Michael Shortland (ed.), *Hugh Miller's Memoir: From Stonemason to Geologist* (Edinburgh, 1995), 107.
97. HCA, Tain Royal Academy, Admissions Register; OPR 685/01 0540 0205.
98. NAS, GD23/6/527.
99. *Inverness Journal*, 17 November 1826; TNA, T71/432, fos 1301 and 1305.
100. HCA, D238, Fraser of Boblainy papers, Fraser to Simon Fraser, 24 April 1801.
101. OPR 080/0010 0059; burials registered in the Methodist Episcopal Church, Buenos Aires, 1871–80 at www.argbrit.org/Methodist/MethFunls1871–80.htm (accessed on 2 June 2014).
102. *Demerary and Essequebo Royal Gazette*, 19 August 1815; *Guiana Boundary, Arbitration with the United States of Venezuela. The Counter-Case on behalf of the Government of Her Britannic*

Majesty (London, 1898), 3; *Statistical Report on the Sickness, Mortality, and Invaliding among the Troops in the West Indies* (London, 1838).

103. *Demerary and Essequebo Royal Gazette*, 8 June 1816.
104. *Inverness Journal*, 19 September 1817.
105. Fortrose Academy, Minute Books; *Inverness Journal*, 21 June 1822.
106. King's College, London, Foreign and Commonwealth Office Library, Land Claims, British Guiana, 256–9.
107. General Register Office, Register of Births, 1837, Quarter 4, St George in the East, vol. 2, p. 91; GROS 080/S00 0012.
108. Genealogy of Rev. Francis Neville Lett (who married the Junors' daughter Agnes) at http://genforum.genealogy.com/lett/messages/2145.html (accessed on 2 June 2014); British and Foreign Bible Society, BSAS/1/J Foreign Correspondents 1804–97; Justice C. Anderson, *An Evangelical Saga – Baptists and their Precursors in Latin America* (Xulon Press, 2005).
109. William Pole (ed.), *The Life of Sir William Fairbairn, Bart.* (London, 1877); James Burnley, 'Fairbairn, Sir William, first baronet (1789–1874)', rev. Robert Brown, *Oxford Dictionary of National Biography* (Oxford, 2004); Gillian Cookson, 'Fairbairn, Sir Peter (1799–1861)', *ODNB*.
110. Duncan Wu, *William Hazlitt: The First Modern Man* (Oxford, 2008), 343.

BENNACHIE, THE 'COLONY', BALQUHAIN AND FETTERNEAR – SOME ARCHIVAL SOURCES

COLIN MILLER

Introduction

Located nineteen miles (thirty kilometres) north-west of Aberdeen, the distinctive silhouette of the hill of Bennachie is visible from many parts of Aberdeenshire. In 2012–14, with funding from the Arts and Humanities Research Council, the Bennachie Landscapes Project – a partnership between the Bailies of Bennachie (an amenity group founded in 1973) and the University of Aberdeen – researched many aspects of the hill.[1] Initial work focused on site investigations for archaeological digs, and on selected archives relating to north-east Scotland. This provided familiarisation with methodology and subject matter, both on the ground and among the archives. The archival focus, spanning several centuries of documents, featured place-names, typical land-related manuscripts, and legal phraseology, and culminated in an exhibition at the Sir Duncan Rice Library, University of Aberdeen, in summer 2012. In 2013, work included field and documentary research into soil science, botany, peat resources, quarries and trackways, and archaeological excavations at the 'Colony' on the 'Commonty of Bennachie', which was popularly considered to be common land. (The true status of this land, at that time, seems to have been variously interpreted and intended future research will seek clarification on the matter). In effect a crofting settlement, the Colony evolved during the first half of the nineteenth-century on the previously uncultivated hillside with the spontaneous arrival of households seeking an independent livelihood at a time of rural and social dislocation in the era of agricultural 'Improvement'.

In parallel with the 2013 fieldwork, archival research was conducted by an 'archives group' of community volunteers, including the present author. This work benefitted significantly from locally available collections, notably those at the University of Aberdeen and the archives of the Bailies of Bennachie, in addition to family history research using online resources. Inventories of previously unlisted papers in relevant University of Aberdeen collections were compiled by post-doctoral research fellow, Thomas Brochard,[2] and were of considerable assistance.

This paper focuses on three collections of direct benefit to the project's archival research, namely:

- The Leslie of Balquhain collection – ninety-three bundles of mainly legal documents, held at Aberdeen University Library's Special Collections Centre.
- The Davidson and Garden collection – papers from a legal firm, held at the Special Collections Centre. Within this extensive corpus, covering many estates in north-east Scotland, there is a large body of papers pertaining to Balquhain and Fetternear, to Westhall and to Overhall. The current paper examines those relating to Bennachie in particular.
- The Bailies of Bennachie archives and library, housed at the Bennachie Centre, near Inverurie in Aberdeenshire.

Brief reference is made to other relevant sources. The current paper reflects the project's emphasis on the Colony, with which land the Leslie of Balquhain family was closely involved until the early twentieth century. The author wishes to acknowledge the valuable assistance and encouragement received from the University of Aberdeen and the Bailies of Bennachie.

Aberdeen University Library Special Collections Centre

Located at the Sir Duncan Rice Library in Old Aberdeen, the Special Collections Centre (hereafter SCC) holds the University's historic collections of books, manuscripts, archives and photographs. Among many other significant functions, the collections cover all aspects of the history and culture of north-east Scotland.[3] Many estate papers have been gifted or loaned to SCC, either by landowners or by legal firms for whom the materials had ceased to be of business significance. Consequently, according to Andrew MacGregor, Deputy Archivist at SCC, 'The Centre holds the largest collection of family and estate papers relating to north-east Scotland to be found together in one resource'.[4]

Balquhain and Fetternear

The barony of Balquhain was held by the influential Leslie family from at least the fourteenth century.[5] In 1566, the barony and mansion of Fetternear were gifted to the family by the bishop of Aberdeen.[6] By the 1870s, these Leslie lands consisted of two domains stretching, with only a short break, more than eleven miles (seventeen kilometres) from the Colpy area in the north to the River Don at Fetternear in the south. The estates were finally broken up in 1932.[7] The estate archives from earlier centuries are dominated by charters, titles, land transaction documents and papers arising from occasional legal disputes. Although the majority of these early documents concern Aberdeenshire, some relate to former Abbey lands at Lindores in Fife which were at one time in Leslie ownership.

During the agricultural 'Improvement' era of the first half of the nineteenth century, the ancient farmtoun system of multiple sub-tenancies gave way to self-contained holdings leased by individual farmers and crofters. A significant part of the SCC's nineteenth-century Leslie of Balquhain holdings consists of material connected with rental and leases, as well as routine estate management. Of particular relevance to the project is the legal process known as the 'Division of the Commonty of Benachie' which in 1859 formally divided 4,042 acres (1,636 hectares)[8] of the hill among the adjoining estates. 316 acres (128 hectares),[9] nearly eight per cent of the overall area concerned, were allocated to Balquhain, including the land comprising the Colony.

SCC: Leslie of Balquhain collection (MS 3043)

The papers comprise of ninety-three numbered bundles, deposited in 1980 by the bishop of Aberdeen, having been surveyed in 1979 by the National Register of Archives (Scotland) (NRAS). The resulting handlist, available at SCC,[10] and in abbreviated form via the on-line SCC catalogue,[11] briefly describes each bundle, although individual manuscripts were not catalogued by NRAS. Historically, the documents had evidently been sorted into bundles according to topic. According to the on-line description, 78 of the 93 bundles concern land ownership, with 65 of these containing land titles. Eight bundles concern church matters; four contain 'legal papers' relating to the family; two pertain to specific legal disputes (one regarding the casting of peats and one a remission in connection with a 'slaughter'). Finally, one bundle concerns debts, and one a marriage contract. Marriage contracts also feature in two of the bundles classified above under land ownership. A narrative summary of the contents of MS 3043 is available via the SCC on-line catalogue.[12]

Following on from researching a single MS 3043 document during the familiarisation phase of the Bennachie Landscapes Project in 2012, and under SCC's supervision, the present author was encouraged to take the first step towards full cataloguing of the collection. For each bundle, a spreadsheet was compiled, describing each of the manuscripts therein. This process was considerably boosted by a helpful note in the handlist, advising that many of the documents had been described by Colonel Charles Leslie of Balquhain in his 1869 work *Historical Records of the Family of Leslie*.[13] Colonel Leslie compiled this three-volume work with a team of associates. Fortuitously, large parts of it, especially Volume III, are essentially a calendar of many of the family archives, each briefly described within the historical narrative. This is of particular value to the aspiring archivist, because: (a) the documents are described, with translation from the Latin where necessary, and in some cases transcribed; and (b) today, some of the manuscripts included, and present in MS 3043 have become illegible, at least regarding the critically important short title and/or date on the reverse.

In most cases, the reverse of each document also carries a reference number in a running series from one to 1010. This numbering corresponds in many (but not all) instances to the approximately 364 footnoted reference numbers (termed 'Balquhain Charter' or 'BC' numbers) in Leslie's work. Leslie's phraseology suggests that he himself did not originate the numbering system.[14] By noting these references, page by page, and sorting the resulting list by number and by date, tables were created, enabling many of the numbered manuscripts in the collection to be cross-referenced to Leslie's work, assuming that the document in question can be identified in the hand. For the present author, the compilation of descriptive spreadsheets would have presented insuperable challenges without Leslie's work and the coincidence of his use of the above numbering system. Copies of the aforementioned tables have been lodged with SCC for public use.

Regarding the total quantity of manuscripts, the highest reference number cited by Leslie is 1010, although many numbers in the one to 1010 range are not actually mentioned. A further four documents are footnoted but without a reference number. SCC places the quantity in MS 3043 as around 1,000.[15] Listing by the present author shows that MS 3043 contains approximately 919 manuscripts, including 49 un-numbered documents, and excluding pages apparently misplaced from documents counted elsewhere in MS 3043. Scope exists for expert work in further 'tidying' of the collection.

The above numbering system was clearly in existence by the conclusion of Charles Leslie's research, but there is reason to suggest that it was a system established in 1778 (see below). A number of the manuscripts contain other reference numbers, probably from an earlier system. In the current paper, wherever possible, specific manuscripts are cited using the 'BC' numbering, here termed 'former reference' (FR) to distinguish them from the SCC catalogue numbering to be applied in due course.

Physically, the contents of MS 3043 comprise:

- Parchment (i.e. animal skin), sometimes too stiff to unfold without good reason; with occasional sheets having remnants of animal hair still attached.
- Paper, sometimes fragile; reinforced with translucent onionskin paper. The backing appears to have been applied long before the collection came to SCC. Without this backing, some of the sheets would have fragmented beyond repair.
- Paper, without reinforcement.

Some material may be too fragile to produce for consultation. Most documents had been folded, before they were grouped in bundles. Individual bundles generally contain manuscripts whose FR numbers form a more or less continuous block within the range '1–1010'. In some instances, the block of numbers is spread irregularly across adjacent bundles. Furthermore, as a general pattern, the higher the FR number, the higher the bundle number in the '1–93' bundle sequence, while the documents of most significance, such as 'Titles of the lands of Balquhain', are grouped early in the sequence. This suggests that the documents and bundles were numbered at the same time, with no subsequent rearrangement. Generally, there is no clear relationship between bundle number and the dates of the documents therein, although within any one bundle the span of dates tends to be limited to a few decades.

The majority of the manuscripts are of sixteenth- and seventeenth-century date, with some from the eighteenth century. There are several fifteenth-century documents and, notably, one dated 30 May 1391. The latter (Bundle 30, FR254) is a parchment charter which, according to Leslie,[16] was 'granted by Sir Andrew de Leslie, VIII. Dominus Ejusdem, to his Brother-in-law, David de Abercrombie, and Margaret de Leslie his Spouse'. It appears to be the oldest document in the collection. Identification is supported by the title on the reverse, which has the unusual letter combination 'auq' discernible, part of the usual historic spelling of the place-name uncharacteristically rendered as 'Achquhorthy' in Leslie's transcription of the text of that document.[17] Languages are generally Latin or Scots, with charters and sasines continuing to use the former when other papers had moved on to the use of Scots. A few notarised documents incorporate both languages in the same manuscript. A number of the manuscripts have seals attached, some virtually complete.

Readers familiar with family and estate papers of the period will find that the collection contains the predictable range of land-related documents ranging from charters under the Great Seal (issued in the name of the monarch or, briefly, Oliver Cromwell) to numerous records of wadsett, disponing and redemption. A Charter of 1511 (Bundle 1, FR1) granted Balquhain and certain other lands in the Garioch to William Leslie, seventh baron of Balquhain.[18] As Balquhain was already in the possession of the Leslies at this time this charter is therefore, in effect, confirmation of the fact. A particularly significant document (Bundle 46, FR456) is, from the internal evidence, almost certainly the feu-charter dated 1566 by William Gordon, bishop of Aberdeen, to William Leslie, ninth baron of Balquhain of the 'Bishop's shire or barony of Fetternear', as translated by Charles Leslie.[19] He gives the historical context for this charter,[20] which was essentially a post-Reformation transfer of church lands in recognition of a supporter. In 1670, Pope Clement X confirmed this charter in a concise, highly legible document with attractive calligraphy (Bundle 63, FR490).[21]

Other papers of note include:

- The marriage contract dated 1679 (Bundle 93, FR863) between Count Patrick Leslie, laird of Balquhain, and Mary Irvine, eldest daughter of Alexander Irvine of Drum.[22]
- Evidence dated 1713 regarding the administration of the peat moss on the hill of Bennachie, compiled in relation to a legal dispute over the extraction of peat or turf from low ground at Tullos (Bundles 70, no FR; and 85, FR951).

In this case, the parish minister was in dispute with the laird. Both were Leslies. Bundle 70 contains the presbytery's evidence, while FR951 has the laird's side of the argument. Both sets of documents are extensive and require careful handling, but have the potential to reveal valuable material on the historical management of peat resources on Bennachie.

- A table of teinds for the parish of Logie Durno (subsequently re-named Chapel of Garioch), for 1643 with their 'augmentation' of 1709 (Bundle 70, FR921). As well as its significance in terms of the local economy, church administration, and agriculture, this table is of interest in its delineation of place-names, and the use of Scots terminology for farm produce, measures and money (Figure 1).

This summary of MS 3043 concludes with an enigma. Leslie reports[23] that 1010 documents and 'fourteen bundles of miscellaneous papers' all pertaining to the barony of Balquhain, were listed in an inventory of 1778. His ensuing text implies that this corpus of documents could not be found at the time of his compilation of the *Historical Records*. While working with MS 3043, the present author noted that the range of FC numbers comprised 1–1010, of which FR1010 is dated 1778. The coincidence of dates suggests that the inventoried manuscripts were from the same collection as seen by Leslie. The reference numbers in the range 1–1010 written on the folded documents appear to be in the same hand and the same ink. Although it is impossible to give precise figures, in a process prone to ambiguities of evidence, inconsistency of interpretation, and minor error, it is useful to explore how many documents Leslie may have seen, and how many additional ones are present in MS 3043. Of the documents presumed to have been numbered in 1778, some 364 numbered manuscripts were cited by Leslie and therefore presumably seen by him. Examination of the ranges of FR numbering of these particular documents shows only small gaps (defined here as less than ten numbers) in the sequence within these ranges. These gaps may represent documents seen by Leslie but not cited, or perhaps incidental losses (as distinct from wholesale disappearance). Allowing for these possibilities, the overall number of manuscripts thus accounted for rises to about 775. There remain around 240 numbers falling within large gaps (ten numbers or more) in the sequence. Of these, about 189 are present in MS 3043, bringing the number accounted for to around 964 and suggesting that some documents deemed to be missing by Leslie in 1869 may subsequently have reached MS 3043. There are also the 49 un-numbered manuscripts referred to previously.

Finally, of the approximately 364 numbered documents cited by Leslie, in around 263 cases, the reference number coincides or makes a near match (allowing for ambiguous referencing) with Leslie's footnoted reference for that particular document, the manuscript's title or content confirming this association. In sixteen or so cases there is a definite mismatch, perhaps due to confusion between different historic numbering systems used at different times, or merely to error.

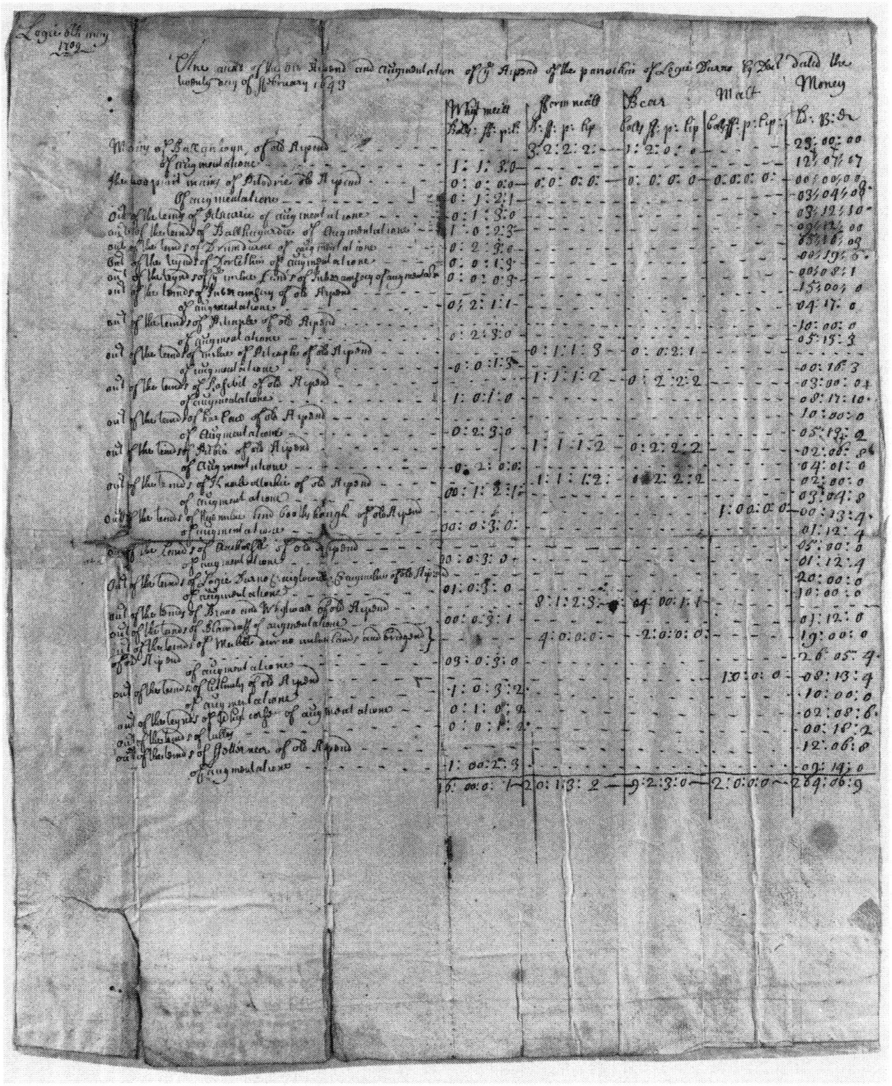

Figure 1. Stipend for the parish of Logie Durno, updated by the minister in 1709; AU MS 3043/70 (former reference 921). Image © University of Aberdeeen 2014

In a further approximately 21 cases the relationship to Leslie's referencing was unclear (due to factors including confusion with older reference numbering systems, manuscript identification issues, and duplication of reference numbers by Leslie). For the remaining 64 or so documents out of the approximately 364, it can only be concluded that these are either broadly encompassed by the 49 'un-numbered' manuscripts found in MS 3043, or are simply not present in that collection. Nevertheless, the around 263 matches or near-matches with Leslie's numbering support the view that the manuscripts seen by Leslie were in fact a portion of those included in the 1010 documents of the £778 inventory. Leaving aside the 'fourteen miscellaneous bundles' and allowing for incidental losses, it seems reasonable to suggest that the two corpora, namely the 'Leslie' and the so-called 'missing' collections, may in fact be one and the same.

SCC: Davidson and Garden collection (MS 2769)

These papers, deposited in the University in 1970 by Davidson and Garden, solicitors in Aberdeen, comprise an extensive archive relating to the firm's many clients over a period covering the fourteenth to the twentieth century.[24] MS 2769 is a major repository of material relating to landed estates in the north-east of Scotland, among these being Balquhain and other Leslie lands, Westhall (near Oyne), and Overhall (near Auchleven). A summary listing of the contents of MS 2769 is available in the SCC on-line catalogue.[25] The individual manuscripts are not formally catalogued although the material is in sufficiently good condition to be fully available for consultation.

With the most recent records in MS 3043 being from the 1790s, it has proved fortunate for current research purposes that MS 2769 covers much of the nineteenth-century affairs of the Leslie estate, albeit at an estate management level rather than at the level of the high status legal documents contained in MS 3043. For example, there are numerous rental and lease records, which have proved to be of particular relevance to the 2013–14 research into the Colony and its context in the surrounding farming landscape. Thomas Brochard has compiled inventories for the MS 2769 holdings most closely connected with the Leslie family's interests at Balquhain and Fetternear, and with the estate of Overhall, near Auchleven on the north side of Bennachie. The inventories, together with Brochard's additional inventories of parts of MS 3482 and MS 3665 (see below) are available for consultation at SCC. Those most useful in the context of the current paper are described below.

MS 2769/I/76/1-4

Box One contains leases and related correspondence; newspaper clippings relating to the 1889 demonstration in favour of the former Bennachie 'colonists'; and reports and memoranda by the estate overseer etc., illuminating estate and farming practice of post-Improvement land management in the second half of the nineteenth century. Of particular note is the printed document listed by Brochard as 'Articles and conditions of lease of lands and barony of Balquhain and others, 1883'.

Box Two has the estate rental book for 1852–90; a report on the various farms and crofts on the estate, 1879; leases and related correspondence; and financial papers relating to farms and the estate. At the back of the estate rental book, Bailies researcher Ken Ledingham made the discovery of a single handwritten sheet, folded and gummed in place. Entitled *Conditions of Letting Crofts, along the Clochie Burn and Kewlie How on Benachie*, this proved to be a key piece of primary evidence concerning the Bennachie Colony at the time of the Division of the Commonty in 1859. The discovery of an apparently unrecognised document of such importance is a perfect example of the unexpected rewards which may await the diligent researcher.

Box Three has leases and related correspondence; plans and contract correspondence for various buildings and other improvements; estate overseer's papers; papers relating to tenants' request for revaluation in 1886; and papers of 1887 concerning arrears of rent. Of particular note is the printed document listed by Brochard as 'Articles and conditions re lease of Balquhain's lands in parishes of Inverurie, Chapel of Garioch and Insch and added pen notes re special conditions, 1853'.

Box Four contains a large and somewhat flamboyant loose document in manuscript entitled 'General regulations for the estate of Balquhain, 1828' which is of note because as an example of estate governance it appears quite early in the post-Improvement era, and can be compared with similar documents of 1853 and 1883 (see above). There is also a note dated 1886 regarding arrears of rent. Of family history interest is an envelope containing, as listed by Brochard, 'Pedigree of Leslies of Balquhain and Gordons of Aberlour as descendants of Patrick or Peter, Count Leslie, first half of the seventeenth-century to post-1858'.

MS 2769/II/22/1-3

Boxes One and Two contain the rental of Balquhain estate for 1875–83 and 1885 respectively, including references to the tenancies on Bennachie. Box Three contains a statement of rents of the estates of Balquhain, Fetternear, etc., including Bennachie, 27 May 1870; also other rental documents.

Selected other material

MS 2769/I/31/1-3, MS 2769/I/41/1-3, and MS 2769/I/108/1 have extensive records for Overhall, a few of which relate to the Division of the Commonty of Bennachie. MS 2769/I/32/1 is largely devoted to papers connected with the Leslies' Drumrossie property at Insch. However, among these is another rewarding discovery, for it also has informative documents concerning the 'Division of the Commonty of Benachie'. MS 2769/I/32/2 contains a list of registered poor in the parish of Oyne for 1872–73, which may be of relevance to Bennachie. A comprehensive study of the records of the Parochial Board of Oyne, in relation to the Bennachie 'Colony', has been provided by Fagen.[26] MS 2769/II/17/1-5 lists letter books for the Grant family's estate of Ardoyne, on the north side of Bennachie, for 1891–1901. MS 3665/14-15 relates to Westhall, including papers concerning Oyne.

SCC also holds the George Washington Wilson & Co. photographic collection (MS 3792), which includes many glass plate negatives of landscapes and buildings in north-east Scotland and further afield, captured between around 1850 and 1905. This includes several images of buildings at Fetternear. The collection is accessible on-line and searchable.[27] As of June 2014, cataloguing of SCC's extensive MacDonald collection of estate maps and plans, MS 3860,[28] was ongoing. Covering the late-eighteenth to the mid-twentieth centuries, this collection will be of considerable interest to those researching the cartographic records of north-east Scotland. No doubt, as additional records are researched, other relevant SCC material will be found. For example, the William Douglas Simpson collection of archaeological, monumental and architectural plans (MS 3759) has recently been more fully catalogued and added to the on-line catalogue. Among these papers was found a copy of a base map prepared in connection with the 'Division of the Commonty of Benachie' (Figure 2).[29]

Finally, the early Ordnance Survey maps at the scales of six inches and twenty-five inches to one mile, have proved invaluable. These maps are now fully accessible on the National Library of Scotland website.[30] The current project has been fortunate in that the Colony area of Bennachie was surveyed for the first edition of the six-inch map in 1866–67, at a time when the layout of the structures and enclosure boundaries remained evident, and a number of the dwellings were still occupied. By the time of the revised second edition, surveyed in this area in 1899, all but one of the dwellings had fallen vacant and the map shows that the enclosures, except at Boghead of Tullos, had been planted with trees.

The twenty-five inch scale was derived from the same survey as the six-inch, and shows virtually the same detail, but on a larger canvas. Unlike the six-inch map, its coverage is limited to populated areas. Its significance is that its second edition gives unique reference numbers to enclosures, together with their acreages, enabling comparison with documentary sources such as rental books. (The first edition gives no acreages, and uses a different enclosure-numbering series). In the case of the Colony, it is fortunate that, although the enclosures on most of the former crofts are shown as tree-covered, their acreages are still depicted. In researching these maps, the author nearly encountered a pitfall of which readers may find it useful to be aware. In the first edition, the rectangular sheet covering the Colony area is divided by a parish boundary. Two separate sheets were published, one for each of the parish areas, with the area outwith the relevant parish left blank. It is therefore advisable to check for a separate sheet covering the 'blank' area, or for an extra sheet combining the two parish areas in one full sheet. Fortunately, by the time of the second edition, this practice had been discontinued.

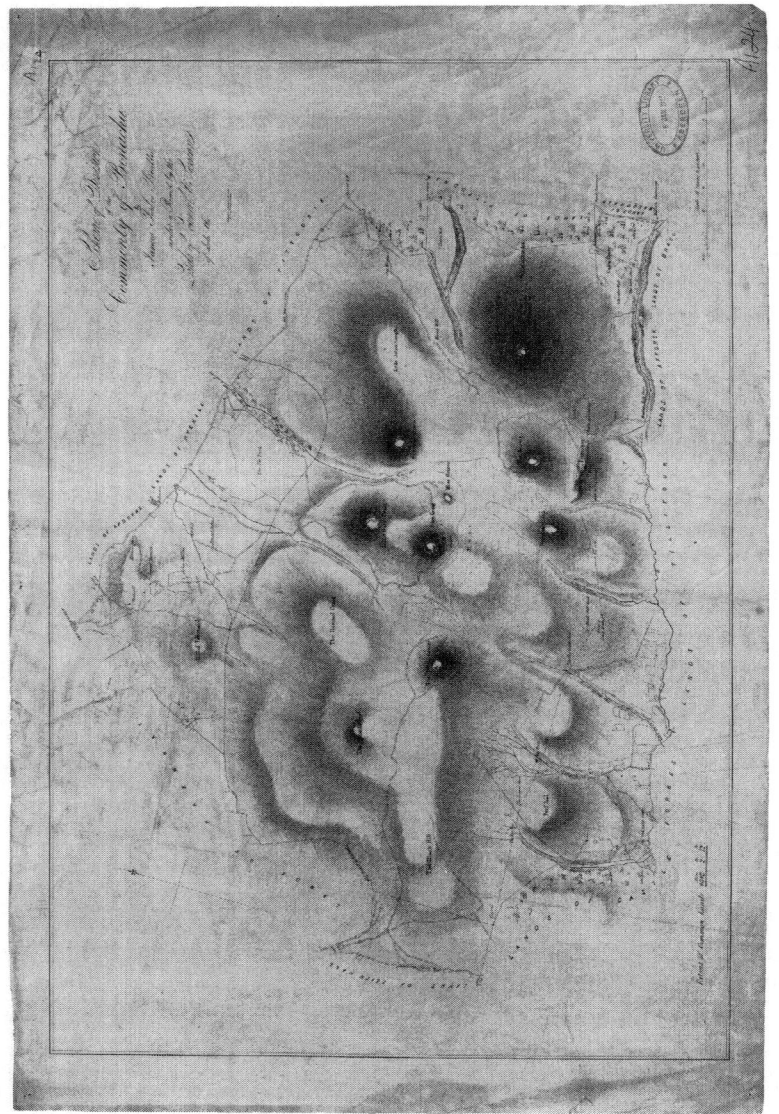

Figure 2. Scheme of Division of the Commonty of Benachie; AU MS 3759/1 (Alternative reference: A1/24). Image © University of Aberdeen 2014

Bailies of Bennachie: Library and Archives

Since its foundation in 1973, the Bailies of Bennachie has amassed a large collection of relevant books and archives. These are housed at the Bennachie Centre, near Chapel of Garioch, and may be consulted by arrangement.[31] The library has an extensive collection relating to north-east Scotland, including works specifically related to Bennachie. The archives include newspaper clippings, the Cormack collection of early twentieth-century photographs, and unique correspondence. Some of the archived material has been published in two volumes, *The Book of Bennachie*[32] and *Bennachie Again*[33] which are excellent introductions for anyone interested in the hill. To date, the Bennachie Landscapes Project has published two volumes for the Bailies of Bennachie in its Bennachie Landscapes Series, namely: Jennifer Fagen, *The Bennachie Colony Project: Examining the Lives and Impact of the Bennachie Colonists* (2011); and Colin Shepherd (ed.), *Bennachie and the Garioch: Society and Ecology in the History of North-East Scotland* (2013). Both can be purchased direct from the Bailies of Bennachie and are available for consultation in the Bailies' library and at SCC.[34] The Bailies' archives include a 1995 bibliography of sources for all topics connected with Bennachie,[35] and (prepared as part of the project) two research guides highlighting, respectively, Colony-related material in the organisation's library and selected portions of the archives.[36] All three documents are indexed by keywords.

Conclusion

Subject to the normal constraints, the papers described above are available for public consultation. They exemplify the vast and largely untapped resource for historical research available in archives such as those of SCC and the Bailies of Bennachie. The fascinating results of such research demonstrate the benefits to community volunteers and academics alike. While the work so far has assisted the Bailies of Bennachie in particular, the many other local heritage groups in Aberdeenshire and beyond have the potential to benefit likewise. The Special Collections Centre welcomes approaches by interested parties, and seminars can be arranged for groups according to their particular interests. The Bailies of Bennachie offers similar assistance to individuals in respect of their collections.

The core ethos of the project is to engage the community at large, as an ongoing process, with the landscapes of Bennachie. Archival research has a key role, offering almost unlimited opportunities for volunteer involvement and the Bailies of Bennachie website provides contact details and further information.[37] In addition, the SCC welcomes members of the public wishing to consult its materials and a guide to visitors is available on its website.[38]

Notes

1. AHRC Connected Communities, Community Heritage Grant, AH/J013447/1, awarded 2012 (Gordon Noble PI); AHRC Development Grant, AH/K007750/1, awarded 2013 (Jeff Oliver PI).
2. Contracted for archival research support on the 2012–13 AHRC Development Grant.
3. http://www.abdn.ac.uk/library/about/special (accessed 22 June 2014).
4. Personal communication, Andrew MacGregor, January 2014.
5. C. J. Leslie, *Pedigree of the Family of Leslie of Balquhain: Extracted from Public Records, Family Charters, Deeds, and Other Authentic Documents, from 1067 to 1861* (Bakewell, 1861) [*PFL*], 9.
6. *PFL*, 12. See also Charles Leslie (ed.), *Historical Records of the Family of Leslie from 1067 to 1868/9 Collected from Public Records and Authentic Private Sources*, 3 vols (Edinburgh, 1869) [*HRL*], iii,, 41, 478.
7. Personal communication, J. R. Trigg, June 2014.
8. Aberdeen University Special Collections [SCC], MS 3759/1/37/4, James Forbes Beattie 'under a Remit by the Lords of Council & Session', map *Scheme of Division of the Commonty of Benachie*, n.d. – possibly 1858 [hereafter *JFB*]. Acreage rounded down to nearest whole acre.
9. SCC, MS 2769/I/32/1, *First Division/ February 24, 1859/ Additional joint minute for Sir J. Dalrymple Horn Elphinstone, Pursuer, and for The Right Hon Walter Forbes, Baron Forbes, and others – Defenders; in action of Division of the Commonty of Benachie*. Acreage rounded down to nearest whole acre.
10. National Register of Archives (Scotland), *Interim Summary List of the Legal and Ecclesiastical Papers of Leslie of Balquhain, Aberdeenshire (MS. 3043)* (Aberdeen, 1982).
11. Search reference 'MS 3043' in SCC Manuscripts & Archives Catalogue. See http://www.abdn.ac.uk/library/collections (accessed 22 June 2014).
12. Ibid.
13. *HRL*.
14. *HRL*, iii, 516–21.
15. Search reference 'MS 3043' in SCC Manuscripts & Archives Catalogue. See http://www.abdn.ac.uk/library/collections (accessed 22 June 2014).
16. *HRL*, i, 155. Leslie's capitalisation has been modified by the present author.
17. Ibid.
18. *HRL*, iii, 466–7.
19. Ibid., 478 ff.
20. Ibid., 41.
21. Ibid., 483 ff.
22. Ibid., iii, 128.
23. Ibid., 520 ff.
24. At http://www.abdn.ac.uk/library/collections search reference 'MS 2769' in Manuscripts & Archives Catalogue (accessed 22 June 2014).
25. Ibid.
26. Jennifer Fagen (for the Bailies of Bennachie), *The Bennachie Colony Project: Examining the Lives and Impact of the Bennachie Colonists* (Aberdeenshire, 2011).
27. http://www.abdn.ac.uk/historic/gww/index.htm (accessed 22 June 2014).
28. SCC, MS 3860, Maps and plans comprising part of the records of F. A. MacDonald and Partners, engineers and surveyors (incorporating Walker & Duncan, Aberdeen).
29. *JFB*.

30. http://maps.nls.uk/geo/find (accessed 22 June 2014).
31. Contact details at http://www.bailiesofbennachie.co.uk/contact-us [*BB*] (accessed 22 June 2014).
32. Archie W. M. Whiteley (ed.), *The Book of Bennachie* (Aberdeenshire, 1976).
33. Archie W. M. Whiteley (ed.), *Bennachie Again* (Aberdeenshire, 1983).
34. *BB*.
35. *Bailies Information Audit* (unpublished, 1999) in Bailies of Bennachie archives, Bennachie Centre, Folder 13.
36. Colin H. Miller (ed.), *Bailies of Bennachie Library: A Research Guide* (unpublished, 2013), and *Bailies of Bennachie Archives: A Research Guide* (unpublished 2013).
37. *BB*.
38. https://www.abdn.ac.uk/library/documents/guides/hcol/qghcol001.pdf (accessed 22 June 2014).

CROFTING: A CLEAN SLATE

SIR CRISPIN AGNEW OF LOCHNAW BT

Introduction

The author presents the case below that croft land is now akin to a random patchwork of property within the crofting counties, this arising from the historical operation of the Landholders (Scotland) Acts 1886 to 1931. Consequently, crofting regulation is applied in a non-uniform way to crofts and croft land alone even though neighbouring holdings display similar characteristics. Further, the effects of the lack of a clear and consistent policy over the years, along with bad drafting, in the Crofters (Scotland) Act 1955, the Crofters (Scotland) Act 1961 and the Crofting Reform (Scotland) Act 1976 (consolidated in the Crofters (Scotland) Act 1993), together with the confusing amendments made to the 1993 Act by the Crofting Reform etc Act 2007 and the Crofting Reform (Scotland) Act 2010, are examined. The suggestion is made that the Crofting Acts should, ideally, be repealed and that, if there is a social need for crofting, then it should be applied to all similar landholdings in the crofting areas by way of a new act. Alternatively, there should be a radical amendment of the Crofting Acts in conjunction with a clear and consistent policy that is fit for the twenty-first century, should it apply to current crofts only.

Historical background

The land which the Crofters (Scotland) Act 1993 and the Crofting Reform (Scotland) Act 2010 cover today is an accident of history, which has created a patchwork of holdings with some as crofts and others nearby not subject to the same regulation. A consequence of this is that crofters and crofting communities are considered to be either a privileged class or, alternatively, a strictly regulated group compared to the rest of the inhabitants of the crofting counties.[1] A starting point for the discussion must be the 'battle' of the Braes in 1882, when the Portree crofters asserted their right to graze their stock on Ben Lee. The crofters' defiance of the sheriff and the dispatch of a police force to Skye was a trigger for the Napier Commission and provides essential background also to the Crofters Holdings (Scotland) Act 1886 ('the 1886 Act') and the establishment of the first Crofters Commission. The Napier Commission had recommended security of tenure for holdings with an annual value of £6 or more with thirty-year leases and a programme for improvement, while holdings of less than £6 annual value were to remain outside the scheme and be catered for by encouragement of voluntary emigration.[2] The 1886 Act, instead, gave security of tenure to all holdings as defined in the Act. Troubles continued, in any case, not helped by the different policies for the Highlands promoted by the Conservative and Liberal administrations, with the military used in Tiree, and then disturbances in the Isle of Lewis and other parishes in the north-west. The Congested Districts (Scotland) Act 1897 established the Congested Districts Board, the intention being to deal with congestion and the lack of land for crofting by giving compulsory powers to acquire land for such a purpose. As the 1897 Act did not fulfil its promise, more agitation led to proposals for a Small Landholders Act that was to apply to the whole of Scotland. The Small Landholders (Scotland) Bill was first introduced on 28 July 1906 but withdrawn by the Government and re-introduced bills of 1907 and 1908 were defeated in the Lords. It was reintroduced and eventually passed on 16 December 1911. The Board of Agriculture replaced the Congested Districts Board and the new Scottish Land Court took over from the Crofters Commission on 1 April 2012.[3]

Analysis of the Landholders Acts reveals that their application in this regard applied arbitrarily to certain classes of holdings in specified, defined locations. The 1886 Act related to holdings with a rent not exceeding £30 and situated in a 'crofting parish'.[4] For example, on Speyside, some parishes were 'crofting parishes' and others were not. Section 33 excluded holdings let to a person 'during his continuance in any office, appointment or employment of the landlord' thus leading to a township of crofts where there were crofts, for example, the 'ferryman's croft'[5] or the 'ghillie's croft'[6] which were almost identical to other holdings but were not under the Act. Similarly under Section 33, a holding let as a pension or let to a person such as a minister of religion or to an innkeeper or tradesmen located in the district was not under the Act.[7] An amendment to include Arran and Bute in the 1886 Act was opposed by the Lord Advocate on the grounds that 'I should not feel warranted in asking Parliament to extend the area of this Bill to places not visited by the Royal Commission.' It was also opposed by the MP for Bute because the Isle of Arran was considered free from 'the grievances which the Royal Commission was appointed to inquire into', and the proposal was defeated on a vote.[8]

The Small Landholders (Scotland) Act 1911 extended 'crofting' to the whole of Scotland and applied it to all landholdings with a rent not exceeding £50 or an acreage not exceeding fifty acres (or in Lewis a rent of £30).[9] Crofts existing in 1886 came under the Act and two new categories of holdings were created:

the 'small landholding', where the landholder 'or his predecessors in the same family' had provided the greater part of fixed equipment, and the 'statutory small tenancy' where the landlord had provided the fixed equipment.[10] There was a residence requirement that only holdings where the tenant 'resides on or within two miles of the holding' came under the Act[11], but, unfortunately, the Court of Session determined that this only applied at the commencement of the Act and that, thereafter, there was no requirement for the tenant to continue to live on or within two miles of the holding.[12]

There were numerous exceptions set out in Section 26 in addition to those outlined under the 1886 Act, which continued to apply.[13] Many of these exempt holdings effectively became occupied as crofts or landholdings following the First World War when the original reasons for the exemptions ceased to hold, but these did not legally became crofts even under the Crofters (Scotland) Act 1955, which added to the patchwork.[14]

The main difference between a small landholding and the statutory small tenancy was that when the tenancy of a small landholding came to an end the vacant holding could only be re-let under the 1911 Act or added as an enlargement of an existing holding, unless the Board of Agriculture consented,[15] whereas the statutory small tenancy ceased to be subject to the Act. This difference was recognised by Section Three of the Crofters (Scotland) Act 1955, because small landholdings 'whether occupied by a landholder or not' came under the 1955 Act, whereas only statutory small holdings that were occupied as such at the 1955 point came under the Act. Thus, it can be seen that the 1886 and 1911 Acts created a patchwork of holdings under the Acts while leaving a number of similar holdings outside the scope of the Acts.

A substantial number of new small landholdings were created under the Land Settlement (Scotland) Act 1919, the purpose of which was 'to facilitate and secure the settlement of suitable persons upon the land, preferably persons who have served in the forces of the Crown in this or in any previous war.'[16] However, the agricultural depression after 1918 saw a substantial number of landholdings and statutory small tenancies, as well as some common grazings, fall out of the protection of the Landholders Acts.[17]

Where a statutory small tenancy was given up, it ceased to be under the remit of the Act. Landholdings remained under the Act, but frequently these were then re-let as agricultural tenancies under the Agricultural Holdings (Scotland) Acts without objection by the Board of Agriculture, objections having to be made within six months of the re-let.[18] They then also fell out of the remit of the Act. Similarly, if a landholder bought his small landholding, and many were sold on the break-up of estates after both world wars, then the landholding ceased to be considered under the Acts.[19] In consequence of these holdings falling outwith the Landholders Act, the patchwork created by the 1886 and 1911 Acts was further confirmed.

As a consequence of the right to buy, introduced by the 1976 Act, together with the absolute right to have the croft house 'de-crofted',[20] many former croft houses have been taken outwith the Act. Often, banks would not lend the purchase price unless the house site was de-crofted.[21] Frequently, this left the croft land without a house unless the landlord agreed to a new one being built.[22] The Act also allowed, probably unintentionally, for the backhand creation of new crofts by separating the grazing right from the croft either on purchase or on assignation. Normally, when croft land is bought, the crofter does not buy the grazing right so the latter is no longer 'deemed to form part of the croft' but instead the crofter is then 'deemed to hold the right ... in tenancy and that right ... shall be deemed to be a croft'.[23] Section Eight allows a crofter to assign the grazing right on its own. The effect of these provisions is that the grazing right is separated from the croft land and may be transferred as a right on its own as a 'deemed croft'. As the grazing right is an incorporeal right it 'floats' in the sense that the grazing right can be used, in common with those of the other crofters, over the whole of the common grazings.[24] The crofter of the deemed croft then has the right to seek an apportionment of the common grazing, which converts the grazing right to be that of a croft over a defined area of land.[25] Where a crofter tenants only an apportioned deemed croft then he or she does not have a statutory right to buy that croft because it is not 'adjacent or contiguous to any other part of the croft', although it may be bought by agreement.[26] Thus, the 1976 Act allowed new crofts to be created even though it had specifically repealed the right to create new crofts under Section 2(1) of the Crofters (Scotland) Act 1961 and created a class of croft that, in certain circumstances, cannot be purchased. As the grazing right is an integral part of the viability of the croft, the effect of the 1976 Act, continued by the Crofters (Scotland) Act 1993, has been to make some crofts now less viable agriculturally, given that the grazing right has been separated from the croft.

The consequence of the patchwork

A major consequence of the creation of the patchwork is that, in current crofting counties, there can be similar holdings, grazings and houses in the same township or area which are not under the Crofting Acts, alongside crofts, grazings and houses that are still regulated by the Acts. This is perhaps most pronounced on Speyside and on the east coast as well as in Shetland and Orkney where there are areas in which crofting townships were not established and it was only individual holdings that came under the 1886 and 1911 Acts. The result is that some holdings and houses are under the new and stricter regulation of the 1993 Act (as amended by the 2007 and 2010 Acts), while others in the same area are not so regulated. Equally, the crofts have the benefit of a 'fair rent', the absolute right to buy, and also to various crofting and housing grants which are unavailable for non-crofts and non-croft houses in the same area. Similarly, the patchwork impacts on communities' rights to buy, whether crofting communities or not: a crofting community has an absolute right to buy under Part Three and a non-crofting community has only a pre-emptive right to buy on a sale of the land under Part Two of the Land Reform (Scotland) Act 2003.

Another problem is that the policy of the 1886 and 1911 Acts, reflected in the 1993 Act, is not wholly relevant today. The 1886 and 1911 Acts gave agricultural tenants, on a yearly lease, security of tenure, as well as the right to a fair rent and to compensation for improvements, provided they abided by the statutory conditions and allowed for rights of succession. At the time, these holdings were agricultural and could, more or less, provide a living for the family that occupied them, even if the crofter was expected to have a supplementary occupation, such as fishing, kelp collecting for sale, or weaving. The 1911 Act gave landholders the right to use the holding 'for subsidiary or auxiliary occupations as in the case of dispute the Land Court may find to be reasonable'.[27] Most of the country was agricultural and supported the population that lived on the land. However, the value of a croft as a unit sufficient to provide for a family has declined over the years. It probably fulfilled this role until the mid-1930s but, in the present day, it is the case that, except in a 'good life' context, a croft alone generally cannot support a family.

It can be argued that few active crofters farm a single croft, unless it is a large croft, and that, for the purpose of providing for a whole family, a holding is no longer a viable unit on which they can live. Multiple occupation of crofts is a problem and varies from place to place. The balance is between providing the farming crofter with a viable agricultural unit and having crofts available for new entrants.[28] In many townships, one or two crofters are the 'farmers' and farm the majority of croft land on various formal or informal arrangements,[29] while the rest of the crofters just live on their crofts. In areas where there are single crofts, as is quite common on the east coast, the croft is usually farmed as part of a larger agricultural holding.

Croft rents have not kept up with comparable open market rents. In 1886, the fair rent for a croft, although often reduced from 1886 by the Crofting Commission,[30] was generally equivalent to the rent that could be obtained for an agricultural holding. In one case, under the Congested District Act 1897, a landowner was only too pleased to offer agricultural holdings for division into crofts, because the rent of the four crofts derived from the farm was more than the farm rent.[31] As a result of crofting rents not keeping up with market rents, crofting tenancies offered no financial return to the landlords, resulting in a lack of investment by the landlords. Further, this led to the neglect of croft land because there was no financial imperative for the crofter to get an economic return from the land.[32]

It is difficult to discern a clear policy in the 1993 Act, which consolidated the earlier legislation and was amended in 2007 and 2010, because the original policy of giving agricultural tenants security of tenure on a yearly lease, the right to a fair rent and to compensation for improvements, was continued by the 1955 Act but no longer generally reflects the reasons for occupying a croft. Additionally, since 1955, further and often competing policy objectives have been tacked onto the Crofting Acts without proper amendment of the legislation and then sometimes discarded by the next legislative round.

Section Two of the Crofters (Scotland) Act 1961 allowed for new crofts to be created or existing crofts to be enlarged. In the mid-1960s, the Crofters Commission appeared to have had a policy of encouraging the amalgamation of crofts into larger and more economical holdings when one became vacant, thus reducing the number of crofts.[33] This was consistent with Sections 26 to 29 of Part II of the Agriculture Act 1967 which promoted the amalgamation of uncommercial agricultural holdings to form a commercial unit by way of grant aid or loans. The Shucksmith Report noted that, between 1960 and 1994, there was a decrease of 10.4% in the stock of crofts.[34]

Subsequent acts have been unclear in approach as regards the creation of new crofts. The Crofting Reform (Scotland) Act 1976 gave crofters the right to buy their crofts and to de-croft the house and garden; the right to create new crofts was abolished, except in the unforeseen situation of creating them via separating the grazing right from the croft on purchase or through an assignation of the grazing right as noted above. However, the right to create new crofts was reintroduced by the Crofting Reform etc Act 2007 which added a new Section 3A into the 1993 Act and also provided for the conversion of some landholdings and statutory small tenancies into crofts in areas outwith the crofting counties designated by statutory instrument.[35] Thus, in effect, crofting has been extended beyond the original crofting counties. The present policy generally requires each croft to be used individually and prevents multiple occupation of crofts formally or informally, although the Commission will consider allowing one person to hold multiple crofts provided 'this is in the wider interests of crofting and the crofting community and can contribute to more viable crofting agricultural activity.'[36]

The post-1998 devolution consultation by the Land Reform Policy Group (hereafter LRPG)[37] appeared, in part in relation to crofting, to be carried out on the basis that crofts could be used to provide house sites in the crofting counties. The advice in 'Recommendations for Action' from January 1999 included, 'CR4 Creation of new crofts' and 'CR 8 End controls over subdivision'.[38] However, the Shucksmith Report and the 'Government Response' expressed concern that the 'amount of land in crofting tenure is declining with more and more land being resumed and de-crofted, most commonly for the purpose of building new housing.'[39]

Nevertheless, the 2007 and 2010 Acts encourage the use of croft land for housing.[40] A difficulty is that paragraph 8 of Schedule Two of the 1993 Act provides that:

8. The crofter shall not, without the consent in writing of the landlord, erect or suffer to be erected on the croft any dwelling-house otherwise than in substitution for a dwelling-house which at the commencement of this Act was already on the croft:

Provided that, if at the commencement of this Act there was no dwelling-house on the croft, the crofter may erect one dwelling-house thereon.[41]

The effect of this provision is that, if the croft house site is de-crofted, then the tenant of the bare land cannot erect another house without the consent in writing of his or her landlord, unless the house site was de-crofted prior to 1993. This provision therefore conflicts with the current Commission policy on 'affordable housing solutions – an incoming crofter of a bareland croft will normally be eligible for the Croft House Grant Scheme.'

Together, these Acts imposed various policies by way of 'regards' to which the Commission must refer in considering any decisions which relate to: 'the desirability of supporting population retention'[42] and residence on or within thirty-two kilometres of the croft; the interests of the estate; the interests of the crofting community in the locality; sustainable development of that crofting community; and the interest of the public at large, as outlined in Section 58A(7), introduced by the 2010 Act.[43]

The reservations in favour of landlords date back to Section 1(7) of the 1886 Act and do not reflect reasonably modern requirements. Paragraph Eleven of Schedule Two of the 1993 Act reserves certain rights to the landlord such as the minerals, the right to use water not required by the crofts, the right to cut timber and peat, the right to open or make roads, fences, drains and water courses, as well as the right to pass to the sea shore, to inspect the croft and the hunting, shooting and fishing rights, these being virtually unchanged since 1886. However, this does not reflect the modern needs of a landlord such as the rights to grant wayleaves for electricity, water and sewerage or telephones, which are required for any new housing and for renewable power developments. This situation can frustrate these developments on or near to croft land with effects on the sustainable development of the wider community.

Some of the policy conflicts in the present Act include:

- the right to buy and de-croft the croft house, which is in conflict with population retention because it allows the house to be taken out of crofting and perhaps sold as a holiday home.
- the requirement that owner occupiers and crofters should live on and use their crofts. On the whole, without employment in the area, the individual use of crofts is difficult to reconcile with sustainable development.
- the requirement for each croft to be used as such, which means that those crofters who have been the farmers of a number of crofts may no longer be

able to do so, this impacting on their financial viability which conflicts with sustainable development.
- the obligation to use a croft, which makes it difficult for the elderly who may not be able to use their croft so are in danger of losing their house, unless they buy it. This would appear to conflict with the interest of the community and the public at large.
- that agriculture is at the heart of crofting, but that allowing crofts to be put to a purposeful use and common grazings used for non-grazing purposes or forestry must impact on the amount of land available for agriculture.
- the right to divide a croft by bequest on succession[44] or under Section Nine, which means that crofts will get smaller and smaller and therefore will become even less economically viable units to provide financial support for the crofter.
- conflicts with a community or a crofting community right to buy where the community becomes the landlord of a crofting township. Often the needs of the community landowners can be frustrated by the rights of the crofters.
- the conflict between Paragraph Eight of Schedule Two, which prevents a new house on a bare land croft without the written consent of the landlord, and the Commission's policy of 'affordable housing solutions'.
- the lack of amendment to the landlord's reserved rights in Paragraph Eleven of Schedule Two, which can frustrate development that would be beneficial to sustainable development in the wider community.

Another problem is the issue of absenteeism. The decision of the Court of Session nearly 100 years ago that the residence provision only related to determining what was a holding, but thereafter there was no requirement to live on the holdings, has led to this.[45] A two-mile residence condition was reintroduced by Section 17(1)(a) of the 1955 Act, amended to sixteen kilometres by the 1976 Act and then to thirty-two kilometres by the 2007 Act. As a result, trying to regulate absentee tenants (something simply not envisaged in 1886 or 1911) and to devise a system that applies both to tenants, as traditionally conceived, and to owner-occupiers (again a category not envisaged at the outset) has led to the present morass. However, this does not address the real issue at the heart of absenteeism. If there were good employment opportunities and provision for young families in the crofting counties, then absenteeism would be less likely. The policy of the Crofting Commission, in enforcing residence in a situation where it has little control over other social and economic policies means that there is no coherent policy providing the social fabric required both to retain the population in crofting counties and to combat the problem of absenteeism.

A further problem with the present Act is that it aims to micromanage crofts and their occupation, without regard to the needs of different areas. It comprises blanket policy for the whole of the crofting counties and does not address the internal conflict that exists between the right to buy, to de-croft croft houses and the duty imposed on the Commission to have regard to 'the desirability of supporting population'.[46] Additionally, it does not take on the social and economic requirement needed to encourage populations to remain in the Highlands, nor does it address the relationship that should sensibly exist between a community buyout landlord and the members of the community that it represents, which leads to tensions and is likely to create difficulties in trying to encourage sustainable development and population retention.

The lack of a clear policy running through the whole 1993 Act creates difficulty in implementation and interpretation. Further, the amendments made to the 1993 Act by the 2007 and 2010 Acts are so complex that the Act is becoming unmanageable and almost incomprehensible. This contradicts the LRPG's vision for crofting of 'Much simplified crofting legislation and administration.'[47] For example, the Westlaw version of the Act[48] notes, in relation to Sections 5B, 6, 7 and 8, that they 'are not repealed but have been moved under a new heading', although the legal effect of this has still be to determined. The Crofting (Amendment) Act 2013 had to be rushed through parliament 'to resolve a technical legal problem which is affecting the ability of owner-occupier crofters to decroft land...'[49] Witnesses to the Rural Affairs Committee also raised problems with the Act and the Rural Affairs, Climate Change and Environment Committee stated:

> 4. The Committee notes the significant number of other outstanding issues relating to crofting many believe require to be addressed by the Scottish Government following the conclusion of consideration of this Bill by Parliament.
>
> 5. The Committee was struck by the evidence it received from those knowledgeable in this area of the law, which demonstrated significant frustration and concern with the increasing complexity and layers of crofting law. Crofting law as it stands was described as 'a mess' by more than one respondent to the Committee's call for views.[50]

The Minister agreed to look at these issues and has established the Crofting Legislation Stakeholder Consultation Group. Furthermore, the Crofting Law Group was asked to produce a 'Sump' of problems. At the Crofting Law Group meeting in May 2014 a provisional Sump was produced for discussion, which included notes on sixty-six sections that give rise to interpretation problems. The Act as it presently stands is almost unworkable and is likely to lead to substantial litigation if it is not 'cleaned up' to resolve the many interpretation difficulties.

The clean slate

Historically, crofting has been viewed as an entity in its own right.[51] Politicians have concentrated on the crofting community without any proper consideration of how crofting should fit into the wider community and social context of the

Highlands, so that the Shucksmith Report, for example, focused on crofting alone. There are three ongoing land reform enquiries underway in Scotland, the existing Land Reform Review Group, which has just reported,[52] being joined by the Agricultural Holdings Law Review Group, set up by Cabinet Secretary Richard Lochhead, which is also considering landholdings under the 1911 Act and reported in January 2015, and the Westminster Scottish Affairs Committee which published the 'Land Reform in Scotland: Interim Report' on 18 March 2014 in which the word 'crofter' appears once.[53] Crofting is unlikely to feature greatly as it is the general view that it is best confined to its own policy 'box'. Thus no one appears to have tried to consider crofting in the wider social context of the Highlands and Islands or how it can best serve the requirements of the whole community in any location both in the Highlands and Islands or the new crofting areas established in 2007 by the new Section 3A of the 1993 Act.

The 1886 and 1911 Acts were introduced, against a strongly political background, to provide for a social need, that is, to give small agricultural tenants security of tenure, the right to a fair rent, to compensation for improvements at the end of the tenancy and right of succession. However, that defined social need is no longer appropriate. It was also recognised that further land should be provided for new holdings and for enlargement of common grazings.[54] To start with a clean slate, the Crofting Acts should be repealed and the current houses and landholdings integrated into an overall policy for the area. There should be a clear policy as to what is required in different parts of Scotland to achieve the policy objectives that have been established in any review. If the policy is population retention, prevention of holiday homes, sustainable development of communities, economic regeneration, provision of house sites and diversification of landownership, then that policy should be applied to all houses and/or land of a class in the given area, irrespective of the historical origins of the type of landholding. The Channel Isles have policies that some houses can only be bought or occupied by islanders, whereas others can be purchased on the general market, which poses the question as to whether such a policy should be adopted in the crofting counties.[55] The Shucksmith Report recommended 'that all croft houses be tied to residency through a real burden, which would be deemed to be included in the conveyancing when next assigned or purchased. This would run with the land in perpetuity. De-crofting the house site or purchasing the landlord's interest would not extinguish this burden.'[56] The Government did 'not agree that the proposed burden is the best approach to addressing these problems' and said it would consult on these issues, but has not done so.[57] Similarly, as crofting communities have an absolute right to buy, then that right should apply to all communities in the area, whether formerly crofting or not.

It may also be that different approaches are required in different parts of Scotland. For example, the requirements of the Western Isles and the West Coast may be different from those of the North-East coast or Orkney and Shetland. Perhaps Arran and the other Clyde islands need their own policy? If so, individual approaches should be developed for each area and perhaps the local authority should be the driver for these policies. If this was implemented there would be no need to have a Register of Crofts, because all land in a particular area would be subject to the same regulatory framework.

It is accepted, additionally, that the European Convention on Human Rights may make the clean slate very difficult if not impossible to implement. Article One of the First Protocol protects 'the peaceful enjoyment of his possession' and allows for deprivation or a control of the property rights in the public interest. Therefore, given that the European Court of Human Rights recognises that the state has a wide margin of appreciation, there has to be a strong public interest case made for such a new policy. Nevertheless, there has to 'be a reasonable relationship of proportionality between the means employed and the aim sought to be realised' and a 'fair balance' must be struck between the demands of the general interest of the community and the requirements of the protection of the individual's fundamental rights. The requisite balance will not be found if the person concerned has had to bear 'an individual and excessive burden.'[58]

Conclusion

To conclude, it is this author's view that the Crofting Acts should be repealed and replaced by a new Act dealing with the current crofts and croft land including common grazings, which achieves the LRPG vision of 'Much simplified crofting legislation and administration.' There should be a careful consideration of the policy objective for crofting and there should be a clear theme and objective running through the whole new Act making it one relevant for the twenty-first century and not a hangover policy from the nineteenth century. It is for the government to determine the policy, but it should be seen as a long term one, not to be changed regularly and thereby confusingly. It should aim to provide a social and economic framework for crofting that is coordinated with the surrounding policies and runs consistently.

This author's specific suggestions can be summarised in the following points. The difference between owner-occupiers and tenants should be abolished so that any occupier of croft land, whether as owner, tenant, sub-tenant, or licensee, should be subject to the same rules and regulation; this would be the equivalent of a title condition, perhaps with a right for the Land Court to vary the condition temporarily, in exceptional circumstances. De-crofting of croft houses should cease so that all croft houses remain subject to crofting rules and regulations if the policy intent is to have these houses available for people with a strong local connection (such as having lived in the area for ten years or being able to demonstrate that they will live and work permanently in the area) to buy at affordable prices; a Channel Isles-type policy should be introduced so that croft houses can only be bought or occupied by those who have lived in the area for a designated number of years or are active crofters. In so far as there is an absenteeism policy, it should have regard to the availability of economic and social facilities, such as employment opportunities and schooling that can sustain people living in the crofting area. Resumption of croft land should be stopped except by compulsory purchase for a reason of public interest, so that no more land is taken away from crofting. The rents of crofts should be open market ones so that landowners can be encouraged to bring more land into crofting and, with a reasonable financial return from the crofts, will become more willing to reinvest in crofting land and tenancies. Equally, if the crofter has to pay a market rent, then he or she would have to use the croft to maximise the return from the croft land, as is particularly the case for community landlords where the cost of collecting the rent exceeds the value of the rent so there is no incentive to invest in or for the crofts themselves. It is only reasonable that community landlords, and indeed all landlords, should get an acceptable return from their land, so as to be able to use the surplus for the benefit of the community.

Note

This paper was first given as a talk at the Writers to the Signet & Crofting Law Group Conference in Edinburgh on 27 September 2012. I am indebted to Professor James Hunter who was to speak with me at the conference, for triggering some ideas, which are now reflected in this paper. However, the views expressed in the paper are entirely my own.

Notes

1. The Crofters Holdings (Scotland) Act 1886, The Small Landholders (Scotland) Act 1911, The Land Settlement (Scotland) Act 1919 and the Small Landholders and Agricultural Holdings (Scotland) Act 1931. Section 26 of the 1931 act calls these, together, 'The Landholders Acts 1886 to 1931'. See James Scott, *The Law of Smallholdings in Scotland* (Edinburgh, 1933) for a detailed exposition of the law of smallholdings and statutory small tenancies. The historical and political reasons for the introduction of the Landholders Acts of 1886 to 1919 have been considered by Ewen Cameron. See Ewen A. Cameron, *Land for the People? The British Government and the Scottish Highlands, c. 1880–1925*, (East Linton, 1996).
2. Cameron, *Land for the People?*, 22–3.
3. Walter Mercer (ed.), *No Ordinary Court. 100 Years of the Scottish Land Court* (Edinburgh, 2012).
4. 1886 Act, Section [hereafter 's.'] 34.
5. *Guthrie v MacLean* 1990, Scottish Land Court Report [SLCR], 47.
6. *Executors of A. C. Greg v Macdonald* 1991, SLCR, 135.
7. *Young v Marquis of Lothian's Curator* 1915, Sheriff Court [Sh Ct], 44.
8. Hansard, HC Deb. 19 April 1886, vol. 305, cc 39 to 56.
9. 1911 Act, s. 26(3)(a) and s. 27.
10. 1911 Act, s. 2(i); 1911 Act, s. 2(ii)(a) and (b).
11. 1911 Act, s. 2(ii).
12. *Rogerson v Viscount Chilston* 1917, Session Cases [SC], 453.

13. Sir Crispin Agnew of Lochnaw, *Crofting Law* (Edinburgh, 2000), ch. 3.
14. See, for example, *Guthrie v MacLean* 1990, SLCR, 47 [ferryman placed in district by landlord]; *Executors of A. C. Greg v Macdonald* 1991, SLCR, 135 [river watcher for landlord].
15. 1911 Act, s. 17 – amended a number of times, but the requirement for consent to let outwith the Act remained.
16. Hansard, HC Deb. 15 August 1919, vol. 119, the Secretary of State for Scotland at cc 1806.
17. *Trs of the late Sir J. J. M. Horlick v O'Hara* 2001, SLCR, 125 [enlargement to common grazing ceasing to be under the 1911 Act].
18. *Seafield Trs v Sutherland* 1935, SLCR, 53 [holding ceasing to be under the 1911 Act]; *Trs of the late Sir J. J. M. Horlick v O'Hara* 2001, SLCR, 125 [common grazings ceasing to be under the 1911 Act].
19. *Highland Primary Care NHS Trust v Thomson* 1999, SLCR, 32.
20. 1993 Act, s. 25(1)(c).
21. See, for example, Committee of Inquiry on Crofting – Final Report [Shucksmith Report], issued on 12 May 2008, e.g. paragraphs 1.5.22, 2.5.5, 3.1.6: http://www.croftinginquiry.org/Documents/final-report.html (accessed 29 November 2014). Paragraph 3.7.1 states 'that a commercial loan is now necessary in addition and this requires decrofting of the house site', although this comment was in the context of a new build house on croft land.
22. Crofters (Scotland) Act 1955, Schedule 2, paragraph 7 and Crofters (Scotland) Act 1993, Schedule 2, paragraph 8.
23. 1993 Act, s. 3(4) and 3(5).
24. See *Crofting Commission Reference* 2012, SLCR, 159, paragraph 22.
25. 1993 Act, s. 52(4).
26. Section 12(3)(b) and *MacMillan v MacKenzie* 1995, SLT (Land Ct), 7 followed in *Guthrie v Bowman* 1998, SLT (Land Ct), 2.
27. Section 10 of the 1911 Act continued into the 1993 Act until the concept of 'purposeful use' was introduced by the 2007 Act and continued by the 2010 Act.
28. Shucksmith Report, paragraphs 2.5.4, 3.14.8 and 3.17.1.
29. See *Bain v Crofting Commission*, SLCR, 164 and 165, decision 13/11/13. This was a case where the Commission refused an assignation of a croft to a crofter who had farmed that croft as part of his enterprise for about twenty years.
30. Cameron, *Land for the People?*, 51.
31. Crofters Commission Record Numbers 1824 and 1825, dealing with the breakup of Bourblock and Tarbet farms on the Lovat Estate near Mallaig under the Congested Districts (Scotland) Act 1897.
32. Shucksmith Report, paragraphs 1.5.22, 2.5.5, 3.1.6.
33. This is the author's observation, having come across a number of croft amalgamations in the 1960s and 1970s as part of his practice – a formal Crofting Commission policy has not been unearthed.
34. Shucksmith Report, paragraph 2.5.4.
35. 1993 Act, s. 3A(1)(b). Under the Crofting (Designation of Areas) (Scotland) Order 2010/29, areas of Highland Council outwith the crofting counties – Moray, the parishes of Kingarth, North Bute and Rothesay in Argyll and Bute Council area and the islands of Arran (including Holy Island and Pladda), Great Cumbrae and Little Cumbrae – have all been designated.
36. Crofting Commission Policy Plan Revised September 2014 (approved by the Scottish Ministers), paragraph 84. See: http://www.crofting.scotland.gov.uk/legislation.asp (accessed 9 December 2014).

37. LRPG 'Identifying the Problems', February 1998, section 5; 'Identifying the Solutions', September 1998 and in particular 'Recommendations for Action', January 1999, Annex B Crofting CR4, Create new Crofts and CR8, End control over subdivision.
38. A comment made to the author by a civil servant involved in the consultation process at the time, who remarked that the end of the control on subdivision was to provide additional house sites.
39. Shucksmith Report, paragraph 3.7.4 and Committee of Inquiry on Crofting – Government Response 1 October 2008, 'Overview', paragraph 4. See: http://www.scotland.gov.uk/Publications/2008/09/25154550/0 (accessed 29 November 2014).
40. 'Affordable housing solutions – an incoming crofter of a bareland croft will normally be eligible for the Croft House Grant Scheme' – Crofting Commission Plan 2013, paragraph 21, second bullet point.
41. This wording comes from the 1955 Act, repeated in the 1976 Act, and again in the 1993 consolidation, in error. 'The 1955 Act' should have been substituted for 'this Act' but this was not done. This means that where a house was bought and de-crofted post-1976, should there have been no house on the croft in 1993, then the crofter can build a new house without the consent of the landlord.
42. 1993 Act, s. 1(2A)(a).
43. 1993 Act, s. 58A(7), inserted by Section 48(7) of the 2010 Act.
44. 1993 Act, s. 10(1)(b), introduced by 2010 Act.
45. *Rogerson v Viscount Chilston* 1917, SC, 453.
46. 1993 Act, s. 1(2A) (as amended by the 2010 Act).
47. LRPG 'Identifying the Solutions', September 1998, 87, Crofting 8, 9, 10 and 11, 'Vision for the Future'.
48. Westlaw is an on-line service provided by Sweet & Maxwell Ltd, Law Publishers, which provides instant access to the most up to date amended version of any Act of Parliament.
49. Scottish Parliament Information Centre ('SPICe') Briefing – Crofting Amendment (Scotland) Bill SB 13/25 of 10 May 2013.
50. Fourth Report, 2013 (Session 4). Stage 1 Report on the Crofting (Amendment) (Scotland) Bill 31 May 2013, summary at paragraphs 4 and 5.
51. *Report of the Commission of Enquiry into Crofting Conditions: presented by the Secretary of State for Scotland to Parliament by Command of Her Majesty* (Edinburgh, 1954).
52. http://www.scotland.gov.uk/About/Review/land-reform (accessed 29 November 2014).
53. http://www.parliament.uk/business/committees/committees-a-z/commons-select/scottish-affairs-committee/inquiries/parliament-2010/land-reform-in-scotland/ (accessed 29 November 2014).
54. For example, 1886 Act, s. 11 'Enlargement of Holdings'; Congested Districts (Scotland) Act 1897; 1911 Act, s. 7 'Powers to facilitate the constitution of new holdings', which was radically amended by the Land Settlement (Scotland) Act 1919.
55. 'Jersey Residential Statuses and what they mean' – http://www.gov.je/Working/Contributions/RegistrationCards/Pages/ResidentialStatus.aspx (accessed 29 November 2014); States of Guernsey has 'Local Market Property' and 'Open Market Property' – http://www.gov.gg/buypropertyinguernsey (accessed 29 November 2014).
56. Shucksmith Report Recommendation at paragraph 3.15.3.
57. Committee of Inquiry on Crofting – Government Response, paragraph 61.
58. *James v United Kingdom* (1986), Law Reports of Cases in the European Court of Human Rights, 123.

BOOK REVIEWS

The Kings of Alba, c.1000–c.1130.
By Alasdair Ross. Pp. xvvii, 245.
ISBN: 9781906566159 (pbk).
Edinburgh: John Donald, 2011. £20.00.
DOI: 10.3366/nor.2015.0090

Most periods of Scottish history have particular source problems that complicate the prospects for straightforward reconstruction or narrative. Even so, the eleventh century is a particular headache. To formulate a basic outline, the historian relies most on a scattering of obits and miscellaneous entries in various English and Irish annals. A handful of literary pieces devoted to Scottish kings, such as poems and king-lists, complements such notices. To get a picture of how informative these are, one of the longest, the Gaelic metrical king-list in *Prophecy of Berchán*, omits the names of most of its Scottish kings and replaces them with insider allusions. Then there are extended but late texts such as the Scoto-Latin chronicles and Scandinavian sagas. These have frequently seduced historians with their detailed and lively episodes, but their independent value for pre-twelfth-century Scotland is limited. For political and social structures, much of our understanding also relies on difficult or late evidence. Scholars are forced to draw inferences from the succeeding two centuries, a period of unparalleled administrative and demographic change, using material produced almost entirely by churchmen from England and France. Such sources are themselves a bi-product of this upheaval, and because cross-cultural analogy lies behind much of the terminology, new institutions introduced from the south and pre-existing (or remodelled) features of Scottish society are difficult to distinguish. With the twelfth and thirteenth centuries so problematic, back-projections carry much risk.

Any historian dealing with the period takes on such challenges, and so Alasdair Ross deserves some sympathy. *Kings of Alba* is a collection of discussions about various aspects of Scottish politics and society between 1000 and 1130. As the title indicates, a significant portion of the book is devoted to the careers of Scotland's eleventh- and early-twelfth-century rulers, the focus of chapters four to six and much of chapter three. The book's interests, however, range beyond royal politics. The opening chapter is devoted to environmental and agricultural matters, treating subjects as various as the development of tide mill (p. 12) and the introduction of hemp (p. 11). Source problems mean that the political significance of environmental developments tends to be obscure, but Ross draws attention to many of the known disease- and weather-related hardships suffered by the people of the era, providing a table of annalistic notices (pp. 6–7). As difficult as it is to explore the detail profitably, such information is itself valuable, and important observations may always lie over the horizon.

While not the first book in recent years to discuss the era, Ross's work makes a number of notable contributions. He goes to great lengths to give his audience a picture of earlier scholarship, a feature that will be appreciated by many, not least students hoping to make their own contributions to individual debates. This effort allows the reader to place Ross's suggestions in broader scholarly context. Another important contribution is the focus on the north, notably in regard to the space and consideration given to Moray. Here Ross is acknowledging the realities of early medieval political geography as well as playing to the strengths of his expertise. The attempt to place political events alongside their administrative setting is also an important step in the right direction. Particularly interesting is his discussion of the *davoch*, arguing that it was an important territorial unit of assessment within the Scottish kingdom. Ross's work will be significant for extending the historiographical debate and widening the vision of many enthusiasts of early Scottish history.

The author deserves added sympathy for trying to complete this ambitious work in a little over two hundred pages. Inevitably, perhaps, this limitation has left balance issues. Many readers will probably feel that events and myths from succeeding centuries have received generous consideration; and, partly down to the author's interest in historiography, late sources such as the chronicles attributed to Fordun, Wyntoun, and Bower appear at times to overshadow superior texts. Ross often engages with more contemporary and reliable annalistic matter briefly, via historiography, or via collections made by W. F. Skene and A. O. Anderson. Such sources are very difficult to utilize effectively in short space. Evidence from ordinarily reliable Irish annals is unpersuasively dismissed in asides or on the basis of manuscript date (pp. 34, 90), while material from late Scandinavian saga is incorporated casually (e.g. pp. 182–6). Several times Ross asserts mistakenly that the sources cease to refer to the office of mormaer after the early twelfth century (pp. 50, 220). In fairness, this belief appears regularly in older historiography, and its apparent plausibility is in part due to the dominance of Latin-language sources. People in the twelfth century came to view the mormaer as analogous to the earl and the count further afield, and each was rendered *comes* in Latin charters and chronicles. Nevertheless, a more thorough investigation of vernacular sources would have dispelled this error. For instance, the Deer *notitiae* show continued use of the term in the mid-to-late twelfth century, while a quick search of the online Irish annals would have shown 'mormaer' to have been a vernacular style for *comites* of fourteenth-century

Carrick and fifteenth-century Lennox. These sources are used elsewhere in Ross's work.

Lack of extended focus on sources has other dangers, including inconsistent evaluation. As an example, take the use of Anglo-Latin annalistic tradition. Until relatively recently scholars tended to believe that Earl Siward of Northumbria had placed Máel Coluim mac Donnchada (later Máel Coluim III) on the Scottish throne as part of his campaign against Macbeth in 1054. In 2002, Archibald Duncan undermined the evidence for this. Duncan highlighted the earliest annal witness to the tradition (in the collection currently attributed to John of Worcester), which had identified Siward's dependant as 'Máel Coluim son of the king of the Cumbrians'. Later writers like William of Malmesbury used a similar annal but added detail that specified the famous Scottish king. Although chronology saves Donnchad's son as a possibility, the wording might indicate that the original annalist had been referring to a separate Máel Coluim, perhaps a relation of an earlier Strathclyde king. Ross accepts this argument and goes so far as to state that 'it is now known that the new king of Strathclyde in 1054 was a member of that kingdom's ruling dynasty and not Máel Coluim mac Donnchada' (p. 130). Yet, earlier in the book Ross had sought to use a Huntingdon extract clearly derived in part from same tradition, stating that Huntingdon's twelfth-century Scottish connection 'raises the possibility that all of the information in this extract could be correct' (p. 120). He had been trying to rescue some early information about Macbeth's relationship with Máel Coluim, and his specific proposition that a twelfth-century contributor might have had access to good Scottish information is unproblematic. Nonetheless, the same logic could be applied, say, to William of Malmesbury's *Gesta Regum Anglorum*, a patron of which was King David I, son of Máel Coluim and husband of Earl Siward's granddaughter.

The book has many points that would have benefitted from fuller development, if only to boost the authority of the argument. Ross treats land-units such as the *davoch* (p. 27) and *arachor* (p. 143) like layers of terminological archaeology, whose appearance in sources provides a direct window on an even earlier age. The assumption might prove to be correct, but is not adequately justified and appears implicitly to deny organisational fluidity to populations living after 1100. Given the extent of political and administrative change in the following centuries, this is a surprising assumption. Likewise, Ross uses a fourteenth-century text describing the earldom of Moray, as granted to Thomas Randolph by Robert I, in order to deduce Moray's early territory (pp. 73–82), suggesting that it 'allows us to calculate that the Moray of c.1130 would have been comprised of approximately 250 *davochs*' (p. 79). Even accepting the relative chronology he assigns to the *davoch* and parish, such stability is surely problematized by the intervening centuries of political turmoil and land redistribution, defeated rebellions and outside penetration, as well as the creation of multiple sheriffdoms in the region, not to mention other innovations undoubtedly lost to us by poor documentation.

A much longer version of this book would have done its arguments and subjects more justice, but arguably this would be the case with any work. *Kings of Alba* is a welcome contribution to an understudied topic, and is well worth reading by anyone seriously interested in the Scottish kingdom of the era. Ross's post-1130 'digressions' are justifiable given the nature of the surviving sources and the questions he tries to answer. Indeed, Ross's focus on later material and events means that, with some additions and alterations, this book is a good platform for a monograph on 'Greater Moray' in the period 1000 to 1300. As it stands, it is one of the most detailed and up-to-date works on this important topic, and would be a good purchase for that reason alone.

Neil McGuigan
University of St Andrews

The Stewart Earls of Orkney.
By Peter Anderson. Pp. xvii, 343.
ISBN: 9781904607465 (pbk).
Edinburgh: Birlinn, 2012. £25.00.
DOI: 10.3366/nor.2015.0091

The infamous tenures of Robert Stewart, first earl of Orkney, lord of Shetland, and his son and successor Patrick, were fraught with social and political unrest. Both contemporary and modern observers have attributed the root cause of this turbulence to the ineptness and even the scornful characters of these infamous figures. Peter Anderson's recent work, *The Stewart Earls of Orkney*, addresses the accusations levelled against them and, through careful reexamination of sources, seeks to provide a more nuanced appraisal of both their characters and their careers. His previous works on the two leaders have been combined here to facilitate comparison. This approach is warranted; although Robert and Patrick are commonly viewed as comprising a single, disastrous house, the newest study shows them to be distinct personalities with different skills and shortcomings.

The book begins by surveying events since the impignorations of Orkney and Shetland to Scotland in 1468–9 and traces the growing interests of the Scottish king and aristocracy in the isles through the sixteenth century. 'Foreign rule' is a recurring motif in the late-medieval history of the Northern Isles, and continues to form a crux in the chronicle of the Stewart earls' sordid regimes. Anderson stages this theme by recounting Robert Stewart's illustrious upbringing in royal, aristocratic and clerical circles in Edinburgh. His eventual grant of authority over the isles was largely a credit to his skills of social climbing and alliance-building within Scotland's political elite. In tracing Robert's path to authority, Anderson locates a divide between the Scottish world of Robert's youth and the island environs over which he would assume power, thereby foreshadowing the estrangement that would develop between him, his son and the island communities.

Moving beyond the opulent courts of lowland Scotland, Anderson introduces the reader to the rustic environs of the Northern Isles, a setting that, although in many ways foreign to Robert, would come to form the focus of his and his son Patrick's economic enterprises. Anderson's analysis of surviving rentals here provides perhaps the most succinct depiction of the isles' pre-modern economies to date. He also touches on the important question of law and the key discrepancies between the native Norse customs and the incoming Scottish influences. While only a minor critique, discussion here is quite stinted. While it is noted that island law had its origins in the *Gulathing* of Western Norway, no mention is made of the *Law of the Realm* of the late thirteenth century or its impact on the development of the island judiciaries in the later middle ages and beyond.

The most pressing issue in Robert's early years in the Northern Isles was the opposition posed by other Scottish aristocrats and clerics with ambitions in the north. Anderson describes the precarious situation that existed at the time of Robert's arrival, one in which the scramble for power and the lack of a firm executive made the isles an untamed political milieu. Robert's failure to placate his rivals and win local support is witnessed in the complaints drawn up against him in 1575 and 1577. Anderson's examination of these sources represents an important piece of his study as it draws attention to key differences between the socioeconomic and political structures of the isles. Whereas the 1575 complaint was motivated by Robert's strife with Scottish aristocratic adversaries in Orkney, those from 1577 reveal a more fundamental clash between the native commons of Shetland and Stewart's foreign, heavy-handed governmental entourage.

Although Patrick Stewart continued many of his late father's projects, his regime was notably more sinister, his appetite for land and revenues more insatiable and his methods more corrupt. Anderson demonstrates in wonderful detail how Patrick set out to clip the wings of his rivals, exploit their lands and curtail efforts to oppose him in the future. These efforts, illegal and treasonous, inspired some of the early steps in a long process of litigation against Patrick. While Anderson notes parallels between the complaints against Patrick and those levelled against his father in 1575, he also suggests the younger Stewart's more heinous crimes were more damning and deprived him of most – though not all – avenues of local support. Worse still was his campaign to crush the rights of the isles' *udallers*, appropriate their lands and reissue them in feudal tenure. He assumed liberties that not only defied the native Norse-inspired laws of the isles, but also exceeded the rights granted to him as earl and lord by the king. Anderson portrays Patrick as a man suffering from desperation and megalomania as he continued to make illegal acquisitions despite the growing threat of prosecution. Anderson supports traditional views of Patrick as a spiteful individual, showing that his abuses of the commons were inspired as much by his disdain for the islanders and their laws as by his own economic desperation.

These mounting tensions reach their climax as Anderson traces Patrick's downfall in the final chapters of the book. It is made strikingly clear that his demise was brought about by the sum of his multiple transgressions and championed not only by disgruntled islanders but also political opponents in Edinburgh, including the king. Yet Patrick's twilight years also witnessed a perplexing twist in his story; though indicted for treason and replaced by a new regime under the mandate of King James VI, Patrick and his son, Robert, mustered some support from the islanders. While scholars have suggested that islanders supported the Stewarts in an effort to protect native Norse laws against the Scottish customs of the new regime, Anderson argues convincingly that it had more to do with immediate displeasure with the new administration. Furthermore, Patrick and his son enjoyed the lingering loyalties of a small circle of allies, something which suggests a more nuanced political situation than has previously been appreciated. Although unpopular, Patrick was not completely isolated, nor was he the only object of displeasure at the local level. These shreds of support ultimately failed, however, to save him and his son from the gallows, nor did they have a lasting impact on his posthumous image as a malicious figure.

The Stewart Earls of Orkney is much more than an updated biographical sketch of these ill-fated individuals. For this reviewer, the work is significant and innovative in three respects: first, it sheds light on the kind of social and political avenues pursued by Scotland's aristocrats in order to augment their titles, enrich their coffers and expand the reach of their influence at the margins of the realm. While each of the careers examined was in some respects unique, there are a number of commonalities, including their strategies of alliance-building, which reflect broader characteristics of Scotland's political environment in the early modern era. Second, the book shows how individuals imbued in the mores of Lowland society navigated Scotland's still largely uncharted cultural, social and political peripheries. While the theme has been addressed in previous studies of the isles, Anderson's comprehensive analysis of the rich source material from the Stewart era provides novel perspectives on the process of cultural convergence. Finally, this work brings us closer to appreciating the challenges of incorporating the Northern Isles into the legal and political framework of the kingdom. Although Orkney and Shetland had been within Scotland's sphere of influence since at least the fifteenth century, it was in the Stewart era that elites first made concerted, and at times overzealous, efforts to anchor them within the realm. The efforts did not follow a single trajectory, and diverging strategies and interests continued to hamper the integration process long after the Stewarts' fall from power.

These innovations might not, however, be readily apparent to the reader. The prologue is devoid of research questions or defined methodologies, and individual chapters are rarely rounded off with summary conclusions. Without these cues, the reader is forced to navigate the chapters without knowing which themes will be prioritized and why. Because the book is presented as a (loosely) chronological narrative, it also reads less like a piece of pure historical scholarship and more like a work of popular history aimed at a broader audience. Although this creates excitement in small doses, the book as a whole is anything but an easy read. It weaves through the careers and interactions of multiple individuals and families, some quite obscure, and those not already familiar with the theme may become bogged down in details while overlooking more significant, broader developments. This problem might have been alleviated had Anderson included more explicit questions at the start of each individual chapter. Only in the final five pages does Anderson tie together strands and offer a clear appraisal of the Stewart earls as men and magnates. In Anderson's view, scrutiny of Robert's enterprises reveal much about political conditions of his day, while Patrick, a more provocative figure, embodied the voraciousness so often associated with Stewart rule in the isles.

Although this reviewer had some initial reservations about Anderson's attempts to identify the earls' character traits, it quickly becomes clear that his portrayals rely heavily on comments derived from the rich, original source material. This bespeaks the greatest strength of this work and the point that has been reiterated throughout this review. Its ample integration of tantalisingly descriptive sources piques the reader's interest and imagination about the Stewart earls as individuals while providing a sound basis for objective historical analysis of contemporary sentiment. Anderson, an archivist with intimate knowledge of these documents, uses them to offer a fair, nuanced and credible portrayal of the two most notorious figures in the history of the Northern Isles.

Ian Peter Grohse
Westfälische Wilhelms-Universität Münster

British and Irish Experiences and Impressions of Central Europe, c.1560–1688.
By David Worthington. Pp. xviii, 232.
ISBN: 9780754663423 (hbk).
Farnham: Ashgate, 2012. £74.00.
DOI: 10.3366/nor.2015.0092

The last decades have seen the growing popularity of transnational history. The concept has been embraced by many since it helps to put national developments in context and, consequently, it liberates scholars from the burden of anachronistic categories. This new book by Worthington gives a taste of the rewards resulting from the concept's effective deployment and proves that it should not be dismissed as merely a fashion.

Though the idea of Central Europe is not without controversy, it certainly works as a convenient shorthand. As a result of replacing the state(s) with the region as an analytical unit, a wholly new pattern of cultural transfer, political pressure and religious influence is revealed. Worthington opens up his enquiry also in another sense, for he aims to capture the fullness of the British and Irish experience – not only as the witnesses to, but also the architects of events; the creators as much as the objects of impressions. The inclusion of four national groups of the archipelago is both refreshing and stimulating, for their relationships abroad provide insights into our understanding of domestic affairs.

Worthington's key purpose is to show how the particular circle and the associated networks of those of archipelagic background emerged, and to put this into the wider context of emigration and exile. According to him, one of the main characteristics of this group was its 'multiplicity of involvements'. Partially, this was a natural result of the growing number of expatriates in the region – a phenomenon recorded in contemporaneous accounts, especially those written after the outbreak of the Thirty Years' War. Furthermore, the analysis of those sources indicates that early modern Irish and British commentators – whether tourists, diplomats or literati – were much keener to see analogies between Poland-Lithuania, the Habsburg lands and their own countries, than contemporary scholars. Everyday custom, religious situation or political organization provoked often colourful, if not always well-informed, comments by the likes of Peyton, Moryson, Mundy and others. As Worthington rightly points out, with this range of accounts at hand, it was possible to form opinions about Central Europe without the inconvenience of crossing the Channel. Yet though the author sufficiently proves this point, his treatment of the related sources leaves the reader slightly dissatisfied. This is particularly true with regard to the writings of John Harrison and others who remarked on the Thirty Years' War (pp. 25, 35ff.), for it appears that the potential of those sources, which reflect shifting attitudes to the conflict and the complexity of perceptions of Central Europe so well, is not fully explored.

Worthington's approach is perhaps understandable, since the wide scope of the book leaves no room for fully-fledged textual analysis. The author closely examines the emergence and movements of various circles that operated in the region in the period from 1560 to 1688. A substantial part of the book is dedicated to the activities of the Leslie family, arguably the most successful among those groups, but a fair share of attention is also given to the Taaffees, the Gordons, the Wallises, the Ogilvies, Nicholas Donnellan and numerous other individuals operating in the region. Worthington shows the important role that kinship played in the process of shaping politics, but his analysis also confirms that diplomacy was by no means a domain of the crown. The intensity of both official and non-official agendas that were pursued by the British and Irish convinces that their interest in and impact on the affairs of Central Europe was stronger than suggested by current historiography.

Vivid illustration of such involvement is provided by the lives of expatriates such as James Leslie and Francis Taaffee, who arrived, successfully integrated and became influential figures within the host societies. The latter owed his advancement to his military talents, which was not an unusual career path, and Worthington provides a fascinating narrative of military ventures and adventures of soldiers from the archipelago in the service of the king of Poland-Lithuania, the emperor and the tsar (pp. 85ff.). Efforts of those servants of many masters and supporters of various causes should be interpreted, as Worthington argues, in the context of Christendom. The continual power of this concept is successfully demonstrated, though perhaps the argument would have been even stronger if the book had been expanded to 1699, when the Treaty of Karlovitz was signed.

The pursuits of scholars, mavericks and the "curious", to use Lawrence Brockliss's phrase, turn out to be no less captivating. As in other parts of the book, the author considers individuals' beliefs in order to assess to what extent religion was a stimulus for – or a deterrent to – networking. The evidence he presents dispels any notion that the relationships established by the British and Irish followed any simple Catholic and Protestant divide, but the most interesting of his inquiries are into possible connections between religion, science and commerce. By his own admission, as for the British and Irish commercial presence in the Austrian Habsburg lands, evidence is generally lacking (p. 145), but the cases of Edward Kelly and Johann Becher are very suggestive and, hopefully, will encourage further research into the subject.

The theme of religion appears also in the final part of the book, which looks at the interplay between nationality and religious affiliation. This could be very complex considering that the British and Irish Catholics in Central Europe operated in close proximity with their non-Catholic neighbours from the archipelago. Worthington demonstrates how the orders of the Jesuits, but also the Franciscans and Benedictines, accommodated for the spiritual needs of Catholic expatriates from Ireland and Britain, but also how they helped them to maintain their ethnic identities.

The narrative woven by Worthington is rich and colourful, though not all threads are managed with the same skill; trimming off the excess background information and tying up a concluding knot here and there would make the pattern of the author's argument clearer. The absence of John Peyton's account of the Empire and Bohemia from the multi-linguistic bibliography is striking. The occasional lack of precision (for example, the apparently intermittent use of 'Poland' and 'the Commonwealth [of Poland-Lithuania]') is upsetting as much as it is surprising, given the author's sensitivity to the nuances of language. But those objections should not overshadow what the book has to offer – a much needed fresh perspective on the history of three kingdoms and a comprehensive study of the presence of the British and Irish in Central Europe.

Martyna Mirecka
University of St Andrews

Lordship and Power in the North of Scotland: the Noble House of Huntly 1603–1690.
By Barry Robertson. Pp. xvii, 221.
ISBN: 9781906566340 (pbk).
Edinburgh: John Donald, 2011. £25.00.
DOI: 10.3366/nor.2015.0093

Barry Robertson's *Lordship and Power in the North of Scotland* is a timely addition to the literature on early modern Scotland's nobility. Whereas contemporaries wrote indispensable, if partisan, chronicles of the Gordons of Huntly and nineteenth-century antiquarians published swathes of extant manuscripts, modern scholars have hitherto neglected the patriarchs of this leading noble family.

Robertson argues that the seventeenth-century Gordons of Huntly qualify current understanding about the prospects of noble power in early modern Europe. A previous generation of scholars posited that noble power was in steady decline across the seventeenth century, but more recently Hamish Scott and Ronald Asch have shown that noble power persisted as a force shaping European politics alongside the development of the central institutions of the modern state. According to Robertson, the Gordons of Huntly present an exception to this trend. Considering that they were one of the leading noble families in sixteenth-century Scotland, Robertson concludes that the Scottish aristocracy retained 'its position of pre-eminence in Scottish society but, within its ranks, there had been a noticeable shift in the balance of power' (p. 187). By 1690 the Gordons of Huntly, once colloquially referred to as the 'Cock of the North', had relinquished much of their control over the lands and people of northeastern Scotland. Throughout the seventeenth century, successive leaders of the Gordons of Huntly found themselves on the wrong side of religious or political disputes. In 1629, the first marquess's Roman Catholicism contributed to the Gordons' loss of control over the sheriffships of Inverness and Aberdeen. During the British Civil Wars, the second marquess chose to support Charles I in his fight against the Covenanters, yet the embattled monarch preferred the marquesses of Hamilton and Montrose to lead Scottish campaigns in Huntly's stead. Rather than reconciling themselves to prevailing opinion in the Scottish Parliament or at the royal court in London, leaders of the Gordons of Huntly decided instead 'to depend on their regional power alone' (p. 186). Yet it was precisely this regional power that was being eroded by tectonic shifts in the structure and organization of the Scottish state.

In six chronological chapters Robertson explores the waxing and waning fortunes of the first four marquesses of Huntly, the last of whom, George, was elevated to the dukedom of Gordon in 1684. Chapters situate regional vignettes in the context of the well-trodden high political narrative of seventeenth-century British history. An initial chapter illuminates the Gordons' 'meteoric' rise in power in the sixteenth century, resulting from the manipulation of kin and allegiance networks, but Robertson also draws attention to limits of their power, highlighting the importance of conflicts with the Forbes family, the earls of Moray and Clan Mackintosh. In chapter two, Robertson shows that George Gordon, first marquess of Huntly, was reluctant to support James VI & I's efforts to 'civilise' the Highlands, unless Gordon lordships were directly threatened. The dissolution of a long-standing bond of association with the Hays of Errol in 1616, moreover, was symptomatic of the early decline of Huntly's powers in the north. Chapter three charts the further decay of Huntly's standing at Charles I's court, which Robertson argues resulted largely from his Roman Catholic faith. Huntly's fall from royal favour was compounded by bitter local feuds. Illuminating this decline, Robertson reconstructs a gripping episode wherein the Crichton family held the Gordons of Huntly responsible for a fatal fire at Frendraught Castle in 1630.

Chapters four and five chart the prospects of the second and third marquesses during the tumultuous decades of the 1640s and 1650s. In these two chapters, Robertson successfully re-places Huntly at the centre of a Scottish 'Royalist' movement, the historiography of which has previously been focused on the exploits of the marquesses of Montrose and Hamilton. According to Robertson, Royalist victories were the result of a 'confederation of allies' and they were 'collaborative efforts' rather than the product of Montrose or MacColla's leadership alone (p. 153). Initial missteps and defeats after 1638 led the second marquess of Huntly to lose control of the lordships of Badenoch and Lochaber to his Covenanter brother-in-law, the marquess of Argyll. Huntly's position in the northeast was also undermined by an internecine feud with his son, George, Lord Gordon, who supported the Covenanters. Such local and familial dynamics contributed to Huntly's weak military standing throughout the 1640s and 1650s and more broadly these troubles, Robertson argues, illustrated the manifold difficulties that thwarted Royalist resistance to the Covenanting regime. The Restoration of Charles II in 1660 marked the beginning of a false dawn for the Gordons of Huntly. The forfeiture and execution of Argyll allowed the Gordons of Huntly to recoup their lost lordships, but familial tensions were exacerbated with the elevation in 1660 of Lord Charles Gordon to the earldom of Aboyne, severing Aboyne lands permanently from the Huntly title. The young fourth marquess of Huntly's Roman Catholicism precluded his involvement in central government either in London or in Edinburgh and his attempts at retaining his family's standing in regional politics was challenged by Charles II's elevation of Sir George Gordon of Haddo to the earldom of Aberdeen and the extension of the earl of Moray's power base into Huntly lands. Although the Roman Catholic monarch, James VII & II, initially favoured Huntly, the latter became alienated from James soon thereafter and shrewdly supported William and Mary after the Revolution of 1688–9. Although his wings were clipped, he retained his title and his estates.

On a superficial level, *Lordship and Power* suffers from myriad textual errors that undermine the strength of the work as a whole. For instance, Robertson twice incorrectly dates the execution of Charles I, which occurred at Whitehall on 30 January 1649, not on either 22 January or 26 January (pp. 62, 145). Moreover, as an intellectual historian, I would have liked to have heard something about the fourth marquess's schooling under the French Oratorian priest and Cartesian philosopher, Nicolas Malebranche (considered 'the premier philosopher of our age' by Pierre Bayle), and whether this relationship related to the relatively early importation of Cartesian ideas into Aberdonian intellectual circles. On a deeper level, Robertson characterizes his analysis as 'multi-level,' encompassing regional, British and European perspectives whilst illuminating the political, religious, social, economic and intellectual dimensions of Gordon power (p. 7). In this vein, *Lordship and Power* falls short of its intended aims. Robertson's chronological narrative often necessitates swift and unbalanced treatment of complex events. Whilst Robertson is at his strongest in his analysis of the role of the second marquess of Huntly in the years 1638–41 – a subject accorded an entire chapter – his analysis of the Restoration and Revolution would have benefitted from being divided into two separate chapters. Robertson's account of the complexities of Scottish Royalism may also have benefitted from further analysis of the social, religious and intellectual complexities of allegiance in 1640s and 1650s Scotland. For example, Robertson briefly discusses the 'intellectual case for Royalism' characterized by the writings of the so-called 'Aberdeen Doctors' – a group of theologians and academics based in Aberdeen – and comprising a defence of the Five Articles of Perth and episcopacy (p. 109). Whilst he qualifies the extent to which the Aberdeen Doctors' pamphlets reflected 'Royalist' thought in Scotland generally, his analysis throughout chapters four and five draws an overly-rigid distinction between 'Royalist' and 'Covenanting' Scots. Indeed, taking the Aberdeen Doctors as an example, William Leslie, John Forbes of Corse, and William Guild all at some point submitted to the Covenanting regime and maintained an ambivalent stance towards the National Covenant. Moreover, at various points from 1638 to 1649 the two other noblemen that Robertson identifies as leading 'Royalist' Scots – Montrose and Hamilton – fought for the Covenanters. Following Laura Stewart, it may be fruitful to consider the richly-textured social, political, economic and religious contexts which shaped noble power relations in order to arrive at a more nuanced portrait of Royalism in 1640s Scotland and Gordon power in the northeast.[1] Such errors notwithstanding, *Lordship and Power in the North of Scotland* provides a welcome addition to our understanding of one of seventeenth-century Scotland's preeminent noble families.

Alexander D. Campbell
Trinity Hall, Cambridge

Note

1. Laura A. M. Stewart, 'Power and faith in early modern Scotland', *Scottish Historical Review*, 92: Supplement (2013), 25–37.

Governing Gaeldom: The Scottish Highlands and the Restoration State, 1660–1688.
By Allan Kennedy. Pp. xiii, 404.
ISBN: 9789004248373 (hbk).
Leiden: Brill, 2014. £99.00.
DOI: 10.3366/nor.2015.0094

Attempts by historians to delineate precisely where the Scottish Highlands begin and end rarely lead to consensus. Geographical definitions of the region have, nevertheless, provided a starting point for numerous critiques of Highland (and broader Highlands and Islands) historiography in recent times, many of them by medievalists and modernists, which have thereby outlined the fault lines that can exist between, for example, 'Gaelic History', '*Gàidhealtachd* History' and 'Highland History'.[1] Early modern historians have, if anything, been even more reflective regarding this area.[2] In the last few years Alison Cathcart, and more recently doctoral theses and subsequent articles by Thomas Brochard and Allan Kennedy, have argued that there is limited worth in treating the region as a 'realm apart' both topographically and also in a broader social, economic and cultural sense, at various points during the epoch between the disintegration of the Lordship of the Isles and Culloden.[3] Thus, they assume a geographical definition to be required when identifying the region yet, importantly, also that the boundary or border between it and the Lowlands was often blurred and indistinct. Consequently, 'syncretic elements' and 'hybridity' have found a place in early-modern Highland historiography alongside versions assuming a more hermetically-sealed subject of study. As Kennedy has himself argued, there operated a 'cultural greyscale' across large swathes of the north and west of Scotland that was neither wholly 'Gaelic' nor entirely Lowland, one which he still interprets, though, as 'Highland'.[4]

It is from within this context that this monograph appears and, indeed, terms such as 'mixed', 'multi-layered' and 'cosmopolitan' crop up in the text. The book is split into two parts, each sub-divided into three chapters: Part One is thematic, exploring Scottish and British perspectives on the region, before moving on to interrogate the 'Highland Problem' and the region's experiences at the whims of a growing 'fiscal-military' state. Part Two explores, from a chronological perspective, the 1660–2 'Restoration Settlement', the twenty-eight year period associated, first, with Lauderdale, and, subsequently, Albany, the latter ruling as James VII and II from 1685 to 1658. The introduction and conclusion are brief and solid, the appendices (including fifty-six pages of tables), considerable, while an exhaustive bibliography and reliable index provide additional, and welcome, further points of reference.

The introduction is ambitious, exploring 'imperial' and 'collaborative' approaches to Highland history, within a pan-archipelagic and European context, and includes comparisons, albeit on a different scale, with kingdoms and 'peripheries' in other dynastic polities. Chapter One comprises a robust and original argument that, in contrast to the stark terms of the notorious Statutes of Iona (1609), many seventeenth-century contemporaries sought to put a limit on outside perceptions of the region's 'incivility', with debt, droving, and a diversifying economy more widely, all acting, and being seen to act, to integrate the region to a greater or lesser degree, whether from an Edinburgh or London perspective. Kennedy is at pains not to essentialise the Highlands, to emphasise it having been 'simply another locality' (p. 65). While perhaps a laudable aim, the model of the 'locality' turns out to be slightly problematic, at least as regards the Scottish context. This reader would have hoped for some outline coverage of which other parts of Scotland, the south-west or north-east, for example, might be explored fruitfully in such a trans-regional and comparative manner. If the Highland experience was 'broadly similar to that of any other locality' (p. 255), within Scotland or beyond, surely contemporaries would have commented on this more and reference could have been made to primary sources that made such analogies? As Kennedy himself suggests, a counter-argument could be constructed arguing that linguistic and other factors allowed for the continued propagation of a specifically Highland-Lowland divide that was not perceived to exist to the same extent between Edinburgh and the much more widely Scots-speaking north-east or borders. Chapter Two banishes successfully the notion of the region as having been especially 'lawless', arguing, for example, for a local explanation of accounts of banditry in Lochaber (p. 70). Animal theft, clanship and feuding were all pointed out and addressed in some manner by the region's governors, although the author cautions wisely against the danger of overstating the uniqueness of each of these, in varying extents, to the Highlands. Chapter Three tackles the complex mix of repression and conciliation used to control the region. Independent companies, watches, garrisons, bonding, judicial commissions and the use of lieutenancies, are all explored rigorously. The three chapters in Part Two are even more nuanced and the theme thus more challenging, following three distinct sub-periods, yet certainly providing the best available account of these to date for the Highlands.

The book constitutes a thoroughly-researched, convincing and clearly argued contribution to an increasingly complex historiography of the seventeenth-century Highlands, albeit not all of it available, unfortunately, at affordable prices for those without access to university library resources, an issue which may continue to slow its dissemination. Still, Kennedy's attention to detail and clarity of expression here is exemplary. In the broadest sense, the book comprises a major success in illuminating the part of the region in 'one of the darker stretches of Scottish history' (p. 251).

David Worthington
University of the Highlands and Islands

Notes

1. See, for example, Geoffrey Barrow, *The Kingdom of the Scots: Government, Church and Society from the Eleventh to the Fourteenth Century* (Edinburgh, 1973); D. Broun and M. MacGregor, (eds), *Mìorun Mòr nan Gall, 'The great ill-will of the Lowlander'? Lowland Perceptions of the Highlands, Medieval and Modern* (Glasgow, 2009); Ewen Cameron, 'Embracing the Past: the Highlands in Nineteenth Century Scotland', in D. E. Broun, R. J. Finlay and M. Lynch (eds), *Image and Identity: the Making and Re-making of Scotland through the Ages* (Edinburgh, 1998), 196; John A. Burnett, *The Making of the Modern Scottish Highlands, 1939–1965: Withstanding the 'Colossus of Advancing Materialism'* (Dublin, 2011), 17–18.
2. See, for example, Allan I. Macinnes, *Clanship, Commerce, and the House of Stuart, 1603–1788* (East Linton, 1996); R.A. Dodgshon, *From Chiefs to Landlords: Social and Economic Change in the Western Highlands and Islands, c.1493–1820* (Edinburgh, 1998).
3. Alison Cathcart, *Kinship and Clientage: Highland Clanship, 1451–1609* (Leiden, 2006), 7–9; Thomas Brochard, 'The "Civilizing" of the Far North of Scotland, 1560–1640', unpublished PhD thesis (University of Aberdeen, 2012), 1, 148.
4. Allan Kennedy, '"A Heavy Yock Uppon Their Necks": covenanting government in the northern Highlands, 1638–1651', *Journal of Scottish Historical Studies* 30 (2) (2010), 97. See, also, Kennedy's 'The Urban Community in Restoration Scotland: government, society and economy in Inverness, 1660–c.1688', *Northern Scotland* 5 (2014), 26–49.

Famine in Scotland. The 'Ill Years' of the 1690s.
By Karen J. Cullen. Pp. xiv, 218.
ISBN: 9780748638871 (hbk).
Edinburgh: Edinburgh University Press, 2010. £60.00.
DOI: 10.3366/nor.2015.0095

Towards the end of this long and detailed book, Karen Cullen explains her intention in writing it. Why, she asks, has there previously been so little attention paid to the crisis of the 1690s in Scotland compared to the attention, both academic and popular, devoted to the crisis of the 1840s in both Ireland and the Scottish Highlands? The answer, in part, is that the crisis was not much talked about in the years that followed although it must have left a deep scar in the memory of those who lived through it. And there may have been something of a tendency to talk the crisis down, to minimise it, amongst historians. But as she shows, there has always been uncertainty about the scale of the crisis, its regional incidence and its impact. Now, as a result of Cullen's assiduous work in the archives, there can be no doubt of the scale and indeed gravity of the crisis. In fact she finds that it was longer in duration than others have assumed, seeing signs of distress by 1692 and 1693 in some areas, while she also finds evidence of displaced persons still on the road in 1700.

No obvious stones have been left unturned in the research which covers all parts of Scotland including the western islands and Shetland and Orkney. In chapter two Cullen considers the evidence for the weather and the development of a famine. In chapter three she discusses the grain market (although here I would have liked more on the Commissioners of Supply). The decision to emulate the English and introduce a corn bounty scheme in 1695 was deeply unfortunate, and with echoes of nationalist accounts of the Great Irish famine, the instinct to export grain into southern markets remained strong even when there was obvious evidence of distress locally. This might be an issue within Scotland itself as when a merchant's agent in Dundee sold bear [barley] to bakers in Glasgow who were prepared to offer a better price than brewers based locally. There is some interesting anecdote in this chapter, including the observation in 1698 that high prices and high excise dues made any beer that might be brewed too expensive to buy.

Chapter four considers the limited provision for the poor. In an important correction to the older work of Mitchison, Cullen offers an appendix of parishes in which she has found evidence of a stent or rate being levied on behalf of the poor to supplement those previously identified. It is noticeable, though, that most parishes only introduced relief on the rates very late in the years of distress. Chapter five gathers together the evidence for the scale of the demographic disaster. The extant parish data is well used with interesting material adduced on the regionality of the crisis from year to year, and the proportion of adults and children buried. And, intriguingly, Cullen offers some evidence on the incidence of smallpox. There is good material here to support a thesis that the famine was not the same in every year, nor in every place. Of course, one of the reasons for the decline in population is emigration which forms the subject of chapter six. Good material on the stresses felt by tenant society may be found here, including the debates within estates over whether tenants in arrears should be discharged (but who was going to take on their tenancies?). The Ayr records are used to show the varying directions of the flow of migrants going through its port: strongly from Ireland to Scotland in the early 1690s, but with a strong counterflow in the later years of the decade.

Cullen can be slightly tentative in her conclusions, and sometimes concludes discussion of her own findings by a reference to the opinions of other historians. She is, however, realistic about what it is, and what it is not, possible to know and so, whilst she inclines to think that population loss in the decade may have been in the region of 15 per cent (including those who lived but left), she acknowledges that the lack of records for much of the Highland zone makes proper estimation impossible. My impression is that whilst she appreciates that the root cause of the famine was ultimately the weather, she has not entirely thought through what this implies. Weather is the great variable. There is no such thing as the weather that creates a famine as the weather in a single year may be poor, or may be very poor, but its impact may vary according to the time of year at which the poor weather occurs. Hence there is no single set or combination of conditions that create famine. Those underpinning successive famines will never be the same and this makes comparisons between famines difficult. Moreover, as we know from our own experience in recent years, severe weather, and in particular repeated

Atlantic storms, are actually quite localised in their incidence. That there was no famine incidence in the north of England in the 1690s (so far as we know) is a reflection of where the bad weather was as much as the capacity of northern English society to withstand a succession of extreme weather events.

Cullen is anxious to place the distress of the 1690s in a European frame and this is surely correct. Following her work, there is no excuse for either Scots or those from further afield to ignore the Scottish famine of the 1690s. That they were living through one of the great European famines would have brought no solace to those who experienced terrible things, many of whom died before conditions improved and life returned to a kind of normality. Famine, like war, is increasingly out of the reach of our personal experience; this book shows why we should be grateful that it should be so.

Richard W. Hoyle
University of Reading

From An Antique Land. Visual Representations of the Highlands and Islands 1700–1880.
By Anne Macleod. Pp. xx, 233.
ISBN: 9781906566531 (pbk).
Edinburgh: John Donald, 2012. £25.
DOI: 10.3366/nor.2015.0096

There is no doubting that before the nineteenth century the great majority of people south of the Border knew very little of the Highlands, or indeed of Scotland. They know 'as little of Scotland as of Japan' was Smollett's assertion in the novel *Humphrey Clinker*, which was published in 1771: one of his characters was convinced that to reach Scotland a sea crossing was necessary. Yet things were to change greatly later in the eighteenth century and thereafter. Visitors found their way north in increasing numbers, even before Walter Scott's poetry and prose established Scotland as a key destination for the literary tourist, 'land of the fountain and the flood.' It was the poems of Ossian (courtesy of James Macpherson) that first put the Highlands on the cultural map of Europe. Interest developed in the social structure of the region, both archaic and uncorrupted. Enthusiasm grew for its scenery and rugged landscape, no longer horrid but attractive, as mountains and waterfalls came into fashion. Some visitors travelled north for sport, shooting or stalking, others for geological or antiquarian enquiry. And they wrote about what they found in the Highlands and Islands, about the people and their pursuits. Accounts of travel proliferated, some of which were very influential such as Thomas Pennant's *Tours* (1769, 1772) and William Gilpin's *Observations* (1789). And quite often these texts were illustrated with views and scenes, a significant element in allowing people to see the Highlands for themselves. But visual representation took many forms. Macleod argues that from about 1700 onwards, the Scottish Highlands became one of the most illustrated subjects in the British Isles, as map makers, artists and painters, sketchers, and latterly photographers hastened to bring images of this remote but now romantic region to a wider audience. There was a growing market in Britain for prints, and pictures of Highland scenery or sport drew crowds to art exhibitions. Sir Edwin Landseer was one painter who cashed in on the vogue, as with the painting entitled *Highlanders Returning from Deerstalking*, which was sold to the duke of Northumberland after being exhibited at the Royal Academy in 1827. Well-represented though Landseer's work is, it is slightly surprising that the *Monarch of the Glen* gets no mention; surely it is the most clichéd Highland painting of all time, the ultimate biscuit tin depiction of Highland Scotland. As Macleod remarks, visual images both shape and reflect stereotyping.

Macleod deals with why and how visual images were created, and admixes this with a close analysis of what they captured. Clearly differing forms of visual representation varied in how high a premium they put on exact depiction. Mapmakers wanted the best accuracy that they could achieve, as did antiquarians, recording ruins or brochs or stone circles. Artists, on the other hand, could and did take liberties. Turner, for example, used a vantage point for his view of Fingal's Cave which is simply impossible. We are referred to figures such as: Paul Sandby, chief draftsman to the Military Survey who became a landscape painter; Moses Griffiths, the self-taught genius who produced the drawings which illustrated Pennant's tours; James Skene of Rubislaw, who drew the stone circles on Arran and Pictish towers in Glenelg; and two personal favourites of mine, William Daniell, whose work includes one of the earliest views of a steamboat on the Clyde, and John Knox, whose *Landscape with Tourists at Loch Katrine*, shows that affliction to visitors to any present day tourist trap, the bagpiper. What is well covered by Macleod in a sequence of chapters is the range of subjects that artists tackled. Highland dress, whether of the gentry or the common folk, was an enduring obsession. So also was Highland custom and domestic life: girls washing clothes in a tub, men playing shinty, women carrying peat. One chapter deals with the Highlander at work, whether fishing, distilling (legally or otherwise) and working the land. Droving seems to have been a favourite subject for artists: a disappearing occupation, thanks first to the steamship and then the railway which did away with the need to walk cattle long distances to market. John Milne Donald's 1857 painting, *The Drove Road*, shows a few cattle only, wandering along in an empty landscape where a generation earlier there would have been scores or hundreds being urged along. This is but one of the many excellent illustrations; there are 100 plates in all, of which a third are in colour.

Some interesting issues are raised. Macleod argues that the visual stereotypes of the Highlands were firmly established by the 1850s: glens and bens, stags and cattle, tartan and bagpipes. She suggests that there is a legacy, that perceptions of the Highlands today are for many (particularly for those living away from the region) anchored in these images around notions of a wilderness rooted in its past, unspoilt by modernity. That has had, she suggests, a baleful effect on policy making. Things like wind farms and pylons (or a gold mine at Tyndrum) are seen as unwelcome and unwanted intrusions on an unspoilt wilderness. The past exercises its influence on the present. This is the conclusion to what is a superbly researched but quite densely argued analysis which in places shows its provenance as a doctoral thesis. The decision to use 1880 as the end point is understandable, but it does mean that there is little discussion of the new medium of photography which arrived from the 1850s onwards. A modest extension to 1914 would also have allowed consideration of other new and very popular forms of visual representation such as railway posters or picture postcards. But perhaps that is for a sequel.

Alastair J. Durie
University of Stirling

The Temperance Movement in Aberdeen, Scotland, 1830–1845: 'Distilled Death and Liquid Damnation'.
By Aaron Hoffman. Pp. ix, 585.
ISBN: 9780773425828 (hbk).
Lampeter: Edwin Mellen Press, 2011. £114.95.
DOI: 10.3366/nor.2015.0097

By the end of the nineteenth century temperance politics was well-established in Scotland. This book narrates its far more fragile beginnings. It is a story of success, stagnation and re-invention, beginning in Aberdeen with an anti-spirits society, founded in 1830. It is the more successful Aberdeen Total Abstinence Society (ATAS), formed following a lecture by a Rev. Mason at George Street Congregational Church on 22 September 1838, however, that is the main focus of Hoffman's analysis. ATAS had 3,000 members by January 1840 and over 10,000 by the end of 1841. At this point it could claim 16 per cent of the city's residents, which Hoffman reckons amounted to 24 per cent of adult Aberdonians. At the same time, campaigners were looking beyond Aberdeen. In October 1840 ATAS formed the North of Scotland Temperance Union with the aim of spreading the message across the region. By 1841 it had sixty-three affiliated societies with a membership of 23,215.

So who were these campaigners, and what did they do? Hoffman sees early temperance and total abstinence work as examples of moral suasion. Reformers targeted individuals, whose decisions to forego drink would be reinforced by making a public pledge. There were different reasons for making such a commitment. Plenty of working-class Chartist supporters took the pledge, for example, but ATAS was keen to maintain its independence from Chartism so as not to appear too political. People had different economic and social reasons for signing up, as well as obvious religious motives. With no significant Irish population Aberdeen, says Hoffman, was spared the sectarian tensions that affected the movement's impact in the central lowlands. But temperance was not free from disagreements that were rooted in religious difference. Hoffman's careful analysis of ninety-six ATAS members shows that 46 per cent belonged to the Established Church of Scotland. He contrasts the 54 per cent of his sample who were dissenters with the 26 per cent identified in an 1837 religious census of the burgh. Moreover, 'three-quarters of the tee-totallers connected with the Church of Scotland joined the Free Church after the Disruption' (p. 399). So, in Aberdeen at least, temperance seems to have been particularly associated with evangelical and dissenting Christianity. Some members of the town council objected to the use of council patronised churches for (non-religious) temperance meetings. Campaigners also battled with those who saw temperance as diverting people from the power of the Gospel which, opponents felt, carried a sufficiently strong message to reclaim drunkards. Some saw the pledge as being akin to an oath, which they interpreted as running counter to Biblical instruction. And, as was common across the country, Sabbatarians objected to temperance meetings and activities on Sundays.

This sounded a major note of opposition to a vital temperance tactic the world over, that of providing various counter-attractions to the drink shop. It is clear that there was money to be made from such ventures, even if one such, the Mariners' Temperance Coffee-House and Reading Room, wanted to help seamen avoid the temptation to drink. Temperance societies organised a range of activities, from scientific demonstrations as to the dangers of drink to more participatory activities such as large processions and bands. Some groups also arranged excursions, or events on the links. These shared activities crucially helped bind people to their pledge and to each other. The participation of women, however, was more circumscribed. Though a female society followed in November 1839, women reportedly did not speak at mixed-gender meetings or participate in teetotal processions.

Their significance was clearer in other areas, such as through the establishment of a home for prostitutes in March 1842, while the figure of the female drunkard remained symbolically important in the temperance imaginary. Police statistics for 1840 showed 3,783 cases of women being taken up for being drunk and disorderly, compared to 892 for men. Recidivism was notably important, with 1,400 repeat offences that year. Even taking these recidivists into account, or perhaps precisely by considering them, an important question as to what these statistics shows emerges: what effect was the temperance movement having on the policing, as distinct from drinking, habits of Aberdeen? Was temperance attention responsible for a disproportionate level of concern about female drunkenness? Local papers seem to have considered the problem to be real enough. The *Aberdeen Banner* believed that the public dealt more severely with female drunkards; they were effectively 'banished from society', which made their reclamation more difficult. When the statistics showed a 30 per cent fall in offences between 1839 and 1841 temperance campaigners were apparently quick to claim credit, but this cannot be taken as conclusive proof that their work had changed drinking habits.

Nevertheless, such statistics necessarily drew temperance reformers into the public eye. This was also true over licensing, with ATAS asking the magistrates to restrict the number of licences in order that parents would spend less of their valuable family income on alcohol at the expense of their children. Hoffman divides Aberdeen into five areas to examine the distribution of licenses. In 1828 there were 551 certificates, he notes: 193 in central, 169 in harbour, 105 in west, sixty-six in east, sixteen in north. By 1846–7 there were 104 in central, ninety-eight in harbour, sixty-nine in west, thirty-four in east, nine in north. Hoffman makes an interesting observation, much later in the book, that ATAS did not want to claim too much success in encouraging people to change consumption because of licensing reductions; rather, they wanted to see the reduction in licenses as a product of their campaigns to encourage sobriety. The magistrates' decisions to continue to licence in particular areas of the town, notably the old medieval centre, which was being abandoned by wealthier residents, might be explained by the fact that, in 1843–44, 11 per cent of the city's municipal electors were liquor sellers. These were divided across three wards (first ward with forty-nine of 361 electors, second ward with sixty-four of 498 and third with forty of 483). Frustratingly, it is not abundantly clear how these wards map on to the areas Hoffman selects for his analysis of licensing. There is a missed opportunity here to map churches and temperance meeting venues on to these municipal boundaries to weigh the relative advances of temperance activity.

The temperance movement *seemed* to be building a useful bloc to challenge the municipal influence of the liquor trade. But Hoffman's focus suggests we should not rush to see this translating into widespread political action. In fact, his close analysis of extant membership records and newspaper sources is really rather revealing. It shows the aspirational character of temperance protagonists and subscribers, with 37 per cent in his analysis of 152 members being in the upper working class and 26 per cent in the lower middle class. It would be wrong to assume that these were voters and, therefore, that temperance was an important municipal electoral issue. Instead, it seems the chief ambition of temperance campaigners was individual and associational rather than overtly political.

This does present us with a problem, however. How are we to judge temperance campaigns? Were they distinct from changes in consumption that might be associated with economic processes or urban expansion, for example? By the end of the book we are told that the causes underpinning the temperance battles of the book had been undermined by events such as the effects of the failure of the potato crop, which drove up the price of grain, and campaigns to abolish the Corn Laws. Hoffman usefully situates his study against late-eighteenth and early nineteenth-century debates, but in a couple of places he frustratingly gestures to later events as being outside the parameters of his lengthy study without necessarily signalling just what to take from the period in question. Perhaps this is to miss the point of Hoffman's focus. Indeed, the very differences Hoffman so thoroughly describes reveal both why temperance grew and, paradoxically, gesture at why it stagnated. The 'temperance movement' of the book's title is perhaps better understood as a term that captures a range of different groups variously interested in encouraging people to forego alcohol. Later campaigners were perhaps fighting different battles.

The book's appeal might be limited by its seemingly narrow title and by its price. That would be a pity. It would do a disservice to Hoffman's thorough treatment of the emergence of temperance in the period in question. While historians of Aberdeen and northern Scotland will no doubt enjoy the richness of this local case study, the lack of detailed studies of the history of alcohol and its regulation in Scotland means Hoffman's book deserves to find a broader audience.

David Beckingham
Department of Geography, University of Cambridge

Scotland's First Oil Boom. The Scottish Shale-Oil Industry, 1851–1914.
By John H. McKay. Pp. x, 310.
ISBN: 9781906566500 (pbk).
Edinburgh: John Donald, 2012. £25.00.
DOI: 10.3366/nor.2015.0098

I first met John McKay when we started work together as tutors on an Open University course in 1994. He was a wonderful colleague: thoughtful, generous, and knowledgeable. I soon learnt of his interest in the West Lothian shale oil industry. More of a surprise, I recall, was my accidental discovery that this self-effacing man was a one-time Lord Provost of Edinburgh! It was a great pleasure to be asked to review his posthumously published book. McKay completed his PhD on the social history of the shale oil industry in 1984, but it is clear from some references that he was working on the subject for several years before that. This present book brings together much of his unrivalled knowledge of this localised but nationally important Scottish industry.

The Scottish shale oil industry was always small, and its output was rapidly overtaken by American imports once the Pennsylvania oilfields were connected to transport networks in the mid-1860s. Nevertheless, as McKay explains, the industry was able to survive by shifting its focus to new products: at first the demand was for lubricants for the textile industry, but later burning oil for lighting, paraffin wax for candles, and sulphate of ammonia as a fertiliser, were all important. On the eve of the First World War, the decision of the Royal Navy to switch from coal to oil was an indication of the future significance of oil as a fuel. A major theme of the book is the inventiveness which enabled the industry to adapt to changing markets.

The book covers the history of the industry from the first successful distillation of oil from shale by James 'Paraffin' Young in 1851 up to the outbreak of the First World War. In fact, however, most of the focus is on the decades between the end of the 'oil mania' in 1864–6, already discussed in John Butt's article from 1965, and the consolidation of the industry around 1900. The four chapters in Part 1 review the period chronologically, whilst Parts 2 and 3 focus on the capital and shareholders of the limited companies. The longest section is Part 4 where nine chapters look at the management of the companies and why some were more successful than others. The book finishes with a very brief conclusion and a postscript which traces the history of the industry from 1914 to the closure of the detergent plant at Pumpherston, the last user of wax extract, in 1982. Two long appendices at the end give data on the capitalisation and shareholders of the companies, amplifying the many admirably clear tables in the text. An index and detailed bibliography complete the work.

In contrast to his PhD and his contribution to a 2002 edited collection on the village of Pumpherston, the focus of this present work is not on the social history of the industry, but very much on the finances and management of the companies. For this McKay draws on the records of those among the companies that were absorbed into Scottish Oils Ltd in 1919, so that their papers ended up in the BP Archive now held by the Almond Valley Heritage Trust in Livingston. As is so often the case, however, most of the surviving company papers are formal ones and there are many gaps, so that the overall value of this source appears to have been frustratingly limited. What is really impressive is the way McKay has complemented these internal documents with information from public sources. In particular, he has drawn extensively on the Scottish Register of Company files, held at the National Archives of Scotland in the case of defunct companies and at Companies House for live ones.

The Register of Company files are most detailed on the financial affairs of incorporated companies, and this is where McKay is strongest. He analyses carefully the original capital of the forty-three limited companies and later changes in their capital to explore such issues as how the firms were originally financed, later additions to the capital, and how much capital was lost. The lists of shareholders are used to explore who invested in these early public companies and the relationship between the numbers of shares held by the board and their role in running the company. In this, he makes good use of Peter Payne's *The Early Scottish Limited Companies, 1856–95* (1980), which remains the most thorough study of this new form of capitalism. McKay shows that even though the average life of companies in the shale oil industry was shorter than in Payne's cohort, they had a larger nominal capital than average and called up substantially more of it. Shale oil was a capital intensive industry which relied on public investment. It was also a risky one in which many companies failed, but, as McKay shows, good profits could also be made.

Although the emphasis in this book is very much on describing the shale oil industry, links are made to wider discussions about the development of Scottish industry during the 'second industrial revolution'. As McKay notes, this was an industry that first emerged mid-century and faced formidable foreign competition from the start. He explores the inventions which allowed the industry to keep ahead of rivals and argues that they were based on solid chemical and engineering expertise. He also draws on A.D. Chandler's work on the shift to managerial capitalism to explore the role of directors and managers. He notes that despite the wide distribution of shares in the largest companies, the men who first launched the companies and their descendants usually retained control, even where they only held a small minority of the shares.

There are a few omissions from the book. My reading would have been helped by a map and by a table with data on production. More surprising is the absence of a single list of the enterprises with their locations and dates. As it is, it is necessary to piece together this information from tables that cover only part of the period. A pity too is that McKay's caution makes him reluctant to highlight the significance of his research. In a discussion of company accounts he notes that many historians do not have the expertise to deal properly with them. This is 'certainly true in this case' he continues (p.203), and the ensuing discussion is brief.

This caution, however, and the quality of the underlying research, means that it is likely that McKay's judgements will stand the test of time. This book is set to become an essential resource for scholars interested in Scotland's first oil industry, which will no doubt receive more attention now that interest is turning once again to the use of shale.

Robin Mackie
The Open University

A Swedish Field Trip to the Outer Hebrides: In Memory of Sven T. Kjellberg and Olof Hasslöf.
Compiled and edited by Alexander Fenton with Mark A. Mulhern. Pp. xv, 110.
ISBN: 9781905267651 (hbk).
Edinburgh: The European Ethnological Research Centre/National Museums Scotland, 2012. £25.00.
DOI: 10.3366/nor.2015.0099

Alexander Fenton's fascinating and beautifully produced collection of ethnological notes and photographs details the 1934 visit to the Outer Hebrides by Sven T. Kjellberg (then director of Gothenburg Historic Museum) and his assistant Olof Hässlöf. Kjellberg was the senior scholar – he celebrated his forty second birthday on 22 June 1934, in the midst of a 'stormy and rainy' day in Lochmaddy (p. 55), and he went on to become superintendent of the *Kulturen* outdoor museum in Lund in 1935, where he remained until his retirement in 1961. He was remembered approvingly as a 'cultural historian of the researcher kind', with a great general knowledge, undertaking work of public interest in an increasingly specialised age.[1] Olof Hasslöf was thirty-three years of age when he visited the Hebrides. He had grown up in a fishing family in Bohuslän, between Gothenburg and the Norwegian border, and maintained a lifetime interest in the history and ethnology of the sea and fishing communities. It was this maritime link that provided the main stimulus for the ethnologists' visit. Their mental geography reflected a historical cultural community that stretched from Western Sweden and Norway, through Shetland and Orkney, to the Hebrides and Faroe Islands.

In an interesting and comprehensive introduction, Fenton outlines the relationship between geology, geography, and land settlement in the Outer Hebrides. Cultural connections between Scandinavia and the Hebrides are also stressed – reaffirming the idea that, when seen from the political capital (London), the Western Isles can be considered an underpopulated periphery, but that there are other cultural zones which can be used to contextualise the region. It is also clear that Kjellberg and Hasslöf were maintaining a relatively strong tradition of external inquiry into the society and material culture of the Hebrides, succeeding other Scandinavian scholars such as J. J. A. Worsaae in this regard (p. 10).

If the Hebrides provided an interesting *space* of inquiry, the 1930s were also an important *time* for such an intervention. Fenton argues (pp. xii-xiii) that this decade marked the 'end of an era', when blackhouses were giving way to 'Lowland'-inspired prototypes, contributing to cultural assimilation with mainland Scotland, and Britain more generally (p. 13). The evacuation of St. Kilda in 1930 added to this atmosphere of irrevocable and accelerating social change in the Hebrides. The emphasis placed by Fenton on the blackhouse as symbolic of a society (pp. 15–27) is justifiable as the links between material culture, architecture and 'racial' or 'ethnic' qualities had contributed considerably to discussions around Scotland's identity in the nineteenth and early twentieth centuries. It is interesting to note (p. 10) that the doyen of Irish folklorists, Séaumus Ó Duilearga, asserted that the 'folk traditions of Ireland and Gaelic Scotland' should be taken as a whole, just as plenty of academics within Scotland were foregrounding the Scots' Norse ethnicity. This in turn demonstrates the fluidity of cultural identities, whether internally or externally constructed.

Part Two of the book – about one third of the overall page count – is where we read the Swedes' own observations. In a welcome editorial intervention Hasslöf's diary entries and Kjellberg's notes are interwoven to maintain narrative coherence. As they proceeded north from Lochboisdale on their bicycles they described, echoing observations made in previous centuries, a landscape betraying 'extreme poverty' and farm clusters with 'something of the character of an African village' (p. 30). Various 'characters' illuminate the narrative. A great deal of detail was recorded about Fergus Walker's home at Daliburgh (p. 34), and Walker himself was described as hospitable, despite 'tasteless cheese' being offered. His neighbour, however, possibly a pioneer of the 'full economic costing' model of academic endeavour, was reluctant to allow the ethnologists access without 'some profit' being involved (p. 37). The account of another South Uist resident – Peter MacDonald of Lochboisdale – amply demonstrates the strengths of the book. There are social details: he spoke good English, but his wife only Gaelic; his house had a mud floor and animals 'walked around' freely – but the added value of the volume is highlighted as the biographical and social details are juxtaposed with photographs of the family and the kitchen interior, as well as detailed plans of the domestic layout. These curatorial touches ensure that the book is raised above a mere collection of photographs. In addition to the descriptions of society and material culture, the notes also show something of the thrill that the ethnologists could get: 'you must have some courage to force the smoke', referring to a blackhouse in South Uist, 'but you are rewarded ... the rooms seem to be something for an antiquarian' (p. 47). This can be contrasted with their disappointing day cycling around the Point peninsula later in the month, which they considered to be 'completely modernised and offer[ing] nothing of interest' (p. 64).

As they headed north up the Long Island, other practices received attention – lobster fishing and creel-making in South Uist (p. 45), tweed (rather than fishing) as the primary economic activity in some parts of North Uist (p. 51), and contrasts were made with the Faroe Islands in terms of female load-bearing (p. 57), again supplemented by diagrams and photographs. There is also a hint in the notes that the local community recognised the changing society in which they were living, with MacDonald (Lingerbay) recalling a form of unleavened barley bannock, claiming that it was healthier than the contemporary bread, and that 'at that time we had strong healthy men, who could lift heavy stones' (p. 60).

Part Three of the book is an interesting, if brief, summary of some of the changes that had taken place in (roughly) the century from the compilation of the *New Statistical Account* in the 1830s and 1840s. Fenton notes a 'striking' level of continuity (p. 86) amidst the change after the *NSA*, and this comparative approach also suggests the possibility of examining the material collected by Kjellberg and Hasslöf alongside other important, but later, sources such as the report of the Napier Commission (1884). Overall, the book is valuable as a snapshot of a critical time in Hebridean society. It is sensitively presented and well contextualised. For the historian, it provides some excellent material, and contributes to the ongoing 'decentring' of Scottish history (p. 4). The Hebrides are not seen in the context of London, or even Edinburgh, but as part of a vibrant and viable Northern European 'cultural zone' (p. 4), a context which continues to resonate in the twenty-first century.

Andrew G. Newby
University of Helsinki

Note

1. www.kulturportallund.se

Landscapes of Protest in the Scottish Highlands after 1914: The Later Highland Land Wars.
By Iain J. M. Robertson. Pp. x, 256.
ISBN: 9781472411372 (hbk).
Farnham: Ashgate Publishing, 2013. £65.00.
DOI: 10.3366/nor.2015.0100

Weeks after the end of the Great War in November 1918, civil servants at the Board of Agriculture for Scotland's headquarters in Edinburgh took delivery of a petition signed by fifty-seven people living in North Tolsta, a Lewis township some fifteen miles from Stornoway. The petition not so much requested as demanded that land at Gress, a farm between Tolsta and Stornoway, be purchased by the board and divided into crofts – crofts which, the Tolsta petitioners made clear, should immediately be allocated to some of the many landless families resident in Gress's vicinity. 'We ourselves and our sons', the Tolsta petitioners wrote, 'have fought in defence of our king and country, and we shall also fight ... if steps are not taken to see us settled on the land of our ancestors which we consider is ours by right'. This threat was soon made good. By late April 1919, one of the Board of Agriculture's Lewis representatives reported, much of Gress was in the hands of the men who had announced their intention to seize it. No fewer than eighty-four 'crofts' had been pegged out or otherwise delineated on the farm's fields.

This Gress episode was one of many land raids – the name given to such illegal seizures – that occurred across the Highlands and Islands in the post-1918 period. Those raids constitute the subject matter of this important book by Iain Robertson. His topic, the author comments by way of introduction, has been 'much neglected'. That, perhaps, is not quite fair. While the present reviewer, in *The Making of the Crofting Community* (1976) – where the events of 1919 and subsequently are treated as not much more than a postscript to nineteenth-century developments – certainly dealt cursorily with the land raiding that followed the First World War, this raiding afterwards received a lot more attention from Leah Leneman in *Fit for Heroes: Land Settlement in Scotland after World War I* (1989) and Ewen Cameron in *'Land for the People': The British Government and the Scottish Highlands, c.1880–1930* (1996). That said, Iain Robertson brings new and intriguing perspectives to bear on the mechanics of land raiding and on the motivation of the people (many of them newly demobilised soldiers) who engaged in it. This he accomplishes, first, by meticulous analysis (founded on extensive archival research) of a whole series of separate raids and, second, by exploring the extent to which agrarian protest in the post-1918

Highlands and Islands conformed, or failed to conform, to analogous protest elsewhere.

As his book's subtitle suggests, Robertson regards land raiding of the sort that peaked in 1920 (but which continued intermittently into the 1930s and beyond) as, in essence, a continuation of a struggle launched in the 1880s – when, in the face of rent-strikes and other (sometimes violent) manifestations of discontent, government conceded security of tenure to crofters. This earlier campaign is often called a *crofters' war*. Robertson, like this reviewer, dislikes that term – which fails to recognise the extent to which the 1880s discontents involved people who were not crofters but who wanted to become so by obtaining land from which their parents or grandparents had been removed in the course of early nineteenth-century clearances. Little such land was obtained in the 1880s. During ensuing decades, successive governments (both Conservative and Liberal) began – in response to continuing Highlands and Islands pressure – to concede the principle that areas which had gone into sheep farming around or after 1800 should be acquired by the state and made available for settlement by people of the sort who signed that petition from North Tolsta. But progress in this direction was slow before the First World War and not much faster in the months immediately following it. Hence raiding of the Gress type – raiding which had the intended effect of forcing government and its agencies to accelerate their land purchase and settlement programmes.

The belief – evident in the Tolsta petition – that wartime service somehow gave returning servicemen a right to have, as it were, crofts 'fit for heroes' is seen by Robertson as something of a novel element in the post-1918 situation. Insofar as this sense of entitlement was a response to promises understood to have been made during Great War recruiting drives, Robertson is right. But much the same point had been made a hundred years before by, for example, former soldiers – veterans of Britain's wars with revolutionary and Napoleonic France – who lost homes and landholdings in the course of the clearances. Indeed the roots of this thinking can arguably be traced to a deep-seated notion – one of centuries-old provenance – that clan chiefs were entitled to look to clansmen for military service only for as long as chiefs, in their turn, saw to it that clansmen were left in undisturbed possession of their landholdings. For that sort of reason – and Robertson is clear and illuminating about this – the ideology of land-related protest in the Highlands and Islands, whether in the 1920s, the 1880s or earlier, cannot be understood solely with reference to 'democratic', 'socialist' or other 'modern' modes of thought then spreading into the region from the south. Those played a part of course. But so did the widespread conviction – stemming from the nature of land occupancy in the pre-clearance Highlands and Islands – that the clearances were not so much a wrong as a betrayal that could only be righted by returning, as far as possible, to pre-clearance patterns of occupancy. This was what post-1918 land raiders – with their constant references, as in the Tolsta petition, to 'the land of [their] ancestors' – looked to achieve; and especially in the Hebrides, as

Robertson demonstrates, they were remarkably successful in forcing government and its agencies to do their bidding.

When, more than half a lifetime ago, this reviewer began to research the Highland land wars and their antecedents, the founding fathers of what are now called protest studies – E. P. Thomson, Eric Hobsbawm and George Rudé – were still hard at work. All are now dead. But protest studies continue to thrive and Robertson's book is intended explicitly to contribute to UK and international effort in this regard as well as to understanding of the modern history of the Highlands and Islands. There were times when, in Robertson's more theoretical (and protest study-oriented) chapters, this reviewer felt that unnecessary violence was being done to the English language by the deployment of terms like 'nature-culture binary', 'performativity', 'co-constitutively' and 'fabric of lifespace'. But such sins, if sins they be, can be forgiven a man who has contributed so substantially to explaining how the present-day Highlands and Islands came to be the way they are. At one point in his book, Iain Robertson says of *The Making of the Crofting Community* that 'it led subsequent commentators to believe little more can be said'. I doubt if this was ever the case. But what is certain is that Iain Robertson has elucidated much that I left uninvestigated.

James Hunter
University of the Highlands and Islands

Broadcasting Empire. The BBC and the British World, 1922–1970.
By Simon J. Potter. Pp. ix, 261.
ISBN: 9780199568963 (hbk).
Oxford: Oxford University Press, 2012. £63.00.
DOI: 10.3366/nor.2015.0101

This deceptively slim volume packs a powerful punch. Since the inter-war years the BBC has been an ever-present and opinionated occupant of most British homes, through radio and subsequently television. From the Corporation's inception, however, the influence of the airwaves extended far beyond Britain's shores, and had a particular impact in the dominions and colonies, where the BBC sought to build up a monopolistic communications empire of its own. It was, says Simon Potter, 'motivated by a mixture of institutional self-interest and ideological commitment'.

The roots and repercussions of those objectives are analysed in rigorous and innovative scholarship that draws heavily on the BBC's extensive written archive, as well as British government papers, and the files of broadcasting and government archives in Australia, Canada, New Zealand, South Africa and the United States. Unlike most studies of the Corporation, it does not separate domestic and overseas operations, but evaluates the BBC's influence in the global 'projection of

Britishness' during half a century of programme-making. There are many separate studies of the impact of empire and the impact of broadcasting, but Potter offers a uniquely integrated approach which asks the chicken and egg question of whether the Corporation's imperial role reshaped its institutional nature or simply reflected and reinforced existing domestically-generated attitudes.

This is one of several key issues that are laid out in a lengthy introduction. Even in the 1920s, there was arguably an anachronistic element in the BBC's attempt to use new communications technology to reinforce imperial unity and ameliorate conflict, although the tensions did not become explicit until the 1950s, when the Corporation had to accommodate Britain's obviously diminished world role, coupled with increasing American influence. Its public service function was inextricably bound up with John Reith's determination that broadcasting should inform and educate, rather than simply entertain, but such a philosophy carried clear propaganda risks, especially when coupled with state interference. Meanwhile public broadcasting authorities in the dominions, whose collaboration the BBC required if it was to fulfil its imperial mission, often had their own agendas which conflicted with the BBC's centralising tendencies. Nor was there any consensus, either at home or abroad, about the definition and function of Britishness. As a consequence of these paradoxes and tensions, Potter claims, 'the gap between intention and achievement was significant'.

The main themes are explored in greater detail in seven chronologically-based chapters: Diversity, 1922–31; Discord, 1932–35; Integration, 1935–39; War, 1939–45; Continuities, 1945–59, Challenges, (also) 1945–59; and Disintegration, 1960–70. During the 1920s the BBC concentrated on domestic issues, and on developing links with broadcasters in Europe and the United States rather than the empire, even though it already saw the Americanisation of broadcasting as a potential threat. While hybridisation of the US and UK approaches was the hallmark of broadcasters in the dominions, the American model was prominent, with more emphasis on private enterprise. Meanwhile, poverty in India and the tropical colonies impeded the development of any sort of service in those locations. The 1930s saw some experimentation in empire broadcasting, with the inauguration of Christmas and Empire Day broadcasts, although these developments were beset by financial and technical problems, uncoordinated structures and intransigent attitudes. In particular, the determination of the BBC Empire Service to organise all activities from London incurred resentment and charges of dictatorial imperialism from dominion broadcasters.

The four years before the outbreak of the Second World War were characterised by greater integration and collaboration. The BBC became more involved – not least through staff deployment – in supporting the establishment and consolidation of public broadcasting authorities around the empire and in Europe, at the same time as broadcasters from the empire began to develop their own networks through more frequent travel and consultation. The BBC also invested in reciprocal programming through the development of an 'Empire exchange', bringing material from the dominions back to Britain and transmitting it on to other parts of the empire via short wave. For their part, the dominions collaborated with the BBC through autonomous public broadcasting authorities, which were controlled by the state remotely in Canada, Australia and South Africa, and directly in New Zealand.

Mass communication by radio played a significant part in the war effort, through morale-boosting entertainment, as well as information and propaganda. The collaborative structures developed during the 1930s continued to operate, though with the injection of some decentralisation into the BBC's relations with the dominions. Post-war collaboration was facilitated by the First Commonwealth Broadcasting Conference, held in London over a three-week period in February 1945, although increased mutual understanding among the broadcasters was not matched by audience engagement with imperial issues.

The post-war decade was a period of consolidation and stabilisation, when the collaborative structures were further strengthened and broadcasting materials were freely exchanged on a non-commercial basis. Imperial revival was, of course, illusory, despite cosmetic secondments of personnel, and frustrations sometimes surfaced, notably in the assertion of Andrew Cowan of the Canadian Broadcasting Corporation that the BBC suffered from an 'institutional arrogance' that demanded 'unrestricted export of their culture', combined with 'a high tariff policy towards any incoming material'.

Yet such spats were incidental to the huge new challenge that was looming. The financial demands of television made it impossible for the BBC to fund the one-way flow of recorded material that it had established with radio programmes, opening the door to the erosion of monopolistic public broadcasting by private commercial operators and, ultimately, to full-blown American competition. The book's final substantive chapter charts the abandonment of Reithian principles under the directorship of Hugh Carleton Greene, who argued that commercial competition could be countered only by producing the same types of programmes as the commercial stations, but to a higher standard. His stance reflected – and perhaps contributed to – the permissive culture of the 1960s, but although it led in the short term to some innovative if controversial programmes, Greene's long-term legacy was more ambiguous. As the last vestiges of empire disappeared, Commonwealth broadcasting lost its unifying, nation-building rationale, at the same time as the BBC became increasingly embroiled in an Anglo-American alliance in which it was very definitely the junior partner.

At the time of writing, the BBC is mired in controversy as a consequence of revelations about the sexual crimes of celebrities, and the inflated salaries and egos of executives. Yet internal and external tensions – albeit of a more impersonal strategic hue – have been a concomitant of the broadcasting industry from its infancy, not least in its transnational dimension, which soon became a field of 'geopolitical contest' involving Britain, the empire and the United States. Simon Potter has avoided the whiggish trap of presenting these episodes of conflict in a simple chronological sequence, leading inevitably to the emergence of autonomous national broadcasters in the dominions as they extricated themselves from the BBC's empire-building tentacles at the same time as they marched towards full national independence. Instead, he paints a much more nuanced and compelling picture of the cyclical failures and successes of collaboration, in the context of ever-changing debates about the relationship between external broadcasting, state funding and the free market.

Broadcasting Empire is a perceptive and exhaustive analysis, but the complexity of the concepts, processes and events, coupled with the sheer detail of coverage, ensure it is by no means an easy read. Its value lies in its unprecedented illumination of a neglected but crucial chapter in the relationship between the BBC and the empire in a half-century when both institutions were experiencing constant and sometimes cataclysmic change. Across the former British world, imperial and media historians alike can benefit from and build on this solid and scholarly foundation.

Marjory Harper
University of Aberdeen

The Making of the Modern Scottish Highlands 1939–1965: Withstanding the 'Colossus of Advancing Materialism'.
By John A. Burnett. Pp. 310.
ISBN: 9781846822414 (hbk).
Dublin: Four Courts Press, 2011. £50.00.
DOI: 10.3366/nor.2015.0102

The Making of the Modern Scottish Highlands sets out to examine a relatively under-studied period in Highland history, that from the outbreak of World War II in 1939 to the establishment of the Highlands and Islands Development Board in 1965. While acknowledging that the Highlands saw significant change from the late nineteenth century through to the inter-war years, the author argues that the social and cultural shift towards modernity did not occur until the period after the Second World War. Throughout this volume Burnett aims to trace different 'ways of seeing' the Scottish Highlands during this period, through the eyes of policy makers, residents, and observers. In particular, two distinct strands run through this book, contrasting the views of those from within and outwith Highland culture.

In the introductory Chapter 1, Burnett outlines the issues to be discussed, and explains his definition of terms such as 'modernisation' and 'identity'. In exploring the issue of social and cultural change, the book defines the Highland and Islands culturally, rather than geographically or linguistically, as a region that was perceived to have a 'deep cultural imprint of Gaelic culture and identity', and what is commonly described as a Highland 'way of life' (pp. 17–18).

The main body of the book comprises three parts, each containing two chapters. Part I, 'Image and Reality', looks at the historical background, examining the 'Highland problem' from 1745 until the outbreak of World War II. Parts II and III explore the period from 1939 until 1965. Part II, 'Governing the Highlands', explores the attitudes of successive governments to the 'Highland problem', while Part III, 'Voices "Within", Laments from "Below"', seeks to identify the views of the Highlanders themselves.

Part I documents the emergence and invention of a distinctive Highland tradition following the 1745 Jacobite Rising. Chapter 2 explores post-1745 Highland history from the perspective of the Highlanders themselves. To those readers with a knowledge of Highland history, this covers familiar ground, but it is presented in a format which focuses on specific economic and social themes (clearance, emigration, resistance and resurgence), from which key motifs are extracted. Burnett argues that these motifs (including victimisation, pauperisation, nostalgia, and alienation) have profoundly shaped Highlanders' own concepts of identity and their responses to interventions from outside the region. Chapter 3 complements Chapter 2 by considering the perceptions of those outwith the Highland community. Here the author explores the 'invented traditions' of the Scottish Highlands, and their principal proponents, while tracing the subtle shift from eighteenth century romanticism to the 'Celtic twilightism' of the nineteenth and twentieth centuries.

Burnett persuasively argues that such issues are key to understanding post-1939 government policy in relation to the Scottish Highlands, as well as resistance to these policies from within the Highland community. By the 1930s, it had become clear that land reform alone would not stem the tide of migration from the Highlands or address the matter of economic and social development. Industrial schemes, such as the introduction of hydro-electric power, were opposed by landowners, local politicians, fishery groups and others, who argued that these would cause immeasurable damage to the scenic beauty of the region and thus detract visitors.

Part II is where the book comes into its own. Chapter 4 focuses on the approaches of the various political parties to the 'Highland problem', examining the 'subtle changes in emphasis' (p. 96) that are apparent during the period in question. These saw policy shift from simple reconstruction within the region, to regeneration through the use of natural resources and traditional industries, to planned regional development with the aim of reducing depopulation. Throughout this section of the book, Burnett highlights the different 'ways of seeing' the Highlands and Islands from within the ranks of specific agencies as well as between agencies, in wider government, and the local population.

Chapter 5 looks in greater detail at how government policies during this period were developed and implemented through the creation of various agencies, including the North of Scotland Hydro-Electric Board, the Crofters Commission, and the Forestry Commission. A lengthy section is devoted to the work of the Advisory Panel on the Highlands and Islands, which was set up in 1947 to deal with the social and economic issues affecting the region. Burnett argues that, while successful in many ways, particularly in terms of preserving and expanding transport links to the area, the panel was hindered by government bureaucracy and was slow to address the still significant problem of land-use.

In Part III, Burnett seeks to understand the voices of 'the Highlanders themselves', in order to gain insight into their own views of the changes that occurred between 1939 and 1965. Chapter 6 aims to capture the views of those Highland representatives who served on some of the agencies examined previously. This chapter is assembled almost entirely from the writings of Naomi Mitchison and Neil Gunn, with occasional insights from James Shaw Grant, Frank Fraser Darling, and Adam Collier. Nonetheless, this is an important chapter which explores the concept of a distinctly Highland 'way of life' and highlights the lack of understanding within government of the local realities of the Highland region. The frustrations felt by those who sought to work within the system, such as Mitchison and Gunn, are palpable.

Chapter 7 specifically examines the Gaels' response to the 'colossus of advancing materialism'. The decline in Gaelic language and culture occurred alongside the move towards modernisation and this chapter explores a number of related issues such as the distorted image of the Highlands and the Highlanders that was still prevalent outside the area, the role of language in determining identity, and the diversity of regional responses to the social and economic changes that were enveloping the Highlands and Islands. Despite searching for the 'Gaelic voice', the information in this chapter is drawn almost entirely from the English-language section of *An Gàidheal*, the bilingual magazine of *An Comunn Gàidhealach*. While a highly relevant source, and a 'useful indicator on attitudes within the Gaelic-speaking community' (p. 219), the author concedes that it represents a limited and selective strand of Gaelic opinion.

In the Introduction, Burnett himself raises the contentious issue of whether a scholar with little or no understanding of the Gaelic language can effectively research and write on issues pertaining to the Scottish Highlands and Islands (pp. 22–3). While he has integrated Gaelic 'voices' through translation or through English-language texts, there are a number of relevant Gaelic-language sources which have necessarily been omitted. These include the voluminous records of the *Comuinn Eachdraidh*, the numerous historical societies that were established in the Hebrides during the late 1970s and 1980s to record and document the changing way of life in the Islands from the late nineteenth century right through to the present day.

The author notes in Chapter 7 that some Gaels felt angered that others were making representations on their behalf, including non-Gaelic-speaking Highlanders, while their own voices were left unheard (p. 263). In this book, too, the voice of the ordinary Gael is absent. While it can be difficult to locate such voices, except through oral history, or the records of the aforementioned historical societies, they can be found in an increasing number of Gaelic- and English-language biographical works such as Calum Ferguson's *Children of the Black House*, and through the pages of Gaelic-language publications such as *Gairm*, and would have made a welcome addition to Burnett's discussion.

In summary, *The Making of the Modern Scottish Highlands* elucidates an important, and much-neglected, era in Highland history. This was the period in which many Highlanders started to desire the trappings of modern life, rather than resist such developments. This book highlights the conflict between the reforming desire to improve living conditions and reduce depopulation, and the conservative desire to retain the Highlanders' unique cultural identity, which was in danger of being eroded. In incorporating the views from within and outwith the Highland community, Burnett provides a detailed examination of the issues at play on all sides, and highlights the difficulties and complexities of dealing with a region that has suffered from historic misrepresentation, where there is more than one mother tongue, a diversity of local economies and 'ways of living', and a population that has for many years felt maligned and disregarded by those in authority. As Burnett notes in his conclusion, the divergence between the 'idea' and the 'reality' of Highland life, which intensified during the period under study, is an issue that we continue to grapple with today.

Dr Catriona Mackie
Isle of Man College of Further and Higher Education